Second Edition

QUEST FOR THE PAST

Second Edition

QUEST FOR THE PAST

Great Discoveries in Archaeology

Brian M. Fagan

University of California, Santa Barbara

WAVELAND

PRESS, INC.

Long Grove, Illinois

Cover Photo:

"How Grand, How Wonderful! How Incomprehensible!" wrote an antiquary of Stonehenge in 1812. Stonehenge in southern Britain is one of the world's most famous archaeological sites. Known to the Romans, the stone circles have been the subject of antiquarian and archaeological inquiry since the seventeenth century. Early antiquarians like John Aubrey and William Stukeley attributed Stonehenge to ancient Britons, to people Aubrey called "two or three degrees less savage than the Americans." Stukeley dined with his friends on one of the uprights and theorized Druidic priests had erected the mysterious circles. Modern archaeological researchers and meticulous radiocarbon dating have shown Stonehenge began as a simple earthwork enclosure in about 3000 BC. A circle of pits containing cremations lay inside the enclosure. About 2150 BC, Stonehenge's entrance was aligned with the rising sun at midsummer solstice. During the next century, the great trilithons were erected using stone imported from eighteen miles (twenty-nine kilometers) away. For the next nine hundred years or so, successive generations tinkered with the monument, adding an oval of uprights outside the trilithons and making other minor changes. The Stonehenge we see today is an amalgram of restless alterations made over sixty to seventy generations. The date of its final abandonment is unknown, but it was long before the Roman Conquest of 55 BC.

Great controversy surrounds Stonehenge's function. Some scientists have used elaborate mathematical calculations in attempts to prove it was a sophisticated astronomical observatory. Most experts believe it was a temple aligned on the midsummer solstice, which reflected the cyclical movements of the sun, moon, and stars across the heavens, and the passing, ever returning seasons.

The controversies surrounding this most famous of archaeological sites epitomize the mystery and fascination of scientific archaeology in the 1990s.

For information about this book, contact:

Waveland Press, Inc.
4180 IL Route 83, Suite 101
Long Grove, IL 60047-9580
(847) 634-0081
info@waveland.com
www.waveland.com

10-digit ISBN 0-88133-791-9
13-digit ISBN 978-0-88133-791-4

Printed in the United States of America

13   12   11   10   9   8

To
George Michaels

Because he cares about archaeology, teaching,
and the past—and not least because he comes from Texas . . .

"A man who has once looked with the archaeological
eye will never see quite normally. He will be wounded
by what other men call trifles. It is possible to refine the
sense of time until an old show in the bunch grass or a
pile of nineteenth century beer bottles in an abandoned
mining town tolls in one's head like a hall clock. This is
the price one pays for learning to read time from
surfaces other than an illuminated dial. It is the
melancholy secret of the artifact, the humanly touched
thing."

Loren Eiseley, *The Night Country*

Stanwick Roman Villa excavations from the East.

Contents

Preface

Quest for the Past originated as a volume of popular appeal, written for the general public. It was never the intention that it be used in the classroom, but it is there that it has found a niche since its original publication in 1979. My objective was, and still is, to tell the story of some well-known archaeologists and some remarkable excavations, to throw light on some of the ways in which the founders of our discipline unearthed early civilizations, probed the origins of humankind, and the history of non-Western societies. Thus, *Quest* ranges widely over the world of archaeology, describing excavations of 2-million-year-old hominids, of long-forgotten Native American settlements, and of spectacular civilizations. Each essay stands on its own, an attempt to describe some of the challenges and discoveries made not only by adventurous pioneers like Austen Henry Layard, but by trained scientists like René Millon and Gertrude Caton-Thompson. From them, I hope that you gain some appreciation of the incredible range, excitement, and complexity of the world of archaeology.

This edition of *Quest* has been revised, changed, and updated in response to comments from reviewers and users of the book. I have included a new chapter on how archaeology works and a chapter on early women archaeologists, a subject sadly neglected in the academic literature. The text has been revised and up-dated throughout, to reflect new advances in our knowledge of the history of archaeology. Please note, however, that this is a book about the discoveries of early archaeologists, about excavations that were completed at the latest some years ago. Thus, the chapters offer little more than general descriptions of the sites and discoveries *in the context of their finders' times.* I have not described the very latest perspectives on, say, Nimrud, except insofar as they are relevant to the story in these pages. Readers interested in the latest scientific advances are encouraged to consult the Sources section at the end of the book.

The locations of sites and cities mentioned in the text are indicated on maps found in chapters 3 to 11. A chronological table in chapter 1 places the sites in the book in a general time frame. Place names are spelled according to the usage in the *Times Atlas of the World*, with the exception of ancient Egyptian and Mesopotamian spellings, which follow common archaeological usage. Archaeological sites, where not geographical place names in the formal sense, conform to common scientific convention.

If radiocarbon dates are cited, it should be noted that these are subject to statistical errors, and should be treated for what they are—statistical approximations. Dates after about 4,000 B.C. are tree-ring calibrated.

I hope that *Quest for the Past* whets your appetite for archaeology, for further enjoyment of the rich, and varied, human past.

My thanks to the anonymous reviewers, who commented on the book, and to the late John Staples, who suggested this book in the first place. This present edition results from the encouragement and interest of Tom Curtin of Waveland Press: I am deeply grateful to him.

Brian Fagan
Santa Barbara, California

1

The
QUEST FOR THE PAST

Archaeologists are commonly thought to be eccentric people who wear rumpled khaki shorts and sun helmets and spend their lives unearthing crumbling ruins in the shadow of mighty pyramids. They live in a world of lost civilizations and buried treasure, deep mysteries and unexplained phenomena. The archaeologist of novel and television seems to be continually off on a "dig," searching for missing links and unwrapping innumerable Ancient Egyptian mummies. Sometimes, too, the angry mummies chase the unfortunate archaeologists, intoning dreadful curses that lead to their premature deaths. Many of us, at one time or another, have dreamed of pursuing such a romantic—if, in fact, mythical—career.

This is a book about actual archaeological discoveries, about remarkable archaeologists whose explorations have dramatically expanded our understanding of human history. It is a book about the excitement of archaeological discovery, about a scientific world that many consider to be one of the most engrossing frontiers of science. Its heroes are archaeologists of extraordinary ability who have made fascinating discoveries, often after years of patient effort. Each was a pioneer who pursued a dream, a conviction that spectacular archaeological finds awaited his or her spade.

The face of archaeology has changed considerably in recent years. Archaeologists of the 1840s, and even as late as the 1930s, could hope to uncover hitherto unknown civilizations: the Assyrians and Sumerians of Mesopotamia surfaced in the mid-nineteenth century, the Maya of Mexico in the 1840s, the Mycenaeans of Greece in the 1870s, the Shang civilization of China in the late 1920s. All of these discoveries captured the public imagination, for they were made under conditions of great difficulty, conditions that often required near-heroic efforts. The early archaeologists had few resources and no advanced excavation techniques. By constant improvisation, by drawing on their own wealth, and by acute political maneuvering, they frequently achieved miracles. They learned digging the hard way, made brilliant finds, and, regrettably, sometimes irreparably damaged vital clues to the past.

Some of our archaeologists belong to this heroic era, others to our own generation, where there are simply no lost civilizations left to find. But today's archaeologists still make remarkable discoveries, often as a result of applying such advanced tools as the computer to archaeological data. Modern archaeology is big business; thousands of people all over the

3

world are currently involved in digging up the past. Practically every nation now employs a few archaeologists—as museum curators, university professors, or conservators of national culture. All of these archaeologists use excavation techniques that have evolved over generations of archaeological discovery. The newer techniques enable them to tackle problems that would have boggled the mind even a few years ago.

One of Mexico's earliest cities, Teotihuacán, is a case in point. Early archaeologists could only gasp at the size of Teotihuacán, sample a portion of a pyramid or a few houses, then turn away in despair. They simply did not have the technology needed to carry their explorations further. It has taken a team of modern archaeologists over a decade to map the entire twelve-and-a-half square miles of Mexico's largest prehistoric city. Their task would have been impossible without a mosaic of air photographs and highly sophisticated computer programs that enabled them to store inventories of archaeological finds and millions of other items of information on computer tape. When the time came to put the data together, the archaeologists could recall and classify thousands of data items in a few seconds. The result: a whole new picture of Teotihuacán.

How do archaeologists dig up the past? What makes archaeological excavation different from ditch digging or the treasure-hunting activities of our mythical, sun-helmeted archaeologist? To get some idea of just how far the field of archaeology has progressed, let's look back over its colorful history.

Archaeology has a long and disreputable line of descent: its ancestors were, quite literally, grave robbers and adventurers. A century and a half ago, even serious archaeological excavation was little more than licensed treasure hunting. Everyone, whether archaeologist or treasure hunter, had the same objective—to recover as many valuable objects as possible in the shortest time. Serious archaeologists would not hesitate to use gunpowder to blast their way into a burial chamber or a pyramid. Everything was cast aside in a frantic search for the valuable and spectacular. As a result, most excavations resembled untidy vegetable gardens.

Mummy hunters in Egypt literally waded through piles of discarded coffins to reach their prey. The famous Italian collector Giovanni Belzoni, who worked in Egypt from 1817 to 1820, would crawl hundreds of yards into the rocky hillsides behind Thebes in search of mummies and papyri. Exhausted, he would perch in the darkness for a few minutes on a convenient mummy. Once his perch collapsed in a cloud of smelly dust. "I sank altogether among the broken mummies, with a crash of bones, rags, and wooden cases," he remembered. It was a good quarter of an hour before Belzoni could extricate himself.

Belzoni and his contemporaries were quite open about their efforts to "rob the Egyptians of their papyri." No one thought this either eccentric or wrong. Rather, Belzoni's audiences would be agog as he related his eerie

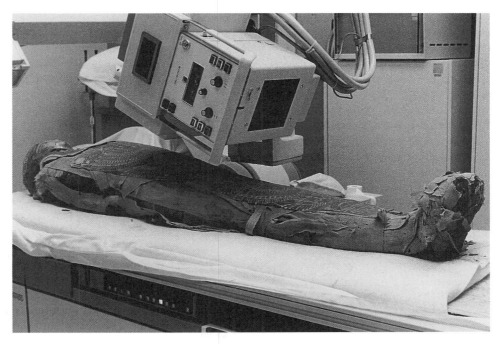

1-1. The Egyptian mummy, Djed Hapi, being x-rayed at the hospital of the University of Pennsylvania.

experiences in the dark burial chambers, where, in the flickering lamplight, the mummies seemed almost to converse with one another and the naked Arab workmen, coated in layers of dust, resembled mummies themselves. The audiences would gasp as Belzoni produced pieces of desiccated ancient Egyptians, remarking casually that "mummies are rather unpleasant to swallow."

In general, the nineteenth century was a time of frantic search for ancient sculptures and fine artifacts, whether from Egypt, Greece, Mesopotamia, or the Americas. Everyone wanted items for their collections and no one had any scruples about the means used to dig up their pet acquisitions. All too often we read in their early reports that such and such a find "crumbled to dust" on discovery or that exposure to the open air caused the finds to "dissolve before our very eyes."

One cannot entirely blame Belzoni and his successors. Basically, they were ignorant. No one had ever tried to dig a large archaeological site at all systematically. Even today, the technology of conservation is in relative infancy and modern archaeologists are still at a loss as to how to preserve many delicate finds satisfactorily. Considering the state of the art, it's a miracle that so much is preserved from early excavations. But the

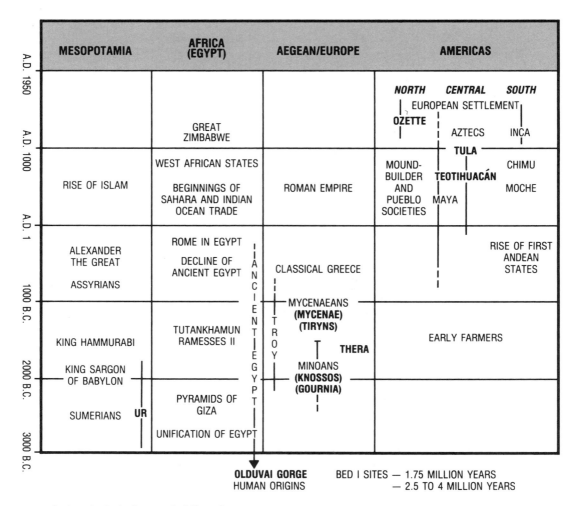

Archaeological sites are **boldfaced**

Table 1.1

Chronological table showing the approximate time periods of the major civilizations mentioned in this book.

This table* covers the main sites, civilizations, and dynasties described in this book which date to after 3000 B.C. It shows, for example, that the Sumerians were in power in Mesopotamia at the time the ancient Egyptians were building their greatest pyramids, and that Knossos was steadily evolving into the powerful center of a far-flung empire while the Assyrians were achieving domination in northern Mesopotamia. Tutankhamun was buried soon after the eruption of Thera and the devastation of Minoan civilization by one of the greatest natural catastrophes to affect humankind. The Mycenaeans rose to power while Troy was still important—like Knossos, an ancient and long-occupied center. As archaeological price of filling the British Museum, the Louvre, and other great museums was simply enormous: witness Austen Henry Layard's excavations in Mesopotamia at ancient Nineveh and Nimrud from 1845 to 1851.

Layard started digging Nimrud with precious little money and absolutely no archaeological experience. He simply tunneled into the huge mounds reputed to be the remains of these ancient cities and went on digging until he hit a fine sculpture or a stone-walled palace room. At Nimrud he was lucky enough to find two palaces. But, as he dug through mud-brick walls and houses, he failed to recognize invaluable inscribed tablets of unbaked clay. To his unskilled eyes, the bricks and tablets were indistinguishable from the brown soil of the mound. Later excavators recovered thousands of these tablets from areas of Nimrud that Layard left untouched. They had developed the skills and techniques to find them.

The deep tunnels that Layard dug along walls or lines of sculptured slabs at least sheltered him from the merciless sun and sweeping winds of the open plains. He would shovel out the contents of each room with dispatch, then sit down to record the intricate details of prancing horsemen and fighting warriors that flickered in the somber shadows. When his trenches were open to the elements, clouds of blinding dust stirred by savage gale-force winds would bombard the workmen. Layard himself would take refuge behind a giant sculpture until the sandstorm subsided. Under the circumstances, it is remarkable that he succeeded in excavating at all.

Austen Henry Layard shifted thousands of tons of soil, discovered nearly two miles of bas-reliefs, and cleared seventy rooms in the Palace of Sennacherib at Kuyunjik alone. Although he did keep some records, he more or less shoveled his way into the past. He tore Nimrud and Nineveh apart and, in the process, wiped out priceless archaeological information— data on daily life and ancient diet, details of houses and storerooms, and, above all, the complex sequence of layers that made up the occupation mounds.

Every Mesopotamian city mound was formed over centuries of occupation through complex processes of rebuilding houses, dumping

Teotihuacán was reaching the zenith of its power and influence, in the Pacific Northwest the Makah Indians were already living at Ozette, a settlement they continued to occupy until modern times. Written records, and hence historical times, began in about 3000 B.C. in Egypt and Mesopotamia and in the second millennium B.C. in the Aegean. Western civilization first encountered the American Indians in the fifteenth century A.D. Olduvai Gorge, of course, dates to a much earlier period than this table shows.

*Dates given in the table are approximations. For more detailed and accurate information, please consult the sources listed at the end of the book.

1-2. Layard's excavations in a tunnel at Nineveh.

garbage, and the natural actions of rain and wind. Many years before Layard came to Nineveh, geologists studying railway cuttings and canal excavations in Europe and America had observed the layered strata of the earth and established the classic principle of superposition. Very simply stated, this means that the lower levels of a succession of geological horizons were laid down earlier than the higher levels. The law of superposition had obvious applications to great city mounds like Nimrud or Nineveh, for every site started as a small settlement on a low ridge. The first occupation levels were soon covered by later settlements built in the same place. A thousand years later, the same city could look down from the top of a high mound of age-old occupation debris. The archaeologist wishing to understand the history of the city would have to dissect this mound layer by layer.

Layard himself was well aware that his mounds had gone through many changes. He knew that many kings had ruled his cities. But his excavation methods were simply too crude to permit him to dig the mounds period by period. One cannot blame Layard. If anything, he was more conscientious than his contemporaries, for he at least wrote popular accounts of his findings.

Many excavations of Layard's time were little more than picnic parties. Wealthy country gentlemen would open Indian burial mounds or Bronze Age earthworks for the sheer fun of it. When the English antiquarian Thomas Wright attended the opening of an ancient burial mound in 1844, he found a large party of interested gentry assembled for the sport. While the workmen opened eight burial mounds, the ladies and gentlemen "continued to spend [their] time, at intervals between digging and picnicking, in games of various descriptions . . . and in other amusements. The weather was fortunately exquisitely fine." When a sudden shower threatened to drench the party, they took refuge in the trench under a shield

1-3. Burial mound excavation—1840s style.

of umbrellas. The burial mounds contained "skeletons, more or less entire, with the remains of weapons in iron, bosses of shields, urns, beads, armlets, and occasionally more vessels." All of these finds vanished into the landowner's private collection, which the party inspected after partaking of a "sumptuous repast." This burial-mound dig was in no way exceptional; rather, it was typical of thousands.

The techniques of excavation were still in their infancy when Heinrich Schliemann began work on the great Hissarlik mound, site of ancient Troy. Schliemann, a millionaire, attacked archaeological problems with the same single-minded intensity he applied to business ventures. His wealth gave him the means to work on a truly grand scale, with resident experts and hundreds of workmen. He arrived on the site in 1871 with the vague notion that the mound contained many different settlements. So he set out to dig to bedrock, on a scale that almost beggars description. In 1872, for example, he borrowed a railroad engineer and employed three overseers to direct over a hundred men. They sliced into Hissarlik with a cutting over 230 feet wide that eventually penetrated over 40 feet into the huge mound. The city walls found in the upper-most strata were ruthlessly cleared away as

1-4. The Hissarlik (Troy) excavations in progress during the 1870s, using techniques employed in digging the Suez Canal.

Schliemann dug his way down through the centuries, toward his Homeric city.

Eventually, Schliemann identified the remains of seven cities, one above the other. His excavations exhibited a notable lack of finesse. In his books, he refers to the clearance of entire ancient streets, to the removal of "older walls which I am also having broken through," and to thousands upon thousands of potsherds, ornaments, and other small finds that were shoveled out as thousands of tons of soil were dug out of Hissarlik. At one point, he boasted that he had removed 325,000 cubic yards of soil from ancient Troy.

Schliemann's motto was speed, more speed, and yet still more. When he dug, he cleared an entire landscape. Every day he described his findings in a comprehensive diary, which he eventually published. Unlike many of his contemporaries, Schliemann kept his finds and recorded all of them, not just the spectacular pieces. And, although he has been castigated as little more than a treasure hunter, he in fact undertook the first large-scale dissection of a city mound where, unlike the situation at Nineveh or Nimrud, there were no sculptures to guide the way to ancient structures. As his digging experience increased, Schliemann began to rely more heavily on expert diggers, who were able to refine his methods drastically.

While Schliemann was working at Troy, German archaeologists had begun a quiet revolution in excavation methods that was to affect both the Troy excavations and many other digs as well. The Austrian archaeologist Alexander Conze dug at the site of Samothrace in Greece between 1873 and 1875. He dug with the help of architects and a photographer, who recorded the progress of the excavations. The Samothrace report was a beautiful production, the first to be illustrated with photographs. Conze's example was not lost on the German Archaeological Institute, which started work at Olympia in 1875. For six winters, Ernst Curtius directed a brilliant campaign of excavations on the site of the original Olympic Games. The Kaiser himself paid for part of the dig. Every find was carefully preserved and housed in a special museum built at the site. No artifacts were exported. Curtius and Wilhelm Dörpfeld worked out every detail of the stratigraphy at Olympia with the aid of new and very precise record-keeping methods. The Olympia excavations set new standards that the ever-energetic Dörpfeld took with him to Troy. In his later years at Hissarlik, Schliemann became what one authority has called "a constitutional monarch among expert ministers." Dörpfeld refined Schliemann's seven cities into the complex history of a mound that, he said, flourished from about 3000–700 B.C., the Homeric city dating from 1500–1000 B.C.

Curtius and Dörpfeld were concerned with the trivial as well as the spectacular. Their excavations were far more meticulous than those of their predecessors, although still crude by modern standards. A retired British general named Augustus Pitt-Rivers revolutionized the art of excavation even further. The general, a formidable personality, spent much of his military career working on the development of army rifles. His experimental research involved him in the history of firearms and the study of different types of primitive artifacts from all over the world. Pitt-Rivers was deeply interested in the evolution of human technology. He became an avid collector of artifacts of all types—masks, shields, weapons, even canoes. His collections became so large that he donated them to Oxford University, where they are to this day.

In 1880, Pitt-Rivers inherited an enormous estate in southern England, an estate littered with ancient burial sites and earthworks. The general decided to devote the rest of his life to investigation of the sites on his property. He did so with ruthless efficiency, diverting enormous sums from his fortune into leisured excavations that lasted twenty years, until his death in 1901. Pitt-Rivers had a mania for records and detail. "Every detail should be recorded in the manner most conducive to facility of reference," he wrote. "I have endeavored to record the results of these excavations in such a way that the whole of the evidence may be available for those who are concerned to go into it." He had realized a cardinal point: all archaeological excavation is permanent destruction and all objects found in a site have a vital context in time and space that is just as important a piece of information as the find itself.

The learned general was far ahead of his time. He trained archaeological assistants, had "before" and "after" models of his sites constructed, built a special museum to display his finds, and even marked his filled-in trenches with special medallions that said, in effect, "Pitt-Rivers was here." His ideas were revolutionary. Consider some of his basic principles of digging: "No excavation ought to ever be permitted except under the immediate eye of a responsible and trustworthy superintendant." "Superfluous precision may be regarded as a fault on the right side." "Tedious as it may appear to some to dwell on the discovery of odds and ends that have, no doubt, been thrown away by the owners as rubbish . . . yet it is by the study of such trivial details that archaeology is mainly dependent for determining the date of earthworks."

Hundreds of man-hours went into each of Pitt-Rivers's sumptuous reports. Each was published privately, complete with detailed plans, accurate measurements of every artifact, and precise information on every aspect of the site from pottery to hut foundations, stratigraphy to animal bones. It was to be years before anyone would equal or surpass Pitt-Rivers's painstaking work. He deplored the destruction of earthworks by plowing, laid out picnic grounds for people visiting his museum, and urged his fellow landowners to follow his example. The general was not a particularly endearing gentleman, but his legacy to archaeology is unquestioned. An interesting glimpse into the man comes from a photograph of the excavations which is tersely captioned: "The figure standing at attention in the foreground gives the scale.'' Evidently Pitt-Rivers was a military man, as well as an archaeologist, to the very end.

Few people followed Pitt-Rivers's example. One could still become an excavator without any training at all, although well-known archaeologists like Wilhelm Dörpfeld and the immortal Egyptologist Flinders Petrie were busy training students to follow in their footsteps. Petrie begged his colleagues to be quit of ''the brandy-and-soda young man . . . of the adventurous speculator. Without the ideal of solid continuous work, certain, accurate, and permanent, archaeology is as futile as any other pursuit.'' He went on to urge informal attire: ''To attempt serious work in pretty suits, shiny leggings or starched collars, would be like mountaineering in evening dress.'' ''It is sickening to see the rate at which everything is being destroyed,'' he once remarked, ''and the little regard paid to preservation.''

Some of the better digging that stemmed from Pitt-Rivers's work took place on Roman sites in Britain. Still, to modern eyes, the efforts appear to have been terribly amateurish and the excavators incredibly ill-equipped. Young Leonard Woolley, for example, later to become famous for his skilled excavations of royal graves at Ur-of-the-Chaldees in Mesopotamia, found himself in charge of a major Roman excavation without any experience at all or the least idea of how to survey a site or make plans.

The early part of this century also seems to have been a difficult period for female archaeologists. When a little-known archaeologist named J. P. Droop wrote a small manual on excavation in 1915, he spent a lot of time worrying about male/female roles. ''I have never seen a trained lady excavator at work,'' he admitted. ''Of a mixed dig, however, I have seen something, and it is an experiment that I would be reluctant to try again.'' His reasons were twofold. ''In the first place, there are the proprieties.'' Excavators should respect the etiquette and mores of the countries they are working in. Droop's other reasons were more personal. It seems that, in his experience, the ''charm'' of ladies vanishes during an excavation, for the dig lays on its mixed participants ''a bond of closer daily intercourse than is conceivable.'' Droop found this irritating. ''The ordinary male at least cannot stand it,'' he added. He cited the strain of ''self-restraint in moments of stress, moments that will occur on the best regulated dig, when you want to say just what you think without translation, which before ladies, whatever their feelings about it, cannot be done.'' Droop was never to know of the key roles played by twentieth-century women in major archaeological excavations the world over.

Nevertheless, there were a handful of women who carried out important work in the field long before female excavators became commonplace. One pioneer was the English novelist Amelia Edwards, a Victorian lady in the classic sense of the word, who embarked on a two-month journey up the Nile in 1874. She traveled in genteel company aboard a sailing ship complete with upright piano and proper chaperones. Edwards was horrified by the looting and destruction of Ancient Egyptian sites on every side, at the blatant forgery of antiquities, and the "black-robed, grave men, who always lay in wait ready to sell you anything." Nevertheless, she was entranced by the Pyramids, the Temple of Karnak, and Abu Simbel, by the columns of ancient temples which she compared to groves of redwood trees. Her *Thousand Miles Up the Nile* (1877) is one of the classics of early archaeological travel and still bears reading today. Edwards devoted the rest of her life to lecturing and writing about the destruction in Egypt and was instrumental in the founding of the Egypt Exploration Society, which works in the Nile Valley to this day.

Harriet Boyd Hawes, a Smith graduate who met Amelia Edwards while in college, was even more remarkable. In 1897, she traveled to Athens to study archaeology, one of the first women to do so. Archaeology soon took a back seat to nursing when Turkey declared war on Greece. For months, Hawes cared for wounded Greek soldiers within sound of artillery barrages, developing a passion for humanitarian causes that guided much of her life. Much to her surprise, she won a fellowship at the American School in Athens from Yale University, but was not allowed to excavate, this being considered a male domain. The British were more encouraging and she went over to Crete, where she combed the countryside for archaeological sites on the back of a mule. Her persistence was rewarded and she became the first woman to excavate a Minoan town. Hawes's monograph on Gournia is one of the classics of early Mediterranean archaeology. Not that Harriet did much more fieldwork, for she threw herself into humanitarian work among Serb soldiers in Corfu and served as a ward aid in American hospitals in France during World War I. But she opened doors into the narrow archaeological world for many talented women that followed in her footsteps.

There were other talented women pioneers, too, among them the redoubtable Gertrude Bell, who became an expert desert traveler and founded the Iraq Museum; Gertrude Caton-Thompson, who discovered what were then the earliest farmers in the world in Egypt's Fayum in the 1920s; and Dorothy Garrod, the first woman Professor of Archaeology anywhere in Europe, who excavated the Stone Age caves on Mount Carmel in the Levant in the 1930s. For the most part, they worked on shoestring budgets and often with few companions. But the discoveries they made contributed to the revolution in archaeological methods that took hold after World War I, in the hands of several capable excavators. Indeed the lax standards of Pitt-Rivers's contemporaries and successors were assaulted by archaeologists of the 1920s and 1930s. "There is no right way of digging but there are many wrong ones," wrote one of Pitt-Rivers's most avid disciples—Mortimer Wheeler. Wheeler, who was ten years old when Pitt-Rivers died, came to archaeology through the good offices of Arthur Evans.

discoverer of the ancient palace of King Minos on Crete. Wheeler spent his lifetime digging large sites with meticulous precision and training new generations of archaeologists in methods that owed their inspiration to the Victorian general.

Wheeler worked first on Roman forts, then on the famous Iron Age fortress at Maiden Castle in southern Britain. From archaeological evidence, he was able to reconstruct a blow-by-blow account of the Roman storming of that fort. After a distinguished military career in World War II, Wheeler was asked to head up the Archaeological Survey of India. With characteristic and flamboyant energy, he took up the task of organizing archaeology out of chaos. He found Roman imported pottery in southern India and dug deeply into the ancient city mounds of Harappa and Mohenjo-daro in the Indus Valley. There he sketched a fascinating picture of a long-extinct Indian civilization that had traded with Mesopotamia and developed its own distinctive, and still undeciphered, script. Mortimer Wheeler's excavations were, quite simply, meticulous, and the results remarkable. Most modern excavations build on the basic principles that he and Pitt-Rivers, as well as a handful of other pioneers, set out.

"The archaeologist is not digging up things, he is digging up people," Wheeler would begin. Good excavation takes imagination, an ability to understand what one is digging up. According to Wheeler, people who do not have this kind of imagination should collect bus tickets instead of digging. He believed the key to excavation was accurate observation and recording of occupation levels and architectural features, of the layout of burials and minute artifacts. The relationship between different objects in the ground can tell one much about the behavior of their makers, he taught his students. Wheeler's excavations were models of tidiness, with straight walls and carefully swept trenches to make the tasks of observation and discovery more precise. The observation of superimposed layers and the features and artifacts in them would give one an accurate chronology to work with, an essential framework for studying the numerous pot fragments and other finds from the dig. He pointed out how buildings should be dissected with great care, so that the foundations could be related to the underlying, dated strata and the contents isolated from those in other parts of the site. The burials Wheeler found were exposed bone by bone and carefully photographed in position before removal.

All of Wheeler's excavations were carefully designed not only to find artifacts but to answer specific questions about chronology or other matters. These questions were formulated in advance or as the dig was in progress. The staff of the excavation was organized into a hierarchy of specialists, led by the director himself, whose task was to "cultivate a scrupulous accuracy and completeness in the observation and record of his factual evidence." Wheeler's ideal director had "the combined virtues of the scholar and the man of action," an ability to achieve accuracy "not

1-5. Sir Mortimer Wheeler's excavation through the mud-brick defense wall of the citadel at the prehistoric city of Harappa in Pakistan. A classic example of superb, scientific excavation.

for accuracy's sake, but as a basis for using his imagination to interpret his finds." "Archaeology," wrote Wheeler, "is primarily a fact-finding discipline." But, he would always add, we have to dig sites as a means to an end, the end being the understanding of humanity's complex and changing relationship with its environment.

Schliemann dug up the past of Troy. He and many other early archaeologists taught us that archaeological sites contain many treasures. Curtius, Dörpfeld, Pitt-Rivers, and Wheeler developed techniques for recording the contents of each site in meticulous detail. And Wheeler himself threw down the gauntlet to his successors—he challenged them to apply these recording methods to such complex problems as "estimating the density and social structure of populations." His words were prophetic, for that is what leading archaeologists are now trying to achieve.

Mortimer Wheeler died in 1976 after witnessing a revolution in digging methods all over the world, a revolution whose impact is still being felt. His students and their students, as well as those of other pioneering archaeologists, have refined his methods even further. Some idea of the complexity of a modern excavation can be gained by a brief look at the investigation of an ancient site at Olduvai Gorge in Tanzania. The site dates to about 1.75 million years ago.

"Archaeology," wrote British archaeologist Stuart Piggott some years ago, "is the science of rubbish." And rubbish is precisely what Louis and Mary Leakey had to dissect when they excavated the scatters of bones and stone artifacts in the lowest levels of Olduvai Gorge. All that remained were small scatters of discarded animal bones, stone tools, and waste chips, lying in irregular concentrations on the very land surfaces ancient people once trod. Often the scatter of artifacts and bones was only a few inches thick and was sealed under dozens of feet of sterile sand and lake clay. How old were these scatters? What activities took place there? Could any information on prehistoric diet and food-getting methods be obtained from the scatters? These and many other questions came to mind as the Leakeys began clearing these small but complicated sites. They had no doubt as to the importance of their excavations: these were probably among the earliest traces of human behavior in the world. To avoid damaging any human fossils and to prevent disturbance of the artifacts from their original positions, only the most delicate methods could be used.

Each scatter lay within a major geological horizon of Olduvai Gorge, one that the Leakeys knew dated to the earliest millennia of the human experience. But dating samples had to be obtained, that is, lumps of lava that could be dated by laboratory tests for their radioactive content. These samples had to come from the scatters themselves, from lava fragments that had actually been carried to the site by those who had lived there. The Leakeys had no choice: they knew they must excavate each entire site, plot all the objects on them, and obtain dating samples from among the finds in the scatter.

One site yielded the famous skull of *Zinjanthropus* in 1959, a discovery we describe in chapter 3. Mary Leakey orginally found a portion of the fossil outcropping from the lower lake beds of the Gorge. A small excavation was immediately undertaken at the site of this discovery to aid both in the removal of the precious skull and in establishing the exact level from which the fossil came. The immediate surroundings of the skull were sifted carefully in case additional fragments had already fallen down the slope on which it was found. The trial excavation yielded broken animal bones, some rodent fragments, and a few stone tools that lay in place near the skull. There seemed a strong possibility that the skull was directly associated with the tools—indeed, its owner might have made them.

It was seven months before Mary Leakey could return to the site, for the skull had been found at the very end of the 1959 season. When the time came for larger-scale excavations, she did not attack the site at once. Her task was to establish the precise position of the artifact scatter in the Olduvai geological strata. To determine this, she dug a six-foot trial trench in steps through the entire forty feet of the geological bed the skull had come from, right down to bedrock. She found that the scatter was halfway up the bed.

Once the stratigraphical position of the fossil skull was established, Mary Leakey set out to determine the extent of the scatter itself. The workmen removed the sterile over-burden of lake bed from the area around the trial trench. This unproductive soil was removed with picks and shovels in rough levels. When they reached a whitish-yellow volcanic-ash zone that Mary Leakey knew directly overlay the precious scatter, they stepped aside. The trench was now divided into four-foot-wide strips that were worked one by one with great care. Skilled workers carefully pared away the volcanic ash to within a few inches of the underlying artifacts and bones. Sometimes bones and other finds protruded through into the ash. So dry was the soil that the excavators had to dampen it before removal to guard against damaging valuable fossils underneath.

The scatter proved to be about a foot thick. With great care, Mary Leakey worked each strip of the trench from one side of the floor to the other. Whenever possible, every find was cleared from the surrounding soil with dental probes and small paintbrushes. Every find of any size, whether a stone tool or an animal bone, was marked with black or white ink and plotted on the floor plan before being lifted. A complete photographic record of the site was maintained as well. Once the larger finds had been removed, the soil was wet- or dry-sifted through one-sixteenth-inch screens so that even the tiniest stone chips and bone fragments were recovered for laboratory analysis. As a result of this painstaking excavation, the position of every significant find on the site was known to within an inch or less. What a contrast to Belzoni's burial chambers or Layard's palaces!

The man-hours expended on the *Zinjanthropus* site were well worth the expense. The amount of detail about early human lifeways that came from the *Zinjanthropus* floor was truly astonishing, all of it the result of meticulous excavation. In addition to the dating samples gathered—which proved the site to be 1.75 million years old—the Leakeys obtained data on the dimensions and layout of one of the earliest archaeological sites in the world. Mary Leakey found and took apart a concentration of stone tools and flakes and over a thousand broken bone fragments covering an area twenty-one feet by fifteen feet near the spot where *Zinjanthropus* was found. This central zone was separated from another concentration of bones by a less densely covered area that she felt might have been the site of a crude shelter. We know that the inhabitants used crude stone choppers and many flakes in the preparation of food and the butchering of small animals. They smashed the limb bones of antelope and zebra and broke open the skulls to remove the brain. But large scavengers like hyenas visited the site as well and chewed up some of the freshly broken bones—presumably after the inhabitants left. None of this information could have been obtained without rigorous excavation techniques. The Leakeys literally drained the site of information.

Each excavation has its own distinctive problems of preservation and recording, but burial sites are among the most challenging of all archaeological problems. Howard Carter spent ten years clearing and preserving the finds from Tutankhamun's tomb in Egypt. In this case, the diggers were more concerned with removal and preservation of funerary furniture than with actual excavation. Still, before removal to the laboratory, the position and context of each piece of grave furniture were carefully recorded.

Cemeteries and even individual burials can provide vital information on the social status of the people buried there. Their costumes, grave furniture, and the circumstances of their burial often reveal a great deal about the individual and the society. Burial excavation involves recording the arrangement of the grave goods and the position of the skeleton even before the find is removed from the ground. Once the presence of a grave is suspected, the first stage is to outline the burial pit and its filling and to identify any surface features that may have marked the ancient grave. Then the pit filling is carefully removed with dental probe and light brush, until the bones and grave furniture appear and the general orientation of the skeleton is established. Many hours later, the complete burial and the pots, ornaments, or other grave furniture are picked clean of clinging soil, so that the grave, its furniture, and the skeleton are all clearly exposed for the eye of the camera. Only when every detail of the burial is described in notebook and recorded on film will the grave be removed. Especially important burials may be lifted in one piece, using a casket of plaster of Paris and steel rods. Less important skeletons are disarticulated and removed piece by piece.

Archaeological literature abounds with stories of remarkable feats of recovery in which extremely delicate or highly fragmentary artifacts have been rescued from oblivion. Water-logged conditions on a site create colossal excavation problems, but often result in spectacular finds. The Danes have recovered two-thousand-year-old corpses from damp bogs, sacrificial victims with clothing, hair, and skin still intact. Richard Daugherty had to use pressure hoses at Ozette in the Pacific Northwest to uncover long-buried cedarwood houses and their highly perishable contents. Dutch archaeologists were able to trace the outlines of corpses in the sandy subsoil under burial mounds, even though the actual flesh and bones had long since vanished. Discolored stains left in the soil from the process of decomposition were exposed by careful scraping of the subsoil.

The Dutch achievement pales considerably beside Leonard Woolley's recovery of the long-vanished wooden harp of Lady Shub-ad of Ur-of-the-Chaldees. Woolley's first clue to the whereabouts of the harp was a gold cap of the upright, found loose in the soil of the royal cemetery. Next, some isolated gold nails came to light. Exploring further, the excavators found a small hole angling steeply down into the ground. A flashlight revealed more gold nails deep in the hole. Woolley inserted a small stick into the shaft and filled the interstices with liquid plaster. As the soil was cleared away, the stem of a harp, preserved in plaster, emerged from its burial place. By using paraffin wax and fine muslin, Woolley was able to recover the mosaic inlay of the sounding box and the gold and lapis lazuli calf's head that had decorated the front of the instrument. Subsequently Woolley could reconstruct a very accurate version of the entire original instrument, simply because he was able to record all the instrument's salient details from the impression they had made in the ground before they decomposed. And he was able to recover fragments of the harp that a less skilled or less experienced excavator would have completely missed.

Archaeology has come a long way since Leonard Woolley performed miracles with plaster at Ur. Today, it is a sophisticated science that calls on experts from dozens of academic disciplines. It owes much to the natural and physical sciences, to revolutionary dating techniques, described in chapter 2, that enable us to date 2.5-million-year-old archaeological sites or tiny fragments of a wooden spear shaft extracted from the socket of a bronze spearhead used three thousand years ago. Computers enable archaeologists to manipulate vast data bases of artifacts and food remains, to plot intricate jigsaw puzzles of waterlogged timbers that once formed a prehistoric house. We can trace the sources of volcanic rock used to make mirrors in three-thousand-year-old Mexican villages, establish whether stone workers making tools in a Belgian hunting camp ten thousand years ago were left- or right-handed. Using minute pollen grains, we can

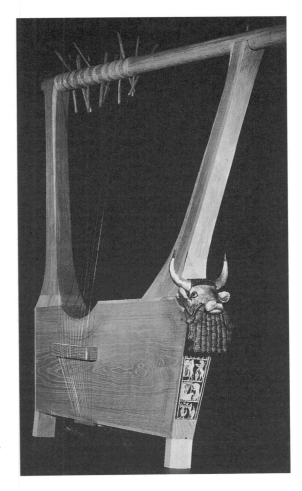

1-6. Bull-headed Lyre from Ur.

reconstruct the landscape around twenty-thousand-year-old Stone Age winter camps. Thousands of bison bones from an ancient mass kill on the American Plains can be reassembled so precisely that we know exactly how bison hunters of eight thousand years ago butchered their prey.

But the greatest advances of all have not been in the field or the laboratory, where all the hi-tech wizardry of archaeology comes into play. They have been in the ways in which we think of archaeology and plan our research. Much early archaeology was designed to recover as many spectacular objects as possible. This is what Layard strove for at Nimrud and Nineveh, and Schliemann at Hissarlik. Today's archaeology has three much more sophisticated goals: to construct the culture history of the past, to reconstruct ancient lifeways, the ways in which people made their living, and, most important of all, to explain how and why ancient human cultures changed through prehistoric times. This is where the most important advances in archaeology have been made—in seeking to explain why humans took up farming and abandoned hunting and gathering, or what caused people to congregate in cities, develop writing, and establish a literate civilization. Studying such topics has involved the development of sophisticated theoretical models for explaining and interpreting the past, models that owe much to evolutionary and ecological theory. Science now realizes that archaeology is about the only discipline that enables us to study human biological and cultural evolution over long periods of time. The development of the tools to do so ranks among the greatest scientific triumphs of this century. Not that archaeology is confined to such topics, for in recent years there has been an explosion of interest in such issues as gender roles in ancient societies, and in such fascinating problems as social inequality in the past. One of the great fascinations of modern archaeology is its sheer range and diversity that accommodates archaeologists who study everything from foraging camps that are millions of years old to Mayan cities and abandoned railroad stations from the Industrial Revolution.

   This book tells the stories of some early archaeologists and makes no pretensions to being a textbook on the sophisticated methods and theoretical approaches of late twentieth-century archaeology. But chapter 2 discusses some of the basic principles of archaeological research, so that you have some understanding of the difficulties and challenges that face not only today's archaeologists, but their illustrious predecessors, who often struggled against much greater practical and scientific odds. After reading it, you may feel that archaeology has become yet another dull and specialized academic discipline, one where mind-numbing detail has taken the romance out of the past. Nothing could be further from the truth, for there is a tremendous satisfaction and excitement in searching out the past. Even today, most talented archaeologists, at one time or another, feel they are in touch with the people they are studying. They seem to have an instinct for discovery, to know where to search and dig, and a sense of identity with their subjects. This sense seems to have been highly developed in Louis Leakey, Heinrich Schliemann, and Howard Carter. Carter experienced an almost eerie bond with Tutankhamun. He summed it up well when he wrote: "I stood in the presence of a king who reigned three thousand years ago." One suspects Carter was not speaking strictly figuratively: he felt he *really had*. Sometimes, as I have stood gazing over a long-deserted prehistoric settlement, silent on a cool evening as the sun casts long shadows over earthworks and eroding occupation deposits, I have experienced a sudden collapse of time. The site comes to life: thatched huts rise from the ground, scented wood smoke ascends in the evening still, dogs bark and children laugh in play. Outside their huts, old men sit and gossip quietly for a brief evening hour. Then, just as quickly, the image recedes and the village once again becomes a deserted archive of archaeological information, a silent complex of mud-hut foundations, dusty pot fragments, and broken food bones. For a moment, the ancient inhabitants of that village sprang to life, shedding their cloaks of anonymity to reach out across the millennia. Heady emotions, perhaps, but, for a moment, one understands why archaeology is so much more than just a set of techniques and tools for digging up the past.

2

HOW ARCHAEOLOGY WORKS

Her skin pricked as she brushed away the last particles of fine dust. A magnificent gold mask gazed up at her, mantling the countenance of the long-dead ruler. Kathy felt as if she was intruding on a private domain. As she reached for her camera, the other members of the team crowding around her, the fragile bones of the skull collapsed softly into dust . . ." Romance, high adventure, gold-decked pharaohs . . . such is the archaeological world of popular imagination, of Indiana Jones and all manner of movie and TV heroes. But what do archaeologists really do? Are they engaged in relentless pursuit of buried treasure, or are they sober scientists, detectives of the past who derive as much satisfaction out of reconstructing a minor village society as they do from finding the richest of royal sepulchers? Today, they are highly trained scientists, who use advanced technology and meticulous research methods to reconstruct the past. This book is about great discoveries, about early archaeologists of flair and imagination, some of them trained scientists, others not. But before we tell the story of these discoveries, we should examine some of the basic principles of archaeology, explore how archaeology works.

What Is Archaeology?

Today, archaeologists study more than 2.5 million years of the human past. They probe for the origins of humanity in East Africa, excavate sites that chronicle the first settlement of the Americas and Australia, record ancient Maya inscriptions, even survey the remains of nineteenth-century factories and railroad stations. Archaeology spans the entire spectrum of human experience, from our origins to the remains of the Industrial Revolution. Some experts even probe modern urban landfills, using archaeological methods to study modern waste discard patterns. Modern archaeology is—simply defined—the study of human behavior in the past. As students of ancient human behavior, archaeologists are anthropologists as well, members of the scientific discipline that studies every aspect of humankind, living and extinct.

We are all familiar with the most spectacular of archaeological discoveries, with household finds like the tomb of the Egyptian pharaoh Tutankhamun, described in chapter 9, or the recent find of a deep-frozen Bronze Age traveler unearthed, his skin and features intact, from a glacier in the European Alps. Most of these unusual discoveries are the result of exceptional preservation conditions, often made in arid, frozen, or waterlogged sites where the local environment halts the processes of natural decay. For the most part, however, the realities of preservation mean that the archaeologist works with less spectacular finds, only with the most durable of artifacts such as stone tools or fired clay vessels. Thus, we can amplify our definition of archaeology by saying that archaeologists use the surviving, material remains of the past to study ancient human behavior and human culture in the past.

The Goals of Archaeology

As the study of ancient human behavior, archaeology has three fundamental objectives:

—The study of the past in time and space—what is often called Culture History (see below),

—The reconstruction of ancient lifeways—how people lived in the past,

—Understanding the processes of culture change in the past—what is sometimes called cultural process (also see below).

Since archaeology studies the human past over more than 2.5 million years, it offers an unrivaled way of examining human biological and cultural evolution over long periods of time.

Prehistory, History, and Anthropology

Archaeologist James Deetz has called an archaeologist a "special type of anthropologist," an apt definition, for, like anthropologists, we are concerned with human behavior. Anthropology is the study of human behavior in the broadest possible sense. Cultural anthropologists study living societies, whereas archaeologists study the societies of the past— ancient human behavior. Archaeology is also history, for much archaeological research into later centuries and millennia is carried out in conjunction with historians.

Archaeology is a highly specialized science, which is hardly surprising, given the great antiquity of humankind. Conventionally, archaeologists divide their discipline into several broad specialties.

Prehistoric archaeologists study prehistory, those periods of the human past that unfolded before the advent of written records. Prehistory begins with the origins of humanity more than 2.5 million years ago, but ends at very different moments all over the world. For instance, the earliest

2-1. Burial from the Behrens site, Kalomo, Zambia, (c. A.D. 1850).

◀ **2-2.** Stela D, Quirigua. Also known as Monument 4. Dedicated 9.16.15.0.0. 7 Ahau 18 Pop. Erected by Cauac Sky to celebrate a *hotun* (5-year) period ending. Numerals are rendered as rare full-figured glyphs. Each cartouche contains two entwined figures, a number god and a time-period god. *Translation:* These three cartouches are a portion of the Long Count date, 9.16.15.0. 0. 7 Ahau 18 Pop.
Top: A smiling god of Zero sits tangled in the limbs of a reptilian *uinal* (20-day month) god. Meaning: no uinals.
Middle: Another Zero-god, this one in profile with a fleshless lower jaw, holds the chin of a *kin*, or day-god. Meaning: no days.
Bottom: Seated figure of the number 7, in profile, looking upwards, next to an elegant day cartouche with a profile of the day, Ahau. Meaning: 7 Ahau.

of all written records come from Mesopotamia and Egypt in about 3,000 B.C. while the Romans introduced writing to Britain in 55 B.C. or shortly thereafter. Although the ancient Maya of Mesoamerica developed a hieroglyphic script, most of the Americas did not enter an era of written documentation until long after Columbus's arrival in 1492. The Chinese were writing before 2,000 B.C., while central Africa remained preliterate until the late nineteenth century.

Few prehistoric archaeologists command the entire prehistory of humankind, so there are specialists in all kinds of prehistoric archaeology. Paleoanthropologists like Mary Leakey study the earliest humans, while others work on the Cro-Magnon peoples of late Ice Age Europe, the Aegean Bronze Age, or on farming cultures in eastern North America—the specialties are endless. In recent years, archaeology has become more and more specialized, to the point that it is possible to find archaeologists spending their entire careers investigating a single valley in Ohio or doing nothing but work with isotopic analysis, radiocarbon dating, or some other specialized method.

Historical archaeologists study sites and cultures that are also known from historical records. This general label, sometimes referred to as document-aided archaeology, covers not only Classical archaeologists, who study ancient Greece and Rome, but experts on Biblical archaeology, Mediterranean shipwrecks, European medieval towns, or Colonial settlements in North America. Industrial archaeology is a flourishing field, concerned as it is with sites from the Industrial Revolution, while University of Arizona archaeologist William Rathje has spent many years studying modern city garbage dumps, as a way of understanding the waste discard patterns of ancient and modern societies.

The Archaeological Record

All archaeologists, whatever their specialty, work not with the historian's documents, but with a myriad of archaeological finds, large and small—simple stone choppers, elaborately decorated clay pots, fine gold ornaments, the remains of a long-forgotten hunt. These make up the archives of the past—the archaeological record.

The *archaeological record* is the data base of artifacts, sites, and other finds found on the surface or excavated by archaeologists. This record can take many forms. The great Pyramid of Knufu at Giza in Egypt forms part of the archaeological record. So does the tomb of the Maya lord Pacal at Palenque in Guatemala and an undistinguished painted potsherd from a two-thousand-year-old village in Illinois. What do a 2-million-year-old stone knife made by an archaic human in East Africa and a fifteen-hundred-year-old South American basket have in common? Both, like millions of other finds, belong in the archaeological record. Like historical archives, whether the records of a recent American president or of an obscure medieval Italian law case, the archaeological record requires care and attention, for it is all too easily destroyed and lost forever.

The archaeological record that has come down to us is a sorry reflection of once vibrant, living cultures. From the moment a site was abandoned or a dwelling burnt down, the forces of human activity and nature have acted on it. Fast-moving floodwaters may flow over a collapsed house, sweeping everything except heavy foundation stones before them. Inexorable ocean winds may mantle a deserted hunting camp with feet of sand within days of abandonment. Acids and other chemicals in the soil leach away organic remains such as bone, leather, or wood and leave only tough organic substances like stone or clay behind. It is small wonder that our knowledge of the past is so incomplete and no surprise that archaeologists have exercised great ingenuity in developing ever more fine-grained methods for conjuring up information about the past from the soil. For example, archaeologist Nicholas Toth of Indiana University has taught himself how to replicate the crude flake tools used by the very earliest humans more than 2 million years ago. Not only did he learn how to make precise copies of the tools, he actually reconstructed the stone technology used by our earliest ancestors to the point where he could tell that some of the tool makers were left-handed.

Many people have likened the archaeologist to a modern-day detective reconstructing intricate developments in the past from a mere handful of clues. The analogy is an apt one, for many archaeologists do indeed spend much of their time following seemingly insignificant clues. For instance, archaeologist Ivor Nöel Hume found a tiny length of twisted gold thread in the foundations of a house at Martin's Hundred, a Colonial settlement

2-3. Archaeologist Nicholas Toth flaking an Oldowan core of basalt.

in Virginia abandoned in 1621. By using historical records and studying pictures of early seventeenth-century dress, he was able to show that the house had once belonged to a man named William Harwood, who was the only person in the village permitted by law to wear gold-thread ornaments (called "points") on his garments.

Imagine trying to reconstruct your own daily life from, say, a spark plug, a frying pan handle, a TV set knob, a needle, and a shoe buckle. This is precisely what archaeologists do every day, sometimes with astounding success. One British archaeologist has described archaeology as "the science of rubbish." In some ways he is right, for archaeologists spend much of their time delving into ancient garbage heaps.

Artifacts, sites, and *structures* are all part of the archaeological record and are terms that we shall refer to frequently in this book. Archaeological sites take many forms. They are locations where archaeological finds have been made, whether an enormous Southwestern Pueblo or a handful of crude stone artifacts from the Australian desert. The Pyramids of Giza in

Egypt are an archaeological site. So is Hadrian's Wall in northern Britain and the Inca settlement at Macchu Picchu high in the Andes. An isolated stone axe found in Africa's Zambezi Valley is technically an archaeological site, a find spot on the map that reveals the existence of ancient human occupation.

While an archaeological site may technically consist of an isolated find, most contain artifacts, tools made by their occupants. The term "artifact" covers a multitude of finds, objects manufactured by humans, or natural items subsequently modified by people for a specific purpose. A sword or a pot are obvious artifacts, but so are minute glass beads, crudely sharpened sticks, and grinding stones.

Artifacts can be distinguished from structures, which are the remains of all forms of construction erected by human beings. These include everything from simple storage pits sunk into the ground to the vast Temple of the sun god Amun at Karnak, Egypt, and the mud-brick houses of Chan Chan in Peru.

Food remains, the remnants of animal and plant foods consumed by our ancestors, are another important part of the archaeological record. They include broken animal bones, like those of late Ice Age mammoth and bison found in twenty-thousand-year-old cave deposits in France, and the domesticated sheep and goats from a nine-thousand-year-old farming settlement at Abu Hureyra, Syria. Thanks to sophisticated flotation methods that pass samples of archaeological layers through water and screens, we know a great deal about the diet of Midwestern Indian communities that existed some four thousand years ago. The microscopic remains of native plants like goosefoot and marsh elder survive by the thousand in the deposits of these long-abandoned communities. Such finds enable us to reconstruct ancient diets and to study an all-important transition in human history, that from hunting and foraging for food to deliberately growing crops and herding domesticated animals.

The archaeological record provides the raw material for the study of the human cultures in the past.

Culture and Cultural Systems

We humans are unique among all animals in that we use artifacts of our own manufacture to adapt to our environment. The arctic fox has a thick white coat that enables it to survive long, sub-zero winters in the far north, and remain invisible to its prey. Monkeys with their long limbs and prehensile fingers and toes survive comfortably in the tropical forest canopy

2-4. The Hypostele Hall at Karnak, by late nineteenth-century photographer Felix ▶ Bonfils.

far above the ground. Only humans adapt to their surroundings by using their own culture to do so. We regulate relationships with the environment through technology and social and belief systems. For example, the Inuit hunter of the Canadian archipelago uses a skin kayak with wood or bone frame and skin covering to hunt seals with a harpoon in open water. The Gwembe Tonga farmer of the Zambezi Valley in central Africa lives in a hut with the thinnest of walls, so that cooling breezes can keep the occupants cool. The technology used to make these artifacts is passed down from one generation to the next, as are all the customs and knowledge a group possesses.

Culture is learned behavior, something unique to humans. More than a century ago, pioneer anthropologist Edward Tylor set down a useful definition of culture: "That complex whole which includes knowledge, belief, art, morals, law custom, and any other capabilities and habits acquired by man as a member of society." This is fine as a general definition, but archaeologists think of culture as the primary non-biological means by which human societies adapt to, and accommodate, their environment. In short, it is the cumulative intellectual resources of human societies. The notion of culture is a theoretical concept that enables archaeologists to explain the products of human activity.

Unlike anthropologists, who study living societies, archaeologists have the means to study changes in human cultures over immensely long periods of time. For instance, the earliest humans, *Homo habilis* (a name that means "Handy person") used the same simple toolkit and enjoyed much the same culture for more than a million years apparently without major change. Thus, their primary concern is with the processes of cultural change over time, the ways in which humans have adapted to changed circumstances over decades, centuries, and millennia. All cultural change is, in the final analysis, cumulative, beginning with the simplest of cultures enjoyed by the first humans and their successors and culminating in the elaborate, ever changing cultures of modern industrial societies.

Anthropologist Leslie White has argued that human culture is made up of many structurally different parts which articulate with one another within what he called a "cultural system." This cultural system is the means whereby human societies adapt to their physical and social environments. They have many interacting components and interact with other systems, such as that of the natural environment. So close are the linkages between cultural and environment systems that changes in one or the other can have profound effects on the other. For instance, the Ice Age hunters who lived on the frigid open plains of the Ukraine eighteen thousand years ago lived in a treeless environment. Therefore, they depended heavily on the hides and bones of large animals like mammoths for building their dwellings.

A major goal of archaeology is to understand the relationships between human cultural systems and local environments, also in the relationships within a cultural system, between, say, grinding stones and the role of wild plant foods in a prehistoric diet. By examining not only artifacts and structures, but their distribution within archaeological sites, an expert can acquire an astounding range of information about ancient life. At a prehistoric farming village at 'Ain Ghazal in Jordan, occupied in about 7,000 B.C., archaeologist Gary Rollefson was able to identify distinctive marks on the leg bones of domesticated goats, which told him that the people tethered their herds within the settlement, a distinctive form of animal husbandry that is commonplace in the region to this day.

Culture History and Cultural Process

Today, we gaze back over a vast landscape of long-extinct and still-living human cultures in every corner of the globe. Until the mid-nineteenth century, scientists believed largely in the literal historical truth of the scriptures, accepting the veracity of the Creation story in Genesis, chapter 1. Under this rubric, Archbishop James Ussher calculated that the world had been created in 4004 B.C., allowing a mere six thousand years for all of human existence. While many religious groups still believe fervently in the historical veracity of the Creation, the theory of evolution and modern dating methods have convinced most scientists that humanity originated at least 2.5 million years ago, giving them a vast period of time in which to study evolving human society in a context of time and space. As we shall see, this context of time and space is vital to archaeology, for it provides us with the framework for what is called culture history, the study of human cultures in time and space.

Culture history is a process of ordering human cultures in time and space, of erecting local sequences of human societies that can be compared one with another from one region to the next. This process of comparison takes place with the aid not only of dates in years, but by sophisticated artifact comparisons as well. Culture history is a descriptive process, one that gives us a chronological and spatial framework for studying ancient societies through time. It is an essential preliminary to the study of early lifeways and to research into the processes of culture change.

Cultural process is the study of the processes of culture change through time. It is not a descriptive form of research, but one that seeks to explain *why* human cultures changed through time. It involves using sophisticated theoretical models that delve not only into the mechanics of changing human adaptations to local environments through time, but also into the intangible factors that affected culture change. Working as they do with material remains, it is hard for archaeologists to reconstruct a long-extinct language or religion, although impressive reconstructions of, say, ancient Egyptian or Maya political history and religious beliefs have been made combining archaeology with deciphered inscriptions.

Very often, archaeologists refer to this form of archaeology as a "culture as adaptation" approach to the study of the human past. It often involves precise measurement of the ways in which human societies adapted to, say, climatic change at the end of the Ice Age, or to environmental deterioration brought about by overgrazing semi-arid grassland, as happened in the central Sudan with the kingdom of Meroe in the fourth century A.D. The study of cultural process assumes that all cultures are in a constant state of change, as their political, social, and technological subsystems adjust to changing circumstances. The challenge for the archaeologist is to *explain* these changes. It is not enough to state, for example, that farming developed first in the Near East, then spread into Europe. What were the mechanisms behind these developments? What were the processes of cultural change within each society before and after the appearance of the new economy?

Explanations for cultural change in the past have ranged from the simplistic to the very complex. Early theories of human development assumed, for example, that all human societies had evolved in a similar direction, from simple hunter-gatherer cultures to the pinnacle of human achievement—modern industrial civilization. Thus, some societies were more "advanced" than others. When it became apparent that such evolutionary schemes were too simple, new schools of thought claimed that the major inventions of human history such as agriculture and civilization had developed in one place, then spread all over the world. Perhaps the most famous of these "diffusionist" hypotheses were those of British anthropologist Grafton Elliot Smith, famous for being the first scholar to X-ray an Egyptian mummy. He believed that civilization and sun worship first developed in the Nile Valley. Then bold voyagers carried these revolutionary ideas across the Atlantic and Pacific to distant lands.

Even in Smith's day, many critics laughed at his ideas for being ridiculously simplistic. But such dramatic theories of the spread of great civilizations persist in popular literature to this day. The Sunken Continent of Atlantis, the Ten Lost Tribes of Israel, ancient Egyptian warships voyaging to the Americas centuries before Columbus, even ancient astronauts from outer space: all have been the heroes of fantasy adventure tales that purport to tell the story of early civilization. None of them are based on rigorous science, for the clues assembled by the authors of these tales come from many places and many lands, linked together to weave a stirring tale. They collapse immediately in the face of generations of archaeological discoveries such as those described in this book, and should be recognized for what they are—pseudo-science, or science fiction.

Studying and explaining the human past involves extremely careful scientific investigation, using procedures and research methods that depend, ultimately, on the fundamental concept of context in time and space.

Context in Time and Space

Consider for a moment a fine bronze sword displayed in a museum case. It is mounted on end, its weathered edges glowing dark green in the soft light. The sword is a finely made artifact that once had a decorated wooden handle and a brightly shining, razor-sharp blade. A label tells us the sword was made in about 1100 B.C. A question immediately comes to mind. How do we know with such confidence that the sword was made in that year? If the artifact comes from a scientific excavation, we know that its context in time and space was recorded on-site.

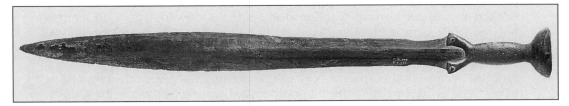

2-5. 1100 B.C. Bronze Age slashing sword.

Archaeological sites are not just collections of tools, structures, and food remains. Each artifact, every broken food bone or tiny seed, every house, has a relationship in time and space to all of the other finds from the same site. This relationship is their "context."

Thus, our fine bronze sword is far more than a magnificent example of a prehistoric artisan's skill. It is a scientifically excavated artifact, whose relationships to other finds in the site and date are precisely established—an artifact in context. Without this vital information, the sword, like so many superb artifacts in the world's museums, is of limited value except as a fine art object. The museums and art galleries of the world are filled with beautiful objects that have been collected by treasure hunters out for a quick profit. Without a known context, they can tell us little about the people who made them.

Time and Superposition

My cat has just walked into my study, as I throw a pile of manuscript (part of this chapter, in fact) on the floor. The white paper stands out against the dark carpet. He flicks his orange tail and settles down comfortably on the documents for a nap. A short time afterward, I need the chapter, so I gently pry some of the pages out from under the protesting feline. After a plaintive miaow, he settles down on the remaining sheets and settles into well-earned slumber. It is, after all, just after breakfast. This is a good example of the Law of Superposition. If archaeologists were to excavate the ruins of my study centuries later, they would find a dark carpet with a pile of paper on it, lying under a cat skeleton that has been disturbed in antiquity. In more technical parlance, the papers are superimposed on the carpet and the cat bones are in turn superimposed on the manuscript.

The Law of Superposition comes into play as the archaeologist reconstructs the sequence of events. It is the principle, derived from geology, that the lowest strata (layers) are earlier than the ones that cover them. Thus, the archaeologist concludes that the papers were left piled on the carpet. Subsequently a cat lay down on them, only to be disturbed later, perhaps by someone removing some documents from the pile. This is known as *relative chronology*, the study of the chronological relationships between different archaeological layers, observed during archaeological excavation by the process of stratigraphic observation.

Note that the archaeologist's observations tell us nothing about the amount of time that elapsed between the manuscript being thrown on the carpet and subsequent events. It could have been seconds, minutes, days, even years. They have merely established the chronological relationships between the finds. The chronology of the human past in Table 1-1 (see chapter 1) is a combination both of thousands of stratigraphic observations of relative chronologies from all corners of the globe and of *chronometric dating*, dating in calendar years.

Chronometric (Absolute) Dating

Four chronometric dating techniques provide at least an outline chronology for the past:

Historical Records date back about five thousand years in Egypt and Mesopotamia, but they are of limited use until about 2,000 B.C., when royal and temple archives proliferated. As we have seen, writing came into use very much later in most parts of the world, making historical records of only limited use, except for studying early civilizations. Sometimes objects of known age, like dated coins, come to light in settlements beyond the frontiers of the historical civilizations. For example, Roman coins of known age were traded over enormous distances and sometimes occur in British villages far from the invaders' garrisons or towns, thereby cross-dating them.

Tree-ring Dating (Dendrochronology) is based on the counting of the concentric growth rings that can be seen in the cross section of a felled

2-6. Pueblo Bonito, Chaco Canyon, New Mexico, dated by dendrochronology to about A.D. 1100. This photograph was taken in about 1954 before recent conservation work.

tree. Such rings are especially useful in areas like the American Southwest, with its sharply seasonal rainfall, indeed it was in this region that astronomer A. E. Douglass first developed dendrochronology. He managed to link sequences of tree rings from ancient Indian beams with those from living trees, creating a master ring sequence that enabled him to date such famous pueblos as Mesa Verde and Pueblo Bonito in Chaco Canyon with great accuracy. Southwestern chronologies go back as far as 322 B.C., but far earlier time scales have come from European oaks, extending back more than 7,262 years in Ireland.

Tree-ring chronologies are extremely accurate, but they are limited to relatively recent times, and to areas with well-defined rainfall patterns. They do, however, provide an excellent way of calibrating radiocarbon dates.

Radiocarbon dating is the most famous of all chronological methods and was developed as a direct result of research on the atomic bomb project in World War II. It is based on the fact that cosmic radiation produces neutrons that enter the earth's atmosphere and react with nitrogen to produce the carbon isotope carbon-14 (C-14). There is a constant ratio of carbon-14 and normal carbon (C-12) in the atmosphere, a ratio that is found in all animals, whether animal or plant. However, when an organism dies, the C-14 is no longer replenished from the atmospheric reservoir. It is unstable and will, in time, radiate its additional neutrons and revert to carbon-12. The C-14 decay starts at death and proceeds at a constant rate that is easily counted with a geiger counter. After 5,730 years, half the original amount will be left, a quarter after 11,400 years, and so on. By calculating the difference between the amount of C-14 originally in the sample and the amount left, and comparing the difference with the amount left, we can compute the number of years that have elapsed since death.

Radiocarbon samples are taken from many kinds of organic samples, among them charcoal, burned bone, and wood. By using accelerator mass spectroscopy, a scientist can now count actual C-14 atoms instead of measuring decay rates. This method has the advantage of requiring samples so small that one can even date an individual tree ring! It also allows one to date such samples as a tiny speck of wood from inside a metal axe socket, so that one can date an actual artifact rather than, say, the remains of a hearth.

Radiocarbon dates are actually statistical approximations that come from the laboratory with plus or minus readings that give a measure of the reliability of the sample. Unfortunately, variations in the strength of the earth's magnetic field and in solar activity have affected the concentrations of radiocarbon in the atmosphere and in living things over the centuries, so radiocarbon dates require calibration against precise chronologies developed from comparing C-14 and tree- ring dates. Such calibrated chronologies go back about six thousand years, while the outer range of radiocarbon dating is about forty thousand to sixty thousand years. Fortunately, however, extreme accuracy is less important for earlier periods, when archaeologists work with dates in millennia rather than centuries.

Radiocarbon dating is of vital importance to the archaeologist, for it enables one to compare the chronologies of widely separated cultures, like, for example, Minoan civilization in Crete with the Olmec civilization of Mexico. It enables one to measure rates of cultural change and to develop a broad framework for all of later human prehistory.

Potassium-Argon dating is a counting method used to date very early human sites situated in areas where volcanic rocks formed by crystallization are to be found. It has been used to date geological deposits tens of millions of years old. Fortunately, many of the world's earliest archaeological sites, like Olduvai Gorge in Tanzania (chapter 3) lie in the heart of volcano country, so it has been possible to date some of the first chapters of human evolution.

Potassium (K) is one of the most abundant minerals in the earth's crust and contains a small proportion of the radioactive isotope K-40. For every one hundred atoms of K-40 that decay, 11 percent will become an inactive gas, Argon-40. As volcanic rocks form by crystallization, the concentration of Ar-40 drops to almost nothing. But the decay of K-40 continues, so 11 percent of every one hundred atoms of K-40 will become Ar-40. By using a spectrometer, one can measure the concentration of Ar-40 that has accumulated since the rock formed. Like radiocarbon dates, potassium-argon dates are a statistical approximation, one that gives us at least a provisional chronology for human origins. They tell us that the first tool-making humans flourished in East Africa at least 2.5 million years ago. Potassium-Argon dating can be used on sites as late as 100,000 years ago, so we have dating methods that provide us with coverage of almost the span of the past.

Space: The Law of Association

Archaeological context has a second dimension, that of space. Imagine yourself at the side of the famous eighteenth-century British navigator, Captain James Cook, aboard his ship, the *Resolution*, bound for Tahiti in the heart of the vast and unknown Pacific. Cook was a remarkable navigator by any standards. Using only the most primitive of navigational instruments and a crude chronometer, he managed to sail from England to Tahiti in nine months and make an accurate landfall without sighting land for weeks. He did so by using the sun and stars to compute his latitude and longitude, which gave him his precise latitude and longitude on earth—his position in space. Archaeologists establish an artifact's context in space by establishing its latitude and longitude in space. They do this by means of precise horizontal and vertical measurements that record the precise position of a find in the trench in which it is uncovered, which, in turn, is tied into a grid reference point on a map with its latitudes and longitudes in the margins.

While some very valuable artifacts, or the scatter of stone artifacts and animal bones on a land surface at Olduvai Gorge, are recorded in position one by one, the fundamental principle when studying space in archaeology is that of the second fundamental law of archaeological context—the Law of Association. The Law of Association states that an artifact found in a specific layer is contemporary with the other objects, be they other tools, hearths, even dwellings, found in the same level. A good example is the burial of the pharaoh Tutankhamun. He was interred in a rock-cut tomb, accompanied by a dazzling array of grave furniture and personal possessions (chapter 9). They were buried with him and are thus, associated with the mummy and contemporary with it.

Doing Archaeology

This is a book about exciting archaeological discoveries, many of them made in days when the archaeologist was more interested in spectacular finds and artifacts than in reconstructing minute details of the past. How, then, do today's archaeologists design their research work, find and excavate sites, and analyze and interpret their finds in the laboratory?

The Process of Archaeological Research

Time was when an archaeologist simply went out to find sites and dig the most promising one, without any advance preparation. In contrast, today's excavators spend many hours developing a research design, defining a specific problem to investigate, and doing background research. They develop carefully formulated hypotheses to be evaluated against data in the field and in the laboratory, raise funds for the fieldwork, and recruit a team of specialist experts to work with them on environmental data, animal bones, and many other topics.

This first stage can take many months and eventually leads into the second, data acquisition in the field. This can take the form of a survey looking for sites, a preliminary dig, or a large-scale excavation. Whatever the kind of data acquisition, no digs these days are on the scale of those conducted by pioneer workers like Austen Henry Layard in Mesopotamia (chapter 5). He could afford to employ hundreds of laborers for cents a day to carry out vast excavations using methods that would set a modern digger's hair on end.

Returning from the field laden with drawings, notes, photographs, and boxes of finds, our excavator now enters a long and laborious chapter in the work, the processing and analysis of the data. Radiocarbon samples are sent to dating laboratories, animal bones and deeds identified, artifacts sorted and classified, everything analyzed in preparation for the final stages of the research: interpretation and publication. The interpretative stage is, perhaps, the most interesting, for it is when everything is brought together to answer the questions formulated in the original research design. These interpretations are made within a theoretical framework, a means by which archaeologists look beyond the finds and material objects for explanations of cultural change.

Finally, the completed study is put on permanent record through formal publication in a scientific paper or monograph. This is the most important stage of all, for it ensures that scientists everywhere can draw on one's fieldwork, on data one has removed from its archaeological context, which is now only recorded in one's field notes. The important point is this: archaeological excavation is also destruction, destruction of archaeological context that can never be replaced in the soil.

Finding and Digging Archaeological Sites

How do you find sites? How do you know where to dig? These questions fascinate newcomers to archaeology intrigued by the apparent ease with which archaeologists find and excavate seemingly invisible sites. No question that instinct, a "feeling" for the past and knowing where to dig, plays a vital role in archaeological discovery, as the stories in these pages show. But most sites are found either by accident or as a result of deliberate archaeological survey.

Many archaeological sites come to light by chance, as the result of farming, road construction, urban renewal, and all kinds of industrial activity. Sometimes, too, archaeologists stumble on sites by accident, as German butterfly hunter Wilhelm Kattwinkel did at Olduvai Gorge (chapter 3). Thousands of Aztec Indian artifacts, even an entire temple, came from the tunnels dug for Mexico City's subway system in the 1970s, while European farmers sometimes dig up spectacular hoards of bronze and gold artifacts buried in times of trouble by their long-forgotten prehistoric owners.

Some sites have never disappeared from memory, like, for example, the Pyramids of Giza in Egypt (chapter 8), Stonehenge in Britain, or the city of Teotihuacán in the Valley of Mexico (chapter 11). But most sites are difficult to identify except with the trained eye; an eye adept at spotting telltale grey patches of ash and potsherds dug out by rabbits burrowing into ancient villages, or the stunted grass growing on four-thousand-year-old Indian shell middens in California. Finding such locations requires carefully designed foot surveys, carried out with the aid of well-designed sampling strategies that allow one to predict and calculate site densities on the landscape while covering only a fraction of the total area. Perhaps the most comprehensive archaeological survey ever carried out was that by a team of archaeologists led by William Sanders of Pennsylvania State University in the 1970s. They surveyed large areas of the Basin of Mexico and studied the changing patterns of landscape use in the heartland of highland Mexican civilization over three thousand years. Most surveys are on a far smaller scale, but they are designed to locate sites of all kinds, to make surface collections of artifacts from them, and to help assess the most likely places where controlled excavation will answer specific questions.

Modern archaeologists rely more and more on "remote sensing" devices, aerial photographs, satellite images, even sub-surface radar, which enables them to locate sites not only within the context of the local landscape, but often when they are invisible on the ground. For example, sub-surface radar revealed buried house foundations at the Maya village of Ceren in San Salvador, which was buried with volcanic ash in the sixth century A.D. Aerial surveys have revealed entire Roman road systems in

2-7. Stonehenge, England

North Africa and long plowed-down prehistoric earthworks throughout Europe.

Archaeological Excavation

Modern archaeological excavation is a highly disciplined process of digging and recording. As we have pointed out, the archaeological record is finite. Once disturbed, archaeological context in time and space is gone for ever. Thus, all excavation is designed in such a way as to do minimum damage to undisturbed deposits while at the same time answering the questions posed in the research design.

Even as late as the 1930s, archaeologists like Leonard Woolley would boast of the enormous size of their excavations, of their veritable armies of workers run by loyal foremen. Woolley shifted thousands of tons of earth from the great city mound at Ur-of-the-Chaldees in southern Mesopotamia. He uncovered entire royal cemeteries and mazes of narrow streets and small dwellings and cut a trench down to the humble village at the base of the mound. These were scientific excavations by the standards of the day, but the information and records from the dig are woefully incomplete by today's criteria. Half a century later, archaeologists dig on a much

2-8. Tollund Man, a Danish sacrificial victim of about 100 B.C., perfectly preserved in waterlogged bog deposits.

smaller scale, working with sophisticated techniques that enable them to sample even a large site without moving large amounts of earth and employing large work forces. The closest analogy is the public opinion poll, which uses what is called probability sampling, a way of relating tiny samples in mathematical ways to large populations. Archaeologists employ somewhat similar methods to plan many excavations.

Excavation involves recording archaeological context in the most economical manner possible. Small scale investigations often employ vertical excavation, to establish the sequence of occupation layers, to locate major structures, and to collect samples of artifacts. The dig consists of a series of small trenches that are designed to acquire relatively limited kinds of information about chronology, the nature of a site, and artifacts, often as a preliminary to larger scale excavations in a later season.

Horizontal excavation involves clearing much larger areas of a site. It is usually used on shallower sites, where the excavators are trying to reconstruct the plan of a settlement, to excavate dwellings, or acquire information about specific activities such as stoneworking or pot manufacture. This technique is especially effective when excavating small hunting camps, places where people have butchered big-game animals, or structures like small burial mounds. Horizontal excavation is, of course, much more expensive than vertical trenching, but is highly effective when research designs call for the acquisition of large quantities of food remains, structural information, stone tools or potsherds. It also allows for the plotting of houses and other features, and of the artifacts in them.

Archaeologists have excavated every kind of archaeological site imaginable, everything from two-million-year-old hominid meat caches to ancient cities and pharaohs' tombs. The approach used varies greatly from one excavation to the next. The Leakeys used horizontal excavation at Olduvai Gorge with great skill, recovering finds as small as mice bones. Richard Daugherty combined vertical and horizontal trenching at Ozette, Washington (chapter 4), for he was concerned to recover not only the remains of collapsed plank houses, but details of the early history of the

2-9. Horizontal excavation of the bath suite of a courtyard house in the Arbeia Roman Fort, South Shields, England. The near figure stands in the hot bath area, while the two figures beyond are in the hot and warm rooms. The far figure stands in the cold plunge bath room.

village as well. At the other end of the spectrum, Egyptologist Howard Carter used picks and shovels to find the hidden entrance to Tutankhamun's tomb (chapter 9), then established the precise context of every find in the sepulcher by measurement and photography. But whatever the challenge, whatever the date of the site, the same basic principles of disciplined recording and infinite care apply. Unlike some of the pioneer archaeologists profiled in later chapters, modern excavators are well aware that archaeology is one of the few sciences that destroys its archives as it investigates them.

Analysis of Artifacts and Food Remains

For every month of excavation there is at least six months' laboratory analysis, a long process of classifying, analyzing, and interpreting the finds from the dig. Such finds come in many forms. Stone tools, clay potsherds, and other artifacts tell us much of the technology of our forebears. Broken animal bones, seeds, shells, and other food remains, even desiccated human feces, are a mine of information on ancient subsistence, and sometimes diet. All of these finds are combined to produce a reconstruction of human behavior at the site.

Artifact Analysis. Human artifacts come in many forms. The most durable are stone tools and clay vessels; while those in wood and bone often perish in the soil. Archaeologists have developed elaborate methods for classifying artifacts of all kinds, classifications based on distinctive features like clay vessel shapes, painted decoration on the pot, methods of stone flaking, and so on. Once they have worked out a classification of artifact types, the experts use various arbitrary classificatory units to help order groups of artifacts in space and time.

These units include the assemblage, which is a diverse group of artifacts found in one site that reflects the shared activities of a community. Then is the component, a physically bounded portion of a site that contains a distinct assemblage. The social equivalent of an archaeologist's component is a community. Obviously a site can contain several components, stratified each above the other. Finally, the culture, a cultural unit represented by like components on different sites or at different levels of the same site, although always within a well-defined chronological bracket.

Archaeological "cultures" are concepts designed to assist in the ordering of artifacts in time and space. They are normally named after a key site where characteristic artifacts of the culture are found. For instance, the Acheulian culture of early prehistory is named after the northern French town of St. Acheul, where the stone hand axes so characteristic of this culture of more than 200,000 years ago, are found.

2-10. Acheulian handaxe from the Thames River, England.

Analyzing food remains.   How did prehistoric peoples make their living? The answer comes not only from artifacts like stone axes and digging sticks, but from food remains of all kinds. Animal bones provide valuable information on hunting practices, on herding and management of domesticated animals, and on butchery techniques. For example, a band of Paleo-Indian hunters drove a large bison herd into a gully at Olsen-Chubbock, Colorado, in 6,000 B.C. By analyzing the thousands of bison bones in the gully, archaeologists have managed to reconstruct the standardized butchery techniques the Indians used after the hunt.

Plant remains survive at many sites and can be recovered by using flotation techniques—floating soil samples through water and fine screens and collecting the light seeds from the surface while the residue falls away. Ancient seeds show us that foraging for wild plant foods was of vital importance to human societies from the earliest times. They also provide insights into ancient agricultural techniques, into the cereal and root crops that sustained early farming societies and early industrial civilizations for thousands of years. Fish bones, freshwater and sea shells, and mollusks, as well as artifacts and ancient rock paintings, tell us much about prehistoric subsistence patterns.

Reconstructing actual prehistoric diets is much harder, for differential preservation of food remains causes many foods to be under-represented in the archaeological record. Desiccated human feces found in dry caves in western North America have told us much about prehistoric Indian diets as early as six thousand years ago. Sophisticated carbon isotope analyses use the ratios between two stable carbon isotopes—C-12 and C-13—in animal tissues to establish the diets of prehistoric populations as they switched from wild plant foods to a predominantly cereal diet.

Interpreting the Archaeological Record

Interpretation of artifacts and food remains provides clues as to ancient human behavior. Archaeologists use three major approaches to interpretation: ethnographic analogy, ethnoarchaeology, and controlled experimentation.

Analogy. Sometimes analogies between living societies and those of the prehistoric past can yield fruitful insights. Such analogies are thwart with difficulty and are carried out under carefully controlled conditions. For example, comparisons of Inuit harpoons from the Canadian arctic can sometimes give insights into prehistoric bone artifacts from the same region, even those manufactured a thousand years earlier.

Ethnoarchaeology. The study of living peoples and their material remains, ethnoarchaeology can provide valuable interpretative information. Some archaeologists have lived for long periods among living hunter-gatherer and subsistence farming societies like the San hunter-gatherers of the Kalahari Desert in southern Africa. They plot the distribution of artifacts and food remains on abandoned living sites of known age, using such data, and other behavioral information, as a basis for interpreting much more ancient societies.

Controlled experimentation. Controlled experiments with ancient technology can yield valuable information. For instance, by replicating the stoneworking techniques used by prehistoric peoples, some prehistorians have been able to reconstruct minute details of ancient stone technology, even establishing that some very early humans were left-handed! Other controlled experiments have felled trees with stone axes and blown replicas of King Tutankhamun's trumpets.

Subdividing Prehistoric Times

The 2.5 million years of human prehistory have seen a brilliant diversity of human societies both simple and complex flourish at different times throughout the world. Ever since the early nineteenth century, archaeologists have tried to subdivide prehistory into meaningful general subdivisions, with varying degrees of success.

The most durable subdivisions of the prehistoric past were devised by Danish archaeologist Christian Jurgensen Thomson in 1806. His Three Age System, based on finds from prehistoric graves, subdivided prehistory into three ages based on technological achievement—the Stone Age, the Bronze Age, and the Iron Age. This scheme has been proven to have some general validity in the Old World, and is still used as a broad label to this day. However, the term "Stone Age"—often called the Paleolithic Age (after the Greek for "old stone age")—has little more than technological significance, for it means that a society has not the use of metals of any kind. "Stone Age" has no chronological significance, for societies without metal vanished in the Near East after 4000 B.C., yet still flourish in New Guinea to this day. We only use the Three Age System in the most general way here. New World archaeologists have never used the Three Age system, largely because metallurgy of any kind was of limited distribution in the Americas. They tend to use more local terms.

In recent years, archaeologists have tried to classify prehistoric societies on the basis of political and social development. They subdivide all human societies into two broad categories: Prestate and State-organized societies.

Prestate societies are invariably small scale, based on the community, band, or village. Many Prestate societies are bands, associations of families that may not exceed twenty-five to sixty people, the dominant form of social organization for most hunter-gatherers from the earliest times up to the origins of farming. Clusters of bands linked by clans, groups of people linked by common ancestral ties, are labeled tribes.

Chiefdoms are societies headed by individuals with unusual ritual, political, or entrepreneurial skills, and are often hard to distinguish from tribes. Such societies are still kin-based, but power is concentrated in the hands of powerful kin leaders responsible for redistributing food and other commodities through society. Chiefdoms tend to have higher population densities and vary greatly in their elaboration. For example, Tahitian chiefs in the Society Islands of the South Pacific presided over elaborate, constantly bickering chiefdoms, frequently waging war against their neighbors.

State-organized societies operate on a large scale with centralized political and social organization, distinct social and economic classes, and large food surpluses created by intensive farming, often employing irrigation agriculture. Such complex societies were ruled by a tiny elite class, who held monopolies over strategic resources and used force and religious power to enforce their authority. Such social organization was typical of the world's pre-industrial civilizations, civilizations like those of the ancient Egyptians and Assyrians, that functioned with technologies that did not rely on fossil fuels like coal.

Archaeological Theory

Archaeologists study human prehistory within broad theoretical frameworks. Such theoretical approaches are a means for looking beyond the facts and material objects from archaeological sites for explanations of cultural developments and changes that took place during the remote past. As we have seen, the most common approach thinks of human cultures as cultural systems interacting with their natural environments—environmental systems of which they are part. This "culture as adaptation" approach is concerned not only with the evolution of prehistoric cultures, but also with reconstructing ancient environments and ways in which past cultures made their living.

At the core of this paradigm is the notion of multilinear cultural evolution, multiple-branched evolution that saw highly diverse human societies evolve from the simple to the more complex in many different ways. It is also based on the doctrines of cultural ecology, which think of human cultures as systems interacting with other human cultures, the biotic community, and the physical environment over long periods of time.

Proponents of culture as adaptation theories argue that each human society pursues its own evolutionary course, determined by the long-term success of its adaptation, via technology and social institutions, to the natural environment. The culture as adaptation approach is now widely accepted as a general framework for the study of human prehistory.

Intense controversy surrounds new generations of archaeological theory that draw on evolutionary biology, behavioral ecology, and studies that focus on the acts of individuals rather than impersonal cultural processes.

New, highly sophisticated evolutionary theories that combine ecological models with biological and cultural developments are likely to dominate the study of early prehistory. As far as later prehistory is concerned, we can expect a new emphasis on research into changing gender roles in ancient societies and into ethnic diversity in complex societies. Of concern, also, are the different ways in which Western and non-Western societies conceive of archaeology and the past, for fundamental cultural and ideological differences can affect the ways in which one interprets the archaeological record.

Such, then, is an outline of the basic principles of modern anthropological archaeology, a hi-tech, extremely specialized science that studies ancient human societies, whether humble bands or great pre-industrial civilizations, in every corner of the world. This sophisticated discipline developed out of the pioneer researches of many remarkable adventurers and archaeologists, whose stories appear in these pages. Today, we may deplore some of their methods, but without their discoveries and insights, today's science would be impossible. Their excavations laid the foundations for one of the great scientific achievements of this century—the development of scientific archaeology.

3

The Leakeys' VALLEY OF BONES

Olduvai Gorge in East Africa was a quiet and warm place on July 17, 1959. The Gorge's steep slopes shimmered in the African heat as Mary Leakey crouched over the dry sands of its lowest geological beds. For weeks, she and her husband Louis had been looking for traces of ancient campsites. Now, while Louis lay sick in their base camp on the lip of the Gorge, Mary continued the unending search for ancient human fossils. This particular day she was working at a place where the Leakeys had found traces of bones and stone tools months before.

Mary worked slowly and painstakingly in the hot sun. The only sounds to be heard were the scraping of trowels and dental picks and the labored panting of the family's two dalmatians, Sally and Victoria. Suddenly, Mary spotted some bone fragments eroding out of the sloping wall of the lowest levels of the Gorge. Electrified, she carefully scraped away the clinging soil from two large teeth. They were unquestionably those of a humanlike fossil, the first to be found in Olduvai Gorge. Mary jumped in the Land Rover and tore up to camp. "I've got him! I've got him," she cried as she burst into the tent. His illness forgotten, Louis leaped into his clothes and, together, husband and wife rattled down the track to the site. With great care, they examined the teeth and prised away more soil. There could be no doubt: Mary Leakey had uncovered a fossil skull of tremendous antiquity. A search that Louis Leakey had begun over twenty-eight years before was finally crowned with success that hot July day.

The destinies of Louis Seymour Bazett Leakey and his wife Mary were inextricably intertwined with a "valley full of bones . . . they were very many in the valley, and lo, they were very dry." The valley is Olduvai Gorge in northern Tanzania, East Africa, and the bones are those of some of the earliest humans ever found. Together, the Leakey family has added more to the story of early humanity than have any other archaeologists. Some of their discoveries resulted from sheer luck, most from dogged hard work, and a few from a sense of vision that only truly great archaeologists possess. The Leakeys displayed an uncanny prophetic sense that enabled them to bring forth bones from the ground and rewrite human prehistory.

The whole of Louis Leakey's long life was linked in some way with East Africa. His father, a pioneer missionary, settled in Kikuyu country near the young town of Nairobi in 1902. Louis was born a year later, the first white baby many Kikuyu had seen. As an infant, Louis learned both Kikuyu and English and was partially initiated into the tribe. For the rest of his life, he called himself a white Kikuyu. The Kikuyu lore that Leakey learned as a child was to prove invaluable later in his life.

Although his father saw to it that Louis had a solid schooling, young Louis's main preoccupations were hunting and trapping small animals. From his Kikuyu mentors, he learned the importance of keen observation and patience, two qualities essential for an archaeologist. "My Kikuyu training taught me this," he wrote in the *National Geographic* many years later, "If you have reason to believe that something should be in a given spot but you don't find it, you must not conclude that it isn't there. Rather, you must conclude that your powers of observation are faulty."

At the age of thirteen, Louis met Arthur Loveridge, curator of the new museum in Nairobi, who encouraged him to study wildlife instead of hunting it. When a loving aunt in England sent Leakey a book about prehistoric stone axes, it was Loveridge who encouraged him to look for similar tools in Kenya. Within a few weeks, Leakey had found several boxes full of stone tools that looked just like the European examples illustrated in his book. Thus was kindled a lifelong interest in archaeology and natural history, pursuits that required all the patience and powers of observation that the Kikuyu had taught Leakey to cultivate.

By the time Louis applied to Cambridge University, he had already decided he would become a great scientist. Since anthropology, his chosen subject, was only studied at an advanced level, two modern languages were required of degree candidates. One was an obvious choice—French. His father had insisted that he study it from an early age. Characteristically, Leakey chose Kikuyu as his second modern language. The university authorities were at a loss. Indeed, Kikuyu filled the modern language requirement, for it was a language spoken by large numbers of people. Furthermore, Leakey's own father had translated the Bible into Kikuyu. It was thus a written tongue. In addition, one competent examiner in Kikuyu resided in England at the time, duly registered with London University—Louis Seymour Bazett Leakey himself! Displaying a touch of genius, Leakey had taken the precaution of registering himself as an examiner a few months before. And his certificate of competence was signed not only by a missionary, but with the thumbprint of a Kikuyu Senior Chief as well.

Leakey started his Cambridge career by teaching his examiner in Kikuyu the language—for the standard university fee. He threw himself into all manner of pursuits and was ejected from the tennis courts for playing tennis in shorts, dress considered to be grossly indecent. He took up conjuring and sawed women in half, and acquired an interest in handwriting that was to stand him in good stead when he became involved with police work in later years. His brand of Rugby football was so violent that, when he was kicked in the head, the doctor advised a year out of school.

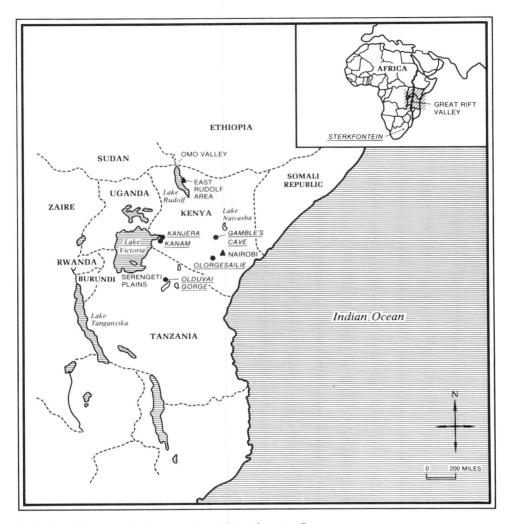

3-1. Locations and sites mentioned in chapter 3.

Instead of moping in England, Louis got himself a job as an assistant on a British Museum dinosaur-hunting expedition to Tanzania. After a hectic year, during which he learned how to lift fossils with plaster of Paris, Louis returned to Cambridge in January of 1925. He was literally bankrupt and supported himself by giving lectures on dinosaur hunting at private schools. For the first time, Leakey learned how to thrill an audience with his tales of exciting discoveries and far-off lands. It was another skill that was to prove invaluable.

Louis went on to study archaeology and anthropology and came under the influence of the great ethnographer A. C. Haddon, a formidable personality with an encyclopaedic knowledge of the world's non-Western peoples. He encouraged Louis to study early technology and, when his young protégé graduated with first-class honors, helped him find money to return to East Africa with his own archaeological expedition.

With Haddon's assistance, Leakey found himself with enough money to support himself and a companion for several months and enough time to find out something about the archaeology of Kenya. There was little to go on. Although a geologist named E. J. Wayland had recovered tons of prehistoric artifacts during geological expeditions in Uganda, Kenya remained a complete archaeological blank. Leakey had corresponded with Wayland for months and was certain he would find similar sites in the Great Rift Valley near Nairobi. In his letters, Wayland had described a sequence of dramatic climatic changes—alternating periods of heavy rainfall and drier conditions—that had persisted in Uganda throughout prehistoric times. Had such climatic changes occurred in Kenya as well? How long had Stone Age people lived in East Africa? These questions were to occupy Leakey's mind throughout his career.

The 1926 expedition had been in the field only a short while when Mr. Gamble, a local resident, showed Leakey two rock shelters that looked promising. So expedition members took up residence in one of Gamble's disused pigsties and proceeded to dig into the deep deposits under the cliff. By the time funds ran out, Leakey had found abundant signs of prehistoric people in Gamble's cave and thought he had evidence of ancient climatic change in the Rift Valley, too. Wayland came, saw, and approved. Louis immediately began to make plans for a second expedition. He obtained a small income for himself and managed to recruit a party of five people to accompany him. He also married Frida Avern, whom he had met in Kenya the year before. Her first home was the Gamble pigsty, which also served as base laboratory for the new excavations.

Gamble's Cave proved to be a prehistoric gold mine, one that took over seven months to excavate. Leakey dug through twenty-eight feet of occupation deposit and was soon finding over seven hundred stone tools a day, each of which had to be catalogued and examined in the evenings. The finds provided a chronicle of prehistoric peoples that went back, Leakey claimed, over twenty thousand years. He found traces of ostrich-eggshell beads, large numbers of small tools delicately fashioned from black volcanic glass, and numerous animal bones from slaughtered game. So complicated were the geological events of the Rift Valley that Louis appealed to the Governor of Kenya for assistance. He was granted a thousand pounds, sufficient for Leakey to cable A. C. Haddon in Cambridge: "Find me a geologist." And Haddon did. Leakey would soon have the evidence for ancient periods of high rainfall that he had been looking for since 1926.

3-2. Louis Leakey

By this time, Leakey's reputation as an archaeologist was well established; he was regarded as an up-and-coming young man in his field. Anyone planning a scientific expedition to Kenya automatically consulted Leakey. The Kenya government used his expertise, too: he served on the Kikuyu Land Commission in 1929 and, while a member, looked into the grievances that erupted ultimately into the Mau Mau rebellion of the 1940s.

One particular archaeological discovery continued to fascinate Leakey during this time, a report of a human skeleton found in 1913 at a remote gorge in northern Tanganyika named *ol duvai* (Masai: "place of the wild sisal"). The Olduvai Gorge was discovered quite by chance: one day in 1911, German entomologist Wilhelm Kattwinkel literally stumbled across it while hunting butterflies. He is rumored to have tripped over the edge and bounced over three hundred feet to the bottom. As he made his way back up the side of the Gorge, he picked up some fossil bones outcropping from erosion gullies. The experts on fossils who examined the bones back in Germany were very excited. Kattwinkel had inadvertently picked up fragments of a three-toed horse and other unknown extinct animals. So the geologists asked Dr. Hans Reck, at that time a member of the Geological Survey of German East Africa, to look for more.

The interior of East Africa was so unfamiliar to Europeans at that time that Reck had considerable difficulty finding Olduvai. He knew it was somewhere on the Serengeti Plain, a vast grassland that teemed with herds of antelope and other game, just as it had for thousands of years. So, outfitted with a hundred porters, he trekked to the Serengeti and, after considerable difficulties, managed to find the Gorge. For three months, Reck searched Olduvai from one end to the other. He recovered hundreds of fossils and spent a great deal of time trying to untangle the geology of the Gorge. At least four distinct sandy beds could be seen in the walls, all dating from several hundred thousand years ago. Millennia before, a large freshwater lake had extended over the Serengeti Plain. Herds of extinct mammals had once drunk from its waters, some of them dying nearby. The lake then rose and covered their rotting carcasses with sand. Much later, a series of earthquakes cut through the deposits of the dry basin, exposing the evaporated lake, along with the bones of the animals that had died on its shores.

Just as Reck was about to leave Olduvai, he made his most dramatic discovery. He nearly stepped on a human skeleton eroding out of a grave deep in the lake beds. Reck was astonished. If the grave actually belonged to this deep level, it must date to hundreds of thousands of years ago. The skeleton lay in a crouched position and was obviously of a modern anatomical type. But why was it lying in such early beds when, presumably, more primitive people were in existence at that time? Was this an early human fossil *in situ*? Reck himself went home and claimed it was, touting "Olduvai Man" as a truly ancient find. Most scientists disagreed with him. The German Kaiser himself was so interested in the finds that he sponsored a new expedition, a venture that was aborted by the First World War. So Olduvai Man remained a mystery until Leakey came along.

Leakey first heard of Reck in Munich in 1925. The two men—the one ambitious, fast talking, and excitable, the other tall, fair, and more easy going—struck up a friendship at once. When Leakey finally saw the Olduvai human remains, he was struck by the close resemblances between Reck's find and the skeletons he had discovered at Gamble's Cave. He was convinced that the burial was much more recent than Reck claimed. Without further ado, he invited Reck to accompany him to Olduvai in 1931—and this, long before he had obtained the money to go! With his usual luck, however, Leakey soon raised some twenty-five hundred pounds from various sources and obtained the support of the British Museum, which was interested in fossil mammals from the Gorge. The museum sent

A. T. Hopwood, a fossil expert, along with the party.

Getting to Olduvai in 1931 was a major undertaking. Leakey hired an ex-Indian officer as a guide to blaze a motor track to the Gorge. Captain Hewlett was also an expert shot, which, as it turned out, was extremely fortunate—he shot two lions while protecting members of the party. Leakey himself had to kill a wounded rhinoceros that charged him. In late September 1931, Leakey, Reck, Hopwood, and Hewlett set out with eighteen Africans on a four-day trek along Hewlett's pioneer trail. The three trucks and one automobile bounced along the rough track at a snail's pace, a journey that Leakey always recalled with pleasure. When they reached Olduvai, the pools of water that Reck and his men had drunk were dry. Alternate supplies were eventually found twelve miles away.

Incredible as it may seem, Reck had never found a single stone implement in all his weeks at Olduvai. He had seen hundreds of them in museums, all European specimens made from fine-grained flint and very easy to identify. There were no flint deposits in East Africa. Prehistoric peoples used coarser materials like lava and quartzite, and occasionally obsidian if they could find it. Expecting flint, Reck had found nothing. Leakey, however, although interested in fossil mammals, was certain even when he first heard of Olduvai that prehistoric tools would be found there. The German was unconvinced.

"I bet you ten pounds that I find a hand axe within twenty-four hours," countered the brash Leakey.

Quietly the geologist agreed. The bet was a sizable chunk of Leakey's valuable research funds. But only a few short hours after starting down the walls of the Gorge, Leakey gave a cry of triumph. He pointed to a stone hand axe protruding from one of the upper beds of the Gorge. Ten pounds duly changed hands.

Leakey was wild with excitement. For six weeks he and his colleagues combed the sides of what turned out to be a vast treasure house of prehistoric sites, as well as of Pleistocene animals. There were over eighteen miles of main and side gorges to traverse, many of them steep cliffs and sharp rocks. The Gorge was dry and very hot, with a resident population of rhinoceroses who resented human interference. All supplies had to be brought in along incredibly rough tracks at great expense. Yet Leakey was in his element with an archaeological challenge that he realized would take him back earlier into human history than anyone had ever been before. With the extraordinary vision that characterized so much of Leakey's work, he felt certain that one day he would find the bones of early humans in this arid place. He also knew it would take years to locate them.

The first step was to work out the geology of Olduvai Gorge. Even today many features of its complicated strata remain a mystery. Leakey and Reck were able to identify five large geological beds, most of them consisting of fine sands and clays that had been laid down in the shallow

3-3. Olduvai Gorge

water of the now-desiccated lake. It was at the edge of this lake that the many animals whose bones lay in the Gorge had drunk. When the two men looked more closely at the strata, they found that the lowest two beds, which they labeled I and II respectively, were closely similar—indeed, passed into each other with few signs of a break. The lowest lake deposits lay directly on a thick layer of volcanic ash, the result of a large eruption millions of years before. A striking red bed overlay the lowermost two beds. Its red earth could be seen for miles, in marked contrast to the whiter levels above and below it. Originally Reck argued that this bed was laid down at a time when there was no lake at Olduvai, but it is now thought to have been deposited under much the same conditions as the earlier beds. Bed IV lay directly above the red horizons of Bed III and seemed very similar to the lower levels of the Gorge. Fish and crocodile bones came from Bed IV, as did fragments of hundreds of large mammals. But, at the close of Bed IV, major earth movements cut a deep gorge through the long-established lake, in some places right down to the volcanic bedrock under Bed I. The edges of the Gorge were subsequently covered with windblown sands, a thin Bed V that is comparatively very recent.

The four older geological beds were found throughout the length of the Gorge. Reck was able to trace them not only in the main gorge itself but also in a side gorge that extended southwestward from the middle of Olduvai. The lowermost beds were particularly well exposed in the mouth of this side gorge—indeed, it has proved to be one of the richest areas of Olduvai. The floor of the main gorge was affected by several geological faults. A stream ran through Olduvai on the rare occasions when there was any lengthy rainfall. It took Reck weeks to work out the geology, for the four major beds were twisted and convoluted by earth movement and erosion, and often covered with dense scrub vegetation. Then, too, there was always the danger of meeting a stray rhinoceros among the thorn brush. Reck achieved miracles under very difficult conditions. He concluded that the Olduvai lake existed during a prolonged period of relatively dry conditions, during which there were several periods of increased rainfall. The many animals found in the lake deposits told him that the lake had existed during the earlier millennia of the Pleistocene epoch or "age of humanity," the most recent of geological periods. Olduvai lake was several hundred thousand years old. But Reck had no means of knowing actually how old the various beds were. At the time, no one had developed a way of dating sites as early as Olduvai. It was to be a quarter of a century before the earliest beds could be dated at all accurately. And when they were, the readings caused a sensation.

As Leakey and Reck fanned out over the Gorge they found that its many gullies were crammed with fossils and stone tools. Each locality received a name after its discoverer—for example, RK for Reck's Karongo, *karongo* being the Swahili word for gully. They worked over an area within five miles of the camp and found stone tools in all of the four Olduvai beds. Most of the stone implements found in Beds II to IV were axe forms, with sharpened edges that became progressively better trimmed and straighter as time went on. But the lowermost bed contained much cruder tools, coarse choppers formed by chipping off a few flakes from a lava lump to make a very simple jagged cutting edge. These remarkable tools were obviously flaked by a human hand and, in their simplicity, seemed to be the earliest and crudest in the world. The first examples were found in a gully Leakey named Frida Leakey Karongo (FLK), in honor of his wife who was in faraway Nairobi. Twenty-eight years later, his second wife Mary was to find a fossil skull only yards away.

While these exciting discoveries were coming to light, Leakey spent some time puzzling over Reck's ancient skeleton, which seemed such a chronological anomaly. On the face of it, the skeleton seemed to be contemporary with Bed IV, for its find spot was sealed by the dense and very hard deposits of a later Bed V, which would have been hard for anyone to dig through. It was some years before they guessed the truth, that the skeleton had been deposited on the surface of Bed IV before Bed V was deposited, but much later than when Bed IV itself was formed.

The expedition sent over a hundred boxes of stone implements and fossils back to Nairobi. Leakey realized that he was probably sitting on the richest early archaeological site in the world, one that was worth not only extensive excavation but years of careful research. His normal inclination would have been to excavate at once. But on this occasion he held off, determined to get to know the Gorge intimately before putting a spade in the ground. An obvious first stage was to examine the thousands of implements and fossils collected during the 1931 expedition. But it was not until after the Second World War that Leakey could start large-scale work at Olduvai.

By the time Louis returned to Olduvai, his first marriage had ended in divorce. Some time before he had met Mary Nicol, a young woman with a passionate interest in prehistory. Together, they worked at Olduvai and other sites in 1935 and were married the following year. Mary Leakey's introduction to Olduvai was a rough one. Heavy rains turned the streams in the Gorge into raging torrents, the roads were awash with mud, and it took them three-and-a-half days to travel sixteen miles. Once they arrived, their work was complicated by prides of lions and by angry rhinoceroses. But the expedition was a profitable one. In examining the side gorge, they found no less than twenty promising sites in an area that was later found to have been the dried-up shore of an ancient lake, where small bands of hunter-gatherers had camped.

Although Olduvai was still a very promising locality, Leakey faced trouble on other fronts. In 1932, he had led a small party to investigate the fossil-bearing beds on the east shores of Lake Victoria near the Gulf of Kavirondo. The ancient lake beds yielded fossils of similar age to those found at Olduvai and, most exciting of all, some fragmentary human remains from two sites at Kanam and Kanjera. Unfortunately, Leakey was in a hurry to return to Olduvai and failed to double-check where precisely the fossils had been found. Unwisely, he went ahead and published his reports of the new fossils, claiming them as ancestors of modern humanity. His scientific colleagues were a bit dubious and an investigation of the circumstances of Leakey's find was launched. When a geologist named Percy Boswell visited Leakey's sites, Leakey was unable to locate the precise spots where the fossils came from. Boswell returned to England and wrote a scathing account of the incident that nearly ruined Leakey's career. For the rest of his life, Leakey was almost fanatically careful about double-checking his finds in the field.

Leakey had suffered a professional setback, but, fortunately, was offered an unusual opportunity by the Rhodes Foundation, an organization deeply interested in African affairs. In exchange for two years' salary, he was to record the customs of the Kikuyu tribe. Time was of the essence, for many of the older tribe members—those most knowledgeable in tribal customs—were nearing the end of their lives. This proposal was the result of an appeal by a group of anthropologists who knew of Leakey's extraordinary reputation among the Kikuyu. Louis accepted this new job with some reluctance, as it would mean abandoning prehistory for a while, but, once the decision was made, he tackled the assignment with extraordinary energy and characteristic shrewdness. Despite his unique qualifications as a white member of an age-set and a fluent Kikuyu speaker, the project was beset with difficulty. Louis started by consulting the Senior Chief of all the Kikuyu. Chief Koinange put Leakey's proposal to the elders and, to allay their obvious suspicions, appointed a nine-man advisory committee who sifted through all the research materials. The resulting study—recorded in a three-volume monograph that ran to some 700,000 words—must rank as one of the more remarkable achievements of Leakey's career. The first volume deals with Kikuyu history and tradition, as well as with their way of life, the second with the life of a Kikuyu from the cradle to death, and the final volume with social organization, religion, and ceremonial life. The Rhodes Foundation was amazed, but was unable to pay for publication of the study. Leakey, deeply hurt by their response, flatly refused to cut the length of what he considered to be a definitive study. The monograph was not published until after his death, in 1977. It is truly a unique and invaluable work.

The Second World War broke out just as Leakey finished his Kikuyu research. He spent the war years in government service, working in intelligence. During his spare time, he worked at the National Museum in Nairobi. A little archaeology could be managed during leaves, but it was impossible to get down to Olduvai. Meanwhile, one remarkable site came to light in the Great Rift Valley forty miles from Nairobi. Years before, a geologist had reported obtaining some stone axes from a white clay deposit at the foot of a mountain called Olorgesailie, but failed to record exactly where. The Leakeys combed the area on weekends, and their diligence paid off. One day, both Louis and Mary excitedly called out at the same moment: each had made a find. Mary's was particularly spectacular—an unbelievable concentration of stone axes lying on a gentle slope. It transpired that Olorgesailie had been a lakeside camp, used year after year by small groups of hunter-gatherers who preyed on the big game that came down to the water's edge to drink.

As the Leakeys dug into the fine lake deposits, they came across the tools of the hunters lying exactly where they had been dropped. Artifact by artifact, bone by bone, they uncovered the ancient campsites, recording and photographing each object in place. Olorgesailie is now an open-air museum. Potassium-argon dating indicates that the site is more than 400,000 years old.

When the war ended, Leakey was appointed permanent curator of the museum in Nairobi, a post he was to hold for many years. During that time, he built up the museum into a research institution of international reputation, renowned not only for archaeology and palaeontology, but for natural history as well. All the diverse interests Leakey had acquired among the Kikuyu came together in the job of curator. He lobbied long and hard for new galleries and facilities and, with these improvements, the number of museum visitors increased a thousandfold. The Leakeys also found time to lead expeditions to geological beds near Lake Victoria. Here, they made another important discovery—an early ape fossil, which they named *Proconsul.*

Louis also moonlighted for the Kenya police as a forensic expert, an interest he had developed while a student. One case involved a young man accused of murdering his wife with a shotgun. Leakey was able to prove, in the best Sherlock Holmes fashion, that the shooting had been an accident. He took plaster casts of a dent in the woodwork of a piano near the body. The casts fitted the gun butt perfectly, for it had flown from the accused's hands and hit the piano. The young man was eventually acquitted. Louis also played an important role in the government's handling of the Mau Mau emergency, a nationalist uprising that resulted in the death of hundreds of innocent Africans and Europeans. He acted as an interpreter at the trial of Jomo Kenyatta. Kenyatta, a prominent nationalist leader, later became first President of an independent Kenya. Leakey knew him well and was involved in the successful search for him

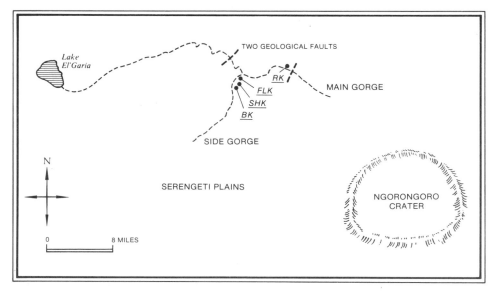

3-4. Map of Olduvai Gorge (Adapted from L.S.B. Leakey, *Olduvai Gorge*, vol. 1, Cambridge. Cambridge University Press, 1965, p. 95).

during the uprising. It is greatly to both men's credit that neither bore a grudge against the other after independence was achieved.

But always at the back of Leakey's mind was the call of the great Valley of Bones. Olduvai Gorge was still unexcavated. A preliminary report on the early expeditions finally appeared after long delays in 1951. Louis described a slowly evolving history of stone-tool technology, from the simple choppers of the very earliest beds up to the finely shaped stone axes of the latest campsites in the Gorge. Obviously, Olduvai had been the scene of a long history of human cultural evolution, one that could be fully charted only through long-term, large-scale excavations. The year the book appeared was the year the Leakeys returned to Olduvai to dig. They were to remain there, on and off, for the rest of Louis's life.

Louis and Mary pitched camp near two sites in Bed II labeled BK and SHK. For seven seasons, between 1951 and 1958, they worked on these remarkable localities. They found an incredible profusion of over eleven thousand stone choppers and other early tools. Both sites were veritable charnel houses of Pleistocene mammals, many of them of enormous size. One such creature was a form of buffalo named *Pelorovis*, an awe-inspiring animal with horns over six feet across. Louis speculated that a band of hunters had one day driven a whole herd of *Pelorovis* into a swamp, where the creatures became bogged down and were unable to escape. Some of the smaller animals were dragged to the shore and cut up. At least one complete skeleton was found upright in the deep clay, standing where it had perished hundreds of thousands of years before.

The entire area was littered with stone tools and waste flakes where the people had cut up their quarry at leisure. BK and SHK were major sources of information on fossil animals, including not only dozens of pigs and other large mammals, but also small rodents, birds, and even frogs. And, unlike many fossil finds, the Olduvai specimens were very often from more or less complete skeletons of animals that had died in the shallows of the ancient lake. But there were no signs of truly ancient human fossils, except for two large teeth found at BK in 1955. Leakey was not worried. I remember hearing him lecture on *Pelorovis* and these two teeth at Cambridge University in 1958. "One day soon we will find more complete human remains," Leakey predicted. How right he was!

The 1959 season crowned nearly a decade of strenuous effort. Exactly a century after the publication of Darwin's *Origin of Species*, Mary Leakey unearthed a large and robust hominid skull on floor FLK in Bed I. The find caused a tremendous sensation. Louis immediately recognized that the new skull was very similar to a series of early hominids found in South Africa, fossils known as *Australopithecines. Australopithecus*, the "southern ape," had been claimed as an ancestor of modern humanity by anatomist Raymond Dart back in 1924, but scientific opinion had laughed him out of court. Although subsequent finds had made people take Dart's claim more seriously, here was additional evidence that *Australopithecus* was close to the human line. But the Olduvai find was of a very robust individual, one with huge teeth and a massive skull. Leakey named it *Zinjanthropus boisei* (African Man of Boise—the name of a Leakey benefactor). Within the Leakey family, the skull was affectionately known as "Dear Boy." The public preferred the catchy "Nutcracker Man," coined because of the skull's huge teeth.

Within a few months, the Leakeys were international celebrities, feted at lectures and public receptions. Olduvai was flooded with visitors. The National Geographic Society and other foundations gave large sums of money that enabled Louis and Mary to put in ninety-two thousand work hours at Olduvai in 1960, more than twice the total number of hours spent there since 1931.

Most of these ninety-two thousand hours were put in by Mary, who spent a whole year at Olduvai. Louis was tied to the museum much of the time. Operating from a camp far more elaborate than they had ever had before, Mary set the workmen to stripping the sterile soil from above the *Zinjanthropus* location. Meanwhile, she sat down to plot the position of every artifact and bone found over an area of five to seven square yards. She found thousands of tiny bone fragments, literally smashed to ribbons for their meat and marrow by hominids. A strip of ground almost bare of finds lay outside this concentration of debris. Outside was a zone where more complete bones and larger tools were found. Since the bare patch lay to windward of the central concentration of occupation debris, Mary theorized that the people had built a simple wind barrier of branches to protect themselves from the prevailing winds. Unfortunately, the jaw of *Zinjanthropus* was nowhere to be found.

In November of 1960, the Leakeys' son Jonathan found some more hominid fragments only three hundred yards from FLK—a jaw and two skull fragments. Although the find came from a slightly lower level than *Zinjanthropus*, the bones were much lighter than those of the earlier discovery and seemed more "human" than Nutcracker Man. When Mary excavated the site, she eventually recovered traces of no less than four individuals, two adults and a juvenile of the less robust form, and some fragments of another creature that resembled *Zinjanthropus*.

Then, only a month later, Louis himself came across a small gully no one had ever examined. There he found a small pile of bones that had eroded out of Bed II. The pile included a thick skull cap with massive brow ridges, obviously from a being less ancient than *Zinjanthropus*. Although the new find was not associated with any artifact concentration, Leakey soon realized that it was the remains of a later hunter-gatherer who had made some of the many stone axes found at Olduvai.

In 1961, the excavations were shifted to other localities in Bed I. Mary started digging at a site named FLK N, near the *Zinjanthropus* floor. She

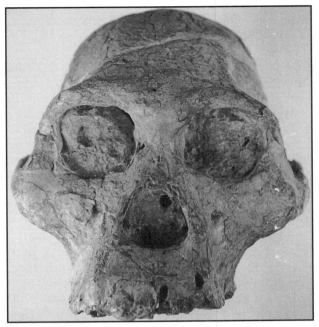

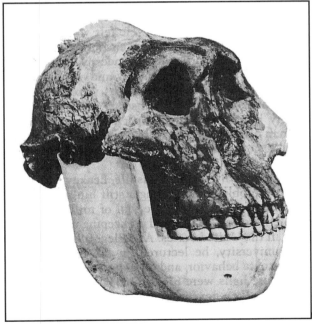

3-5. Gracile *Australopithecus africanus* skull (top, Copyright Transvaal Museum) compared with *Zinjanthropus boisei* (bottom).

came across five artifact and bone scatters stratified one above another. At one of them, the hunters had butchered an elephant where it had fallen. Mary found no less than fourteen thousand rodent bones as well—also lizards and frogs. Fish and bird bones were abundant, the latter from all kinds of wading species that fed by the shores of the ancient lake. Presumably the hunters caught them when the birds roosted after dark.

Mary was surprised to find a strange concentration of rocks on the oldest Olduvai site of all. When she uncovered and plotted them, she found they lay in a circle about twelve feet across. Mary theorized they had served as the foundation for a crude shelter of branches and thorns that protected the inhabitants from the sweeping winds that bombard the Serengeti Plain. This ingenious explanation is impossible to prove.

It was now time for specialist work at Olduvai. Louis himself was overwhelmed with all kinds of commitments—fund-raising lectures, other excavations, and museum work. Mary shouldered most of the excavation and laboratory analysis. Professional geologists and fossil experts were called in to unravel the myriad details of Olduvai's geology and animal life, a job that could be tackled only by specialists. Louis Leakey's greatness lay in his ability to look at the broader picture, to fire other people with his enthusiasm for archaeology and anthropology. He had a natural flair for publicity and made the most of it to gain support for his excavations. Above all, he encouraged younger scientists to engage in bold research, investigations that took the study of human origins in new directions.

How old was Olduvai? No one really knew. The first indication came from two University of California scientists, Jack Evernden and Garniss Curtis, who applied a new radioactive method named potassium-argon dating to the Gorge. This technique was highly effective at dating very old lava beds but had rarely been applied to recent strata. The Olduvai sites, however, were ideal for experimental dating, for the early hominids had used lava for tools and other purposes. After prolonged study of many samples, Evernden and Curtis came up with an average date of 1.75 ± 0.25 million years for the base of Bed I and the early Olduvai sites. The dates caused a sensation, for everyone had guessed that *Zinjanthropus* was about 600,000 years old. At one fell swoop, the scientists had more than doubled the length of time that humans had lived on earth.

Increased resources and worldwide fame meant that the Leakeys were never short of helpers. They were now able not only to excavate but to search for new Olduvai artifact concentrations as well. More hominid fossils came to light, among them a fragmentary skull from the lower levels of Bed II, somewhat later than *Zinjanthropus*. The skull resembled those of the lighter individuals found in 1961. Leakey spent many hours puzzling over the relationship between this new find and *Zinjanthropus*.

By the time the Olduvai excavations ended in 1964, the Leakeys had found some twenty hominid fragments, pieces of an extraordinary anthropological puzzle. What could be made of them? When *Zinjanthropus* was first found with stone tools, Louis claimed that the skull was that of the earliest human toolmaker. But when the lighter and less primitive finds came to light in Bed I, Leakey had to eat his words. Were these the people who made the tools found with *Zinjanthropus*? Did they kill their robust relative at Olduvai? Who was the first toolmaker? The question was still wide open. Leakey characteristically took the bull by the horns. When the anatomists told him that the foot bones of the lighter individuals looked astonishingly human and came from a relatively short primate who walked upright like humans, Leakey was convinced he had found his early human ancestor at last.

Meanwhile, anatomist Philip Tobias of the University of the

3-6. Louis and Mary Leakey at work on a 1.75-million-year-old artifact and bone scatter at Olduvai Gorge, Tanzania.

DATE (in years)	BED IV	
Not less than 700,000	BED III	
Not less than 1.0 million	BED II	*Homo erectus* ("George")
Possible break in sequence		*Homo habilis* finds
	BED I	— *"Zinjanthropus"* — *Homo habilis* — Stone structure
1.75 million 1.8 million c. 2.2 million		Volcanic lava

Table 3-1. Schematic diagram of the geological beds and fossils mentioned in the text.

Witwaterstrand in Johannesburg had started to examine the skull of *Zinjanthropus*. Leakey and Tobias pored over the Bed I fossils and compared *Zinjanthropus* with lighter individuals. Eventually they decided that they did, indeed, have a new genus of human that was contemporary with *Zinjanthropus*. This being had walked upright; stood about four feet, six inches tall; and had a brain somewhat larger than the *Australopithecines*. It was also capable of manipulating its hands to make stone tools and was thus the first toolmaker. Leakey and Tobias named this human ancestor *Homo habilis*.

I remember meeting Tobias as he passed through Livingstone in Zambia on his way back from Nairobi.

"We have a new man from Olduvai," he told me excitedly, "a Handy Man."

"A Handy Man?" I asked. "Why?"

He then explained how they had hit on the term "habilis," a word that implies dexterity of mind and hand. Fittingly, it had been Raymond

Dart, the discoverer of *Australopithecus*, who had coined the label.

The announcement of *Homo habilis* generated yet another heated Leakey controversy, one that rages to this day. Leakey was a confirmed splitter of fossils into new categories. His opponents felt that *Homo habilis* was an *Australopithecus* and that Leakey's argument was based on very slender information. Even Tobias and John Napier, who had studied the feet of *Homo habilis*, were somewhat uncertain about the classification. It was the sheer power of Leakey's personality that eventually carried the day.

By now, son Richard had begun to take an interest in archaeology. After leaving school, Richard had started a successful safari business that had taken him into remote parts of Kenya. Then, in 1967, he joined an international party of scientists who were to look for early humans in the remote Omo Valley of southern Ethiopia. It was Louis who had persuaded the Emperor of Ethiopia to authorize the expedition. American, French, and Kenyan anthropologists were involved in a team effort that brought back thousands of mammal fossils and numerous examples of *Australopithecus*. To Richard's disappointment, the Kenya sector of Omo was rather sparse in fossils. But during the expedition he traveled by helicopter over the eastern shores of remote Lake Rudolf in northern Kenya. Looking down from his lofty perch, he spotted some promising-looking deposits where fossils might be found. The helicopter pilot was persuaded to land for a short look and, sure enough, the locality looked very exciting.

Using the powerful Leakey techniques of persuasion, young Richard managed to convince the National Geographic Society in Washington, D.C., to pay for a season's look at the area. They gave him the money on condition that he would never return for more funds if he found nothing. The East Rudolf area where he chose to work turned out to be a fossil treasure house. There were over two thousand square miles of fossil-bearing beds that, within six weeks, had yielded dozens of mammals and several hominid fragments. A few years later, Richard found an almost complete skull, "1470," which he considered to be from a creature more human than *Australopithecus* had ever been and related, at least in a general way, to Louis's *Homo habilis*. The East Rudolf sites were older than Olduvai, dating from 1.5 to 4 million years old. Another Leakey generation had added a new chapter to the history of humankind.

Louis Leakey's interest turned in other directions in his later life. The study of fossil mammals and early human evolution was becoming an increasingly professional field, one where Leakey's impatient and flamboyant gestures were sometimes counterproductive. He was never good at detail, preferring to leave the minute affairs of excavation to Mary and others. He was particularly fascinated with primate behavior. Surely, he argued, studying living apes in the wild should tell us something about the behavior of early humans who were, in many respects, like apes. He

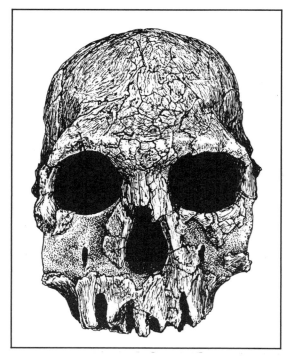

3-7. Reconstruction of *Homo habilis* skull 1470 from East Turkana, Kenya.

felt women were best for this type of sensitive research and encouraged, among others, Jane Goodall and Dian Fossey to undertake what became classic studies of the chimpanzee and the gorilla. Goodall's research showed that chimpanzees were perfectly capable of using small sticks to gather insects. Their behavior was astonishingly human in many respects. The transition from ape to human might have been less of a jump than some people believed. A new field of research was born from this work.

During the last four or five years of his life, Leakey suffered greatly from health problems, including a stiff hip and a bad heart. By this time he had become the idol of millions. Despite considerable suffering, he insisted on keeping up a hectic lecture schedule in the United States. At college after college, university after university, he lectured on the latest fossil discoveries, on primate behavior, and on his African research. Invariably his lecture halls were filled to capacity; hundreds were turned away. Leakey never slowed his pace. In October 1972, while on his way to another lecture tour, he collapsed with a fatal heart attack in London.

The world mourned a great anthropologist and public figure. Even his old adversary Jomo Kenyatta sent a wreath to his funeral.

Louis Leakey must rank as one of the most remarkable archaeologists of all time, a man who, with his family, added whole new dimensions to the study of human origins. When Leakey started digging in the 1920s, no one knew much about prehistoric Africa and the oldest humans were thought to be not much more than a million years old. Leakey's fossil discoveries in the Valley of Bones doubled the time span of human history. He was one of the last of the Renaissance men in archaeology; today, a new generation of specialist scientists have taken over at Olduvai and elsewhere.

The science of paleoanthropology has made giant strides since Louis Leakey's death. Mary Leakey is still active in the field. She has published a meticulous account of the stone artifacts from Olduvai, Bed I, remarkable for its magnificent drawings of simple choppers, flakes, and other very early human tools. She also excavated a 3.6-million-year-old site at Laetoli in northern Tanzania, uncovering not only fossil remains, but the footprints of big game and hominids preserved beautifully in hardened volcanic ash. The Laetoli hominids walked across the ash when it was soft, perhaps after a rain storm. The 3.6-million-year-old tracks cross the dry water course close together, imprints of at least two individuals, the one a step or two ahead of the other. The footprints tell us the hominids walked with a rolling and slow-moving gait, their hips swiveling at each step, their movements a far cry from the free striding of modern human beings. More than any fossil discovery, they bring us face-to-face with our remotest ancestors, people more apelike than human, living at the threshold of prehistory.

Louis and Mary Leakey believed that the scatters of artifacts and broken bones associated with *Zinjanthropus* and *Homo habilis* were temporary campsites, where the very first humans created home bases, sleeping in crude brush shelters by the edge of a shallow lake. They based their interpretations not only on the tools and bones, but on the dramatic field observations of chimpanzee life in the wild collected by Jane Goodall, and on long-term fieldwork by Canadian anthropologist Richard Lee among the !Kung San hunter-gatherers of the Kalahari Desert in southern Africa. From these researches came a portrait of the earliest humans as successful hunters and foragers; the men hunting, the women foraging, just as modern hunter-gatherers do today. The Leakey interpretation enjoyed wide popularity until a new generation of researchers questioned their conclusions, not with excavations, but with microscopes, controlled experiments, and observations of hyenas and other predators on Tanzania's Serengeti Plain. They peered closely at minute cut marks on the Olduvai bones, experimented with the making of Oldowan choppers and flakes, spent long months not only watching lions and hyenas killing and eating their prey, but studying the carcasses they left behind. They believe that

3-8. A chimpanzee uses a stick to remove grubs from an anthill.

our earliest ancestors were scavengers rather than hunters, who ate many species of vegetable foods, seizing meat from predator carcasses when the opportunity arose, especially when they could scavenge in more wooded country near water in the dry season. When they scavenged meat, they would carry the flesh and bones to convenient spots, perhaps under trees or in protected water courses, where they would break up the bones and consume the meat, always with a watchful eye for hovering predators. Then they would move on, leaving a pile of stone tools and broken bones behind them. They believe that *Homo habilis* was more apelike than human in its behavior, that the Leakeys' campsites or living floors were in fact places to which the hominids returned at irregular intervals to consume scavenged meat. And when they departed, the hyenas would move in for their share— hyena tooth marks appear on some of the broken bones over those marks made by stone tools.

　　None of these new advances minimize the remarkable achievements of Louis and Mary Leakey, for science is always advancing, always building on the discoveries of earlier scholars. Without the Leakeys, few of us would be conscious of the immense chapters of human prehistory that stretch back to a past almost too remote to imagine. They made the public aware of its ancestry, an ancestry which, the Victorians had discovered, was among the apes. The Victorians had not liked this; the Leakeys helped us accept it. Today, Richard Leakey carries on the work of his parents and keeps their vision alive.

4

THE MAKAH
FIND THEIR HISTORY

South of Vancouver Island, the rugged pacific coast of North America sweeps southward in a series of wide bays fully exposed to the winter force of the ocean. Rolling swells batter the coast and carry driftwood from far-off lands to its deserted beaches. The mighty fury of hurricane-force southwesterly gales brings high tides and floods to the forested shore. Few spots on this wild coast offer shelter for canoes or small vessels. Yet, for thousands of years, Makah Indians settled on this exposed coast, living off the incredible bounty of the ocean and forest. They selected their village sites with great care, settling where offshore islands and kelp beds offered shelter from the perennial swells and where seals and other sea life flourished in profusion. One such Makah settlement nestled in a sheltered bay behind a small island named Ozette, protected by Ozette from southwesterly gales and from the northwest by two further islands, massive kelp beds, a sandspit, and offshore rocks.

Five hundred years ago, a visitor to Ozette would have found a cluster of weathered cedarwood houses ranged along the sheltered beach, their natural wood tones merging with the greens and browns of the forested slope behind. Viewed from afar, the village would blend almost imperceptibly with the landscape of ocean and forest. Indeed, the naive observer would believe it had nestled there since time immemorial. To get a clearer picture of the Makah way of life, let's pay a visit to the settlement as it might have appeared on a fine summer day five hundred years ago.

As we approach, we can see children playing among the houses and adults working on the fine cedarwood canoes drawn up on the beach. Each plank house is alive with domestic activity, humming with conversation and laughter on this pleasant day. As we near our host's house, we can see a bleached whale skull and a line of vertebrae lined up in front of the dwelling. Our host is a whale hunter, respected for his skills with the harpoon. The weathered planks of the house show signs of constant repair and replacement. Some of them are fresh, obviously recently brought to Ozette from the forest; others have been in place for generations, held in position by regularly spaced uprights. In one place, the side of a long-abandoned canoe has been pressed into service as a house plank. The worn gunwale of the canoe overlaps the plank below it. Two men are clambering around on the planked roof, picking their way through the large boulders that hold the overlapping planks in position on windy days. They lift a roof plank and place it on one side as a cloud of woodsmoke billows upward

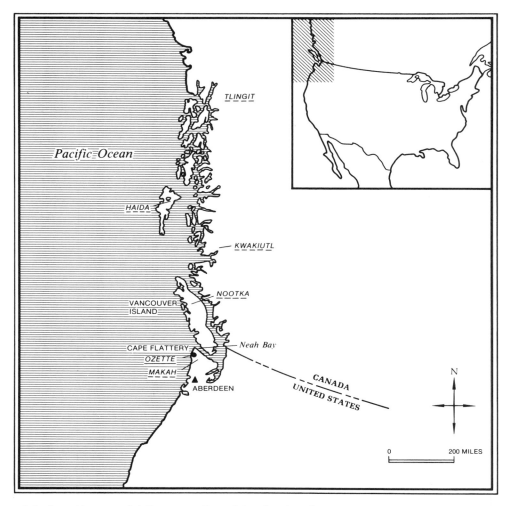

4-1. Locations and tribes mentioned in chapter 4.

into their faces. Laughing voices come from inside the house as the occupants begin passing up salmon to the sunlit roof. The men lay the fish out in the sunshine to dry, all the while keeping up a steady flow of banter with the women below.

The house opens onto the beach and the entrance is open on this warm afternoon. A wooden partition keeps the wind out of the interior, placed so as to act as an effective windbreak. The interior seems very dark to us after the bright sunlight. A few shafts of sun filter through the roof, making their way between the tools, bundles, and skins hanging from the massive rafters. The house is divided into family areas with low partitions, each lined with cedarwood sleeping benches, some decorated with seashells. A young boy, his bow and arrow by his side, sleeps on one of the benches, oblivious to the noise around him. An old women sits with her back against a nearby bench, gazing into the fire, a partially completed basket forgotten on her knees. Under the sleeping bench is a row of cedarwood boxes. A girl squats near an open box, going through the skin-working tools stored · inside. The rafters seem to reach down into the house, festooned as they are with bundles of dried cattails, dozens of dried salmon, and loads of seaweed. A row of large sealskins bulging with oil hangs nearby, blackened with hearth smoke from the cooking fires below. Two large whale-harpoon shafts hang on the walls behind the sleeping bench. A fine canoe paddle lies on top of a sleeping bench near a woven blanket. The smell of dead fish, wood smoke, and seal oil pervades the atmosphere. Everything seems slightly oily to the touch. The wooden oil-storage bowls by the fire glisten with seal oil and everyone's hands and bodies seem to exude oil.

Three women are watching over a pair of fresh salmon spread out on sticks and roasting in front of the fire. A wooden carved seal club lies close by, black with smoke and oil. A young fisherman squats near the hearth, intent on mending a well-used fishing net. His old father sits on his right, binding a wooden barb to the curved halibut fishhook in his hand. At intervals he admonishes the small boy by his side who is poking around in a large storage basket and fiddling with a shell harpoon head wrapped in a fine storage sheath. A murmur of voices, of soft laughter and occasional caustic comments to the men on the roof, keeps the family around the fire in touch with the rest of the house.

Softly the old man greets us and bids us welcome. The talk turns to seals and salmon, and then to whales, as he shows the young boy how he fashioned the harpoon head that lies in the basket. He tells us about the ultimate quarry—the whale. Proudly, he boasts how the Makah are one of the few tribes bold enough to hunt the whale for its rich bounty of meat and oil. He speaks with authority, for he is a whale hunter, a person of high rank in Makah society, closely connected to important spirits.

Whale hunting is surrounded with elaborate rituals and taboos; the whale hunters themselves are important members of the community who inherited their roles from earlier generations. As we listen raptly, the old man tells stories of whale hunts of old and recounts the tale behind the bleached whale skeleton resting in front of the house. When the Makah spotted a pod of whales, he remembers, the whaling parties would set out in eight-man dugout canoes. The whale hunters wore nothing but a coating of oil and red ochre to protect them from sun and rain and, sometimes, woven hats to keep the rain from their faces. They frequently painted their faces with ritual designs. For several days before the hunt all crew members abstained from sexual relations. Magic charms and spirit tokens, perhaps even the skull of a skilled whale-hunting ancestor, went along on the hunt in a wooden box. As the canoe paddled out to the unsuspecting pod, the whale hunter would invite the whales to come and be caught, referring to them as "noble ladies," never as "whales."

Once a blowing whale came into sight, the canoe would paddle up behind it as it cruised along. With silent strokes, the captain would direct the craft to a position above and slightly to the left of the unsuspecting whale. The hunter stood in the bow with raised harpoon. The whale would blow and start to submerge directly under the hovering canoe. At that precise moment, the harpooner would drive his heavy weapon into the whale. The sharp, mussel-shell tip penetrated deeply into the wounded animal as it plunged away from the canoe. For hours the paddlers would follow their wounded quarry, pursuing the bobbing sealskin floats affixed to the harpoon to reveal the position of the whale. As their quarry tired, the whale hunters would approach carefully and attempt to kill the whale with a deep lance stroke aimed behind the great flipper.

Our host also remembers how the whole village would follow the progress of the hunt blow by blow. The captain's wife played out the whale's role, lying quietly at home, willing the whale to do the same. Once the strike was made, she would chant incantations, inviting the whale to visit the village. And, when the rejoicing villagers beached the carcass, the captain's wife would greet the visitor and bring the whale a drink of fresh water. Then the entire community would help cut up the carcass with blubber knives. The meat and blubber were distributed by rank and the entire community enjoyed a feast. Everyone was continually on the lookout for stranded whales, too, for strandings, of course, saved the hunters a great deal of trouble. Every whaling village had its own whale shrine, where the hunters and canoe captains performed the powerful rituals that ensured the continued arrival of whales off the coast.

We listen spellbound as the old man continues his stories of legendary whale hunts, of great ceremonies, of canoes lost at sea, of raging storms, and strange happenings. It seems as if the Makah have been living and hunting at Ozette since time began, living off the bounty of the ocean. On this gentle summer day, we feel that nothing could interrupt the even tenor of life in this remote bay.

But we are wrong. Only a few years later, life at Ozette came to a temporary full stop. Several houses vanished suddenly under a dense blanket of slippery mud. The mud slide arrived abruptly and without warning in the early morning; few people were astir. The planked dwellings vanished completely in a few moments, their loose roofs sliding onto the beach on a conveyer belt of oozing mud. A few muffled cries could be heard, then silence. Much of Ozette disappeared totally and instantly. Although the Makah continued to live at Ozette until as late as 1910, they cherished only a few folk memories of sudden mud slides and terrible tragedy. In

4-2. Cleaning a whale bone found in the Ozette excavations.

effect, their past was buried under a canopy of mud, sealed from the destructive atmosphere so effectively that it survived almost intact until the 1960s.

The Makah continued to hunt whales until the early twentieth century. Like other Northwest Coast Indian groups, they suffered at the hands of white settlers and traders in the nineteenth century until only a fraction of their original population still survived. Ozette itself was abandoned when the Makah moved closer to the public school in Neah Bay in the 1920s. Over a quarter of a century was to elapse before a young archaeologist named Richard Daugherty was lucky enough to find one of the most remarkable archaeological sites in North America.

Richard Daugherty is a native of Aberdeen, Washington, a small coastal town sixty miles south of Cape Flattery. In his youth, he spent many days wandering along the remote beaches north of Aberdeen. He studied anthropology in college and was appointed to the faculty of Washington State University in Pullman, a post he held until his retirement. Daugherty developed a strong interest in the archaeology of the Washington coast and started recording sites along his favorite stretch of the Pacific. His research forays were sporadic, for he was deeply involved in salvage archaeology in eastern Washington and Idaho. Still, by the fall of 1947, Daugherty had already recorded fifty coastal sites, most of them thick concentrations of charcoal, fish bones, and shells. The richest sites lay at the mouths of salmon rivers. Daugherty found time to walk out to a protected beach named Ozette, a hike through dense forest on a muddy trail. Twenty or thirty years before, a Makah community had lived at Ozette, but the inhabitants had gradually moved away. Except for occasional fishermen, Ozette was now silent and deserted. Some of the abandoned houses were still visible, the only remains of a substantial village that was now rotting away into the soil. The ruined structures lay on a low terrace that overlooked a sheltered landing and a sandy beach. The terrace was black with ash, charcoal, and shells. Daugherty knew that hundreds of people had lived at Ozette for centuries. But how long ago? he wondered.

Daugherty had to wait fourteen years before he was able to visit Ozette a second time. This time he took two students with him. They dug carefully into the black soil. Within a few hours, Daugherty was admiring two smooth bone whale-harpoon barbs. Perhaps Ozette was the ancient whaling village he had been looking for. Four years later, Daugherty returned with adequate research funds and plans for a thorough investigation of Ozette. He has been involved with the site ever since.

Daugherty realized at the outset that he was dealing with a complex site whose history was linked to the vast ocean that lapped against its shore. How, for example, had changing sea levels over the years affected the inhabitants of Ozette? Wisely, he invited geologist Roald Fryxell to study Ozette. In addition, Carl Gustafson, a zoologist, was on hand to examine the many animal bones that Daugherty expected to uncover in the trenches.

The extensive occupation levels at Ozette lay above the high tide mark on top of a series of low platforms or terraces overlooking the beach. Fryxell determined that Ozette had flourished at the water's edge for a long period of time, but the occupants had moved their houses several times as the high tide fluctuated. The highest terrace was about forty feet above the present beach. Presumably this was occupied first, while the lower, later terraces were still under the Pacific.

Daugherty began by laying out a 240-foot trench across the deepest

4-3. Excavation of the first trench through the terraces at Ozette, Washington, with screens for sifting soil at the edge of the cutting. Note Cannonball Island close offshore.

4-4. Meri Flynn, Makah student and a member of the Ozette summer excavation crew, cleans a cedarbark basket from House 2.

and widest part of the site to intersect the terraces. The excavations proceeded slowly at first, for dense vegetation masked the rich occupation deposits. But once the twenty students on the crew reached the soil of the ancient village, they dug faster. The diggers worked in teams, some carefully shovelling out the soil, others sifting the damp earth for minute fragments of bones, stone tools, and shells. The uppermost levels of the trench yielded rusty nails and broken glass, some coins, and parts of a muzzle-loader rifle. Most of these finds belonged to historic nineteenth-century Makah villages. The lower levels yielded no European trade goods or traces of contact with foreigners. They obviously predated the eighteenth century.

As the students dug deeper into Ozette, they came across bone fishhooks, stone and shell knife blades, and the whetstones used to sharpen them. One student discovered a bone comb decorated with a human face. Many of the fish hooks lay close to the stone sinkers that once carried the fishermen's lines to the ocean bottom. Thousands of fish bones were scattered through the midden, many of them from deep-water species that could only have been taken with nets or by line fishing from offshore canoes. The hundreds of Ozette artifacts lay alongside the remains of thousands of ancient meals. Clam and mussel shells were piled in heaps. The Ozette people also had feasted on shallow-water fish, on sea birds like gulls, and on geese, ducks, and land birds. But sea-mammal bones were the most common food remains, far more abundant than deer and elk, which, even today, feed near Ozette.

Why were sea mammals so common? Daugherty wondered. As the excavators dug deeper, whole layers of the site composed almost exclusively of whale and seal bones were revealed. Enormous whale bones blocked parts of the trench, indeed passed right across it. Daugherty carefully recorded the location of the bones, then told the students to saw them up so they could dig deeper. Whale bones came not only from the historic levels, but from the very lowest, prehistoric depths of the settlement. People had been hunting whales for centuries at Ozette, far back into prehistoric times. Clearly the locality had some special attraction for people who lived off the sea, one that kept them tied to Ozette for centuries.

Anyone camped at Ozette in a gale can quickly see one good reason why the site was situated where it was. Cannonball and Ozette islands lie close offshore, the former joined to the beach by a sandspit at low tide. These natural features shelter the beach, breaking the full force of the Pacific swells that batter this remote coast. Ozette was a natural canoe landing, accessible even in pretty severe conditions. It also lies on the westernmost point of North America south of Vancouver Island, close to fur seal and whale migration routes. A reef teeming with fish eaten by fur seals can be seen just three miles off the coast. Most migrating seals stay at least ten miles offshore. Between March and May, however, many seals migrating to the Arctic are drawn to this plentiful food supply off Ozette's shore. Thus, they can be killed by the dozens without venturing too far into deep water. Over 80 percent of the sea-mammal bones found at Ozette in the first season were those of fur seals. When Gustafson started identifying the more than eighty thousand bones from the site, he found a similar pattern of hunting from the oldest to the most recent levels of the site. The Ozette people were obviously skillful seamen. Fur seals could only be hunted from a canoe. And whales never come into the shallow water off the Washington coast except when washed ashore or ailing and unable to fend for themselves.

By July 1966, the Ozette trench was over sixty feet long and penetrated deep into the midden. The superimposed layers of successive villages were revealed one after another, a jumble of hearths, charcoal fragments, broken bones, and piles of shells. In one place, a careful student unearthed a cluster of whale barnacles. These golfball-sized barnacles grow only on whale skin. Presumably they were all that remained of a hunk of skin and blubber carried back to the village hundreds of years before. In other places, too, it was possible to identify the packed earth floors of ancient houses, even the dark post holes of the wooden frames. But all the wood had decayed. Clearly, many of the people's tools had vanished forever.

Roald Fryxell spent many hours poring over the complicated geology of the settlement. Dozens of occupation layers, over ten feet deep, could be pieced together to form a continuous history of Ozette life. And this long occupation had to be tied to the complex history of the retreating seashore and of movements of the earth's crust, both intricate puzzles to sort out.

How old was Ozette? The most recent layers could be dated by the coins and other familiar modern objects found in them. And Daugherty knew that the site had been used as recently as the 1920s. The archaeologists recovered charcoal fragments from the lower level of the beach and sent them off for radiocarbon dating at Washington State University. The radiocarbon laboratory dated the lowest levels of Ozette to around two thousand years ago. Since there was every reason to believe that Ozette had been occupied continuously throughout its long history, Daugherty was now able to say that the Makah had been whale hunting on the Washington Coast for at least two thousand years. At the end of the 1966 season, Fryxell used a powerful core augur to bore below the deepest levels of the excavation. He recovered not only beach sand from a long-buried shore but traces of whale bones and perfectly preserved wood as well. The buried midden seemed very fresh. Fryxell noticed that it was covered by a thick mud slide. Had the slopes of the site slid onto the beach year after year? Had Ozette houses been buried by sudden inrushes of liquid mud? More excavations were needed to solve this and other problems.

In 1967, Daugherty and Fryxell returned to Ozette. Their objectives were to learn more about the recent village and to dig into the midden that lay perched on the summit of Cannonball Island close offshore. The foundations of the historic houses yielded a wealth of broken dishes and bottles, as well as the usual seal and whale bones. The Indians had salvaged valuable iron for axes and wedges from the wreck of the barque *Austria* which ran aground off Ozette in 1887.

Cannonball Island was surprisingly interesting, too. The Makah had laboriously carried seal meat and clam shells to the summit over many centuries. Perhaps the island served as a refuge in times of war or as a lookout for migrating whales. But the most interesting finds of all came from a muddy area on the mainland. A test pit dug to test the extent of the ancient village penetrated ten feet into wet mud. Just as Daugherty was about to fill in the hole, a student's shovel hit a solid object in the muck. It proved to be a cedar plank in perfect condition, covered with a cedar-bark mat. Other planks, even some baskets, lay nearby. The probe had hit upon a perfectly preserved house buried beneath a thick layer of sticky mud. Fryxell looked at the pit and checked his measurements of the present slope. It was still oozing slowly toward the beach. The Makah themselves remembered catastrophic mud slides that had buried entire houses, even people, without warning. Regretfully, Daugherty had neither the time nor the money to investigate his remarkable find more fully. So with great reluctance, he was forced to abandon Ozette for the time being.

Ozette lies in the Makah Indian Reservation. Daugherty, with characteristic sensitivity, had not only obtained permission from the Makah Tribal Council to dig at Ozette but had kept the Makah informed of the progress of the excavations. He had developed a close rapport over the years with Ed Claplanhoo, then Tribal Chairman. Claplanhoo, like Daugherty, had connections with Washington State University, where he had majored in forestry. In February 1970, Daugherty received an urgent call from Claplanhoo, urging him to drop everything and come to Ozette at once. A severe winter storm had undercut the bank where the site lay. The precious midden had slumped onto the beach, exposing deep layers of the site. Passersby were astonished to find a wooden canoe paddle, fish hooks, and all sorts of other treasures oozing out of the mud. Could Daugherty come at once and take over? Daugherty could indeed. A day later, he was at the site with the Makah.

The slump was only a small one, from a fifteen-foot-high bank. Groping blindly, but with extreme care in the sticky mud, Daugherty grasped some cedar planks and bone harpoon heads, parts of a carved wooden box, and a complete basketry hat in perfect condition. The mud slide had exposed a collapsed house. Daugherty was thrilled by the new finds, but also worried. Ozette was obviously a unique site, one where ancient Makah life was likely to be preserved in all its fascinating complexity. But how could he obtain the money to dig the site?

At this point, the Makah Tribal Council stepped in. To them, and to Daugherty, Ozette was far more than a fascinating archaeological site. Ozette was a critically important archive of Makah history, equal in importance to the written records of other societies. An emergency meeting of the Council appealed to Senator Henry Jackson of Washington State for help. Within a short time, Jackson arranged for a seventy-thousand dollar grant from the Bureau of Indian Affairs to cover the costs of a new field season at Ozette. From this work, the Makah hoped, their long-lost history would see the light of day.

Daugherty soon realized that the wooden houses could never be excavated by conventional means. The delicate cedar planks would crumble to pulp if even touched with a trowel. The wood was so waterlogged that it had the consistency of soft mud. A thick mantle of dense clay several feet deep covered the wooden objects. This had to be removed before the difficult task of extracting the houses could begin. Some years before, Daugherty had successfully used pressure hoses to clear some ancient baskets from a river bank a few miles away. He decided to try the same technique at Ozette, but on a much larger scale. Jerry Grosso, the Conservator for the Project, devised an elaborate pumping system for the dig, one that enabled the diggers to use jets of varying intensity for different tasks.

The pump rigs were flown in by U.S. Marine helicopter and pipes were extended into the ocean. After a long period of trial and error, Grosso

4-5. Timbers of the old houses are washed free from the mud that had held them for centuries. A whale scapula (shoulder blade) is just to the right of the upper worker. The cabins were used by the archaeologists; they were not part of the ancient village.

managed to maintain a steady 250 pounds of pressurized water through the hoses. Diggers used the torrents of water to wash away the thick clay above the wooden houses. The upper levels explored in 1966 were removed as quickly as possible. It was urgent to get to the older wooden objects before high tides washed them away. The students on the crew worked in pairs, one watching the mud flow as it was hosed away, the other operating the hose. Apparently, the liquid had rushed down the hillside very suddenly, burying within a few moments the houses lying at the foot of the slope. No one knew when the slide had occurred, but it was probably long before whites visited the coast. No European trade goods were found among the many household possessions recovered. Daugherty estimated that the house was buried four hundred years ago.

An extraordinary prehistoric story awaited Daugherty under the clay. It took two years to work from the south wall of the buried house across to the north side of the building. Foot by foot, the students hosed away the clay overburden with pressure hoses. They then used garden hoses to dissolve the mud and free the planks with fine jets and careful brushing. The plank house was nearly seventy feet long and forty-five feet wide. Everything was still in place, including the sleeping benches where twenty to forty people had once slept in the communal dwelling.

Never had archaeologists in the Northwest faced such a formidable challenge of recovery and preservation. Hundreds of small household items lay jumbled among the collapsed walls, everything from bones and storage boxes to baskets and cooking hearths. It took months to sort out the mess, to distinguish the roof and wall planks from the wooden boxes and layers of delicate fiber materials and nets that festooned the collapsed foundations. Some wooden planks were four feet wide and two-and-a-quarter inches thick, split laboriously from huge cedar logs. Every wood fragment had to be lifted with infinite care and treated with the proper chemicals to prevent it from drying out and cracking. Grosso set up a treatment system at the site itself, so that the wooden objects could be taken straight from the waterlogged dig and placed in solutions of polyethylene glycol. The Makah Tribal Council converted a heavy-equipment garage in Neah Bay into a laboratory, where Grosso set up equipment to store the wooden objects as they arrived from the site by helicopter and to treat artifacts that needed special, experimental preservative measures.

The initial excavations yielded over thirteen thousand wood and fiber objects, many of priceless scientific value. Some of the larger objects will be immersed in polyethylene glycol for years as the chemical replaces the water that has soaked into the wood cells over the centuries. This treatment technique has been commonly used all over the world, especially with the Swedish warship *Vasa*, whose timbers were recovered from the bottom of Stockholm harbor and preserved in a special museum.

At the time, the Ozette conservation operation was probably the largest of its type after the *Vasa* project and, like all projects of this type, involved some real headaches. One was keeping track of the artifacts as they passed through the conservation process. Grosso developed a record system and a log that tracks the artifacts right through the laboratory to storage. Another problem was the conservation of wooden vessels heavily impregnated with seal oil. One vessel was airfreighted to Australia for preservation using a new, freeze-drying technique. Others were treated over long periods in an attempt to break down the seal oil. The task of preserving the unique Ozette finds will take even longer than the excavations.

The Ozette house had evidently stood for several generations, for its planks had been eaten by termites and been repaired on several occasions. The roof timbers were bevelled at the edges, so they overlapped to drain off rainwater. One huge, fragile wall plank over twenty feet long took ten students to lift it from the mud. Its underside bore a carving of a whale with backbone and baleful eye clearly shown.

4-6. Effigy of a whale's fin carved of red cedar and inlaid with over 700 sea otter teeth. Here Richard Daugherty looks at the reassembled sculpture, which was found in several pieces within one of the buried houses. The teeth at the base form the design of a huge bird carrying a whale in its talons.

The dominance of whales in Ozette life was reflected in many ways. One day in 1971, one of the crew unearthed a piece of carved wood covered with sea-otter teeth. For four days, the crew labored to free the carving. When they were at last successful, everyone clustered around to admire a truly unique find—a wooden whale's fin inlaid with no less than seven hundred sea-otter teeth. The rear edge bore a row of sharp canines to give it a jagged edge. Not even the Makah elders had seen such an object before. Daugherty finally remembered an etching of a similarly carved fin in an Indian village on Vancouver Island; the etching had been made by an artist with Captain Cook's expedition. Could the two objects be related?

As the excavations proceeded, the students uncovered hundreds of small wooden objects never before found in early Northwest Indian sites. Carved wooden bowls that once held seal and whale oil still carried the smell of their odoriferous contents. One was carved in the form of a man with a braided hairstyle. The Ozette people also made wooden boxes of every size by grooving and steaming single softwood planks in seaweed and then bending them into squares. Each was carefully assembled with wooden pegs.

With the enthusiastic assistance of surviving Makah craftsmen, the students experimented with carpentry techniques, learned how to duplicate the basketry found in the excavations, and tried their hand at traditional wood carving. The incomplete picture of Ozette culture that came from the 1966–1967 excavations was now transformed. The Makah who worked on the dig could admire seal, human, and owl heads carved on heavy wooden clubs and large storage boxes decorated with ornate stylized and geometric designs. Even some sleeping platforms bore shell studs arranged in simple decorative patterns.

4-7. An oil bowl from Ozette carved in the shape of a man, complete with braided hair.

Three complete looms and the remains of several others were found in the house. The Ozette weavers used dog wool on their looms to weave fabric for their coats, a wool shorn from a special breed of woolly fleeced dog. Early explorers to Ozette noted that the Indians bred such now-extinct dogs and segregated them from other breeds to preserve their woolly coats. The weavers also made blankets of wool and cattail fluff. One fine example found in a broken box bore a plaid pattern.

The Ozette house contained hundreds of baskets and boxes, many of them still holding the special tool kits originally stored in them. Some baskets held dried foods, others carried fishing gear and equipment. Baskets and mats were woven from rolls of cedar bark which were stored in the house, ready for use. A weaver's kit, complete with spindle whorl, awls, combs, and fiber lay near one of the walls. When the archaeologists opened another storage box, they found a woven pouch containing a complete tool kit for making fish hooks. One whaler's basket held mussel-shell harpoon heads, each carefully wrapped in a sheath of cedar bark. Daugherty and Grosso opened one package by brushing on hot water to saturate the bark. Inside lay the barbed harpoon head, exactly as originally stored away. Even the wooden wedges for the harpoon barbs lay in perfect alignment. The contents of the single completely dug house give us a fascinating glimpse into the remote past of a community whose livelihood depended on the sea.

The discoveries at Ozette are, of course, of incalculable scientific value. They have given archaeologists a unique opportunity to study the rich prehistoric culture of the Makah, an intricate culture that was enjoyed, with variations, by thousands of other Northwest Indians. Exceptional preservation conditions have revealed almost the entire range of Makah technology and a magnificent art tradition without parallel in North America. The conservation methods used in the Ozette laboratories are being copied by other archaeologists fortunate enough to recover wooden objects in their excavations.

But the excavations have also had an impact that extends far beyond the field of archaeology. Ozette lies just outside the boundaries of a national park. Tens of thousands of visitors have walked out to the site since its discovery. No one leaves Ozette without being stirred by the vivid story of the Makah past that is emerging from the excavations. The educational value of the site is enormous.

Ozette has had its strongest impact on the Makah themselves. During the excavations dozens of Makah of all ages shared in the excitement of discovering their long-lost history. With the aid of federal funds, the Makah Tribal Council built a magnificent historical museum at Neah Bay. The museum has become not only a special place to display their newly discovered history but also a major economic boon for the local community. The admission fees paid by the thousands of tourists who visit the museum

4-8. A whale harpoon head with its mussel shell blade, bone barbs, and lashings, intact inside its storage pouch.

not only pay salaries and operating expenses, they yield a profit for the Makah as well. The story of their past will benefit many future generations of Makah in a unique way.

All too often archaeologists forget that the Indian sites they dig and record for posterity are part of the cultural heritage of peoples who are discounted in our Western society. Their technical reports appear in learned publications that few people other than specialist archaeologists ever read. Frequently, the scholars don't bother to disseminate their findings to a wider audience, to the very people whose ancestors inhabited the sites centuries ago. The story of Ozette is one of exceptional cooperation between the archaeologists and the Makah. As a result, Ozette is far more than a remarkable archaeological site. Thanks to Richard Daugherty's skill and sensitivity, the Makah have not only recovered new chapters of their lost history, they have also shared in the work and excitement of discovery. And that is what good archaeology is all about.

5

Austen Henry Layard of NINEVEH

A rise, go to Nineveh, that great city," said the Lord to Jonah. "Cry against it; for their wickedness is come up before me"(Jonah 1:2). And Jonah obeyed orders and duly rebuked the city, which repented of its sins and was spared from destruction. Jonah's mission to Nineveh is but one of thousands of allusions to great cities and mighty kings in the Scriptures. But did these cities and monarchs actually exist? Was the Old Testament based on historical fact? These questions have preoccupied not only theologists and archaeologists for generations, but many lay persons as well.

A hundred and fifty years ago, at a time when scientists were challenging the historical truth of the Biblical story of the Creation, this preoccupation became almost an obsession. Had Nineveh actually been a great city? Where were Joseph's huge granaries by the banks of the Nile? Did the Assyrians and the Hanging Gardens of Babylon actually exist? This chapter is the story of a man who proved that many of the cities and kings of the Old Testament actually existed and who helped discover the unique and long-lost civilizations of the Assyrians and Sumerians.

Long before Englishman Austen Henry Layard started digging in the desolate plains of Mesopotamia between the rivers Tigris and Euphrates, the area had evoked intense interest among Biblical scholars because of its associations with the Garden of Eden and Noah's Flood. As early as the twelfth century, the celebrated Jewish rabbi Benjamin of Tudela gazed on the desolate mounds of Nineveh and commented on the utter destruction around him. Another traveler, the Englishman John Shirley, referred to Nineveh as a "witnesse to God's judgement." When the seventeenth-century Italian explorer Pietro della Valle returned from the mounds of Nimrud with a few mysterious square bricks bearing strange written characters, scholars from all over Europe flocked to see his find. Yet, until the middle of the nineteenth century, the secrets of the Assyrians and Sumerians remained buried deep in the huge *tells* of Mesopotamia. Nineveh was little more than a shadowy city of legend, marked only by a few dusty mounds and the ruins of palace foundations.

Even a century and a half ago, Mesopotamia was a wild and dangerous place for European travelers. The territory between the Tigris and Euphrates was under the nominal jurisdiction of the sultan of Turkey, part of the huge and slowly decaying Ottoman Empire based in Constantinople. Local rulers held uneasy sway over huge tracts of desolate landscape, under sporadic supervision from far-distant Ottoman officials. The real political force was exerted by nomad tribes who fanned out over the dry plains in constant search of grazing land for their flocks. A long tradition of raiding and tribal warfare, of family feuds and princely hospitality was observed. Woe betide the rash foreigner who ventured into this wild land without either a powerful escort or the money to buy himself out.

Despite its remoteness and legendary wildness, the Great Powers kept

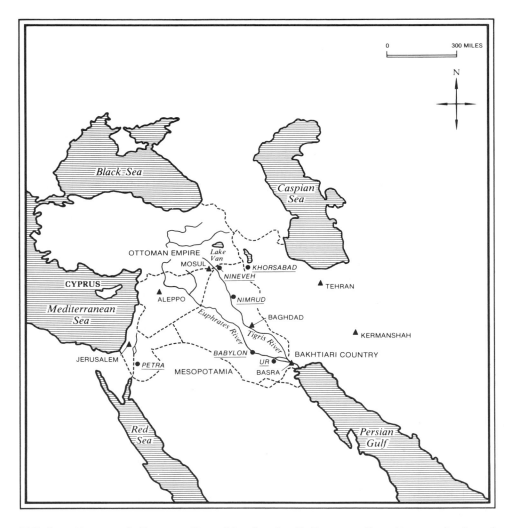

5-1. Locations and sites mentioned in chapter 5. Some earlier sites can be found on the map for chapters 6 and 7.

a keen eye on this distant land, strategically placed as it was to regulate overland commerce to the British colonies in India. Its great rivers presented tantalizing prospects for new, navigable trade routes into untapped markets for foreign wares. The European nations maintained embassies in Constantinople, where they competed for the favors of the sultan. Diplomatic missions were constantly on the move into unknown territory, scouting for military or commercial advantage. Britain and France were farsighted enough to post consuls in Baghdad and other remote cities famous in Biblical times. These officials ministered to the needs of the occasional traveler, kept an eye on local conditions, and attempted to keep abreast of volatile Mesopotamian politics.

In 1840, this harsh and little-known land was still a region of mystery, considered by Westerners to be the cradle of humankind, the most ancient part of the known world. Archaeologists like Austen Henry Layard were among the first to draw aside the curtain of mystery that shrouded Mesopotamia. In so doing, they gave new life to parts of the Old Testament and generated keen public interest in ancient Biblical stories.

"My life has been, in some respects, an eventful one," wrote Austen Henry Layard in his old age. His modest remark grossly understated the truth. By the time he was thirty-five, Henry Layard was not only a traveler of world renown, but he had also discovered an ancient Near Eastern civilization. In addition, he had made his mark as a brilliant popular writer. But this was only the beginning. In later life, Layard was to become a politician, art connoisseur, and diplomat of high repute. He crammed more into one lifetime than most of us could manage in six, giving up archaeology before he was forty.

Austen Henry Layard was born in Paris on March 5, 1817, the son of English parents who enjoyed living on the Continent. Young Henry grew up in an atmosphere of cultured leisure, for his parents were friendly with many writers and artists. By the time he was seventeen, Layard himself was ambitious to move up in the world. His family was so poor, despite their culture, that he was unable to go to college. Instead, he was articled as a clerk to a relative's law firm in London. For a few years he led a miserable life, going without food to buy the hundreds of books he read in his chilly lodgings. Henry hated being a lawyer. The dull and predictable career that lay ahead of him filled his heart with gloom; his bubbling ambition seemed doomed to die under a mountain of legal briefs and dry court decisions. The family worried about what to do with their unconventional son who seemed intent on rising to the top as quickly as possible by blithely ignoring all normal steps on the ladder to success.

During vacations, Layard abandoned his arid studies and traveled all over Europe. He visited Russia and Poland, ventured as far north as Finland, and fell in love with Italy, a country he was to visit again and again. In his diaries and letters, he poured out his feelings, expressing excitement

5-2. Austen Henry Layard

over his many new friends and adventures. He did most of his traveling on foot, with occasional railway journeys, at a time when travel around Europe was far more difficult than it is today. Fortunately, just as Layard's ambitions were getting the best of him and creating family tensions, salvation came along in the form of Henry's Uncle Charles.

In his early life, Layard's father had worked in Ceylon for a while, until forced to return to England because of ill health. Henry's Uncle Charles had gone to Ceylon at the same time and was now a high government official there. When Charles came home on leave, he suggested that Henry consider practicing law in Ceylon. Layard was interested, so Charles introduced him to Edward Mitford, a young businessman of thirty-two who had just returned from a business venture in Morocco and was about to go coffee planting in Ceylon. The two men took to each other immediately and agreed to travel out together.

The normal route to Ceylon was to take a steamer to Alexandria, then travel overland via the Isthmus of Suez (the Suez Canal did not, of course, exist), and then continue on by ship to Colombo. But Mitford was subject to chronic seasickness and was determined to go by another route—overland from Europe to Constantinople, then through Syria, Jerusalem, and Baghdad to Persia, India, and Ceylon. Although one can now go by bus from London to Calcutta, the journey can still be eventful and beset with unexpected complications. In 1839 such a journey was not only dangerous, it was literally an expedition into the unknown. To further complicate matters, Henry Layard had never been to the East, spoke no Oriental languages, and, worst of all, had never ridden a horse. Even Mitford was a little doubtful as to whether Layard would survive the journey.

With feverish eagerness, Layard threw himself into preparations for the trip. He passed his law examinations, took lessons in surveying, and consulted the few English diplomats and travelers who had visited Persia. The family thought he was crazy and said so in no uncertain terms. But they soon realized their objections were falling on deaf ears. So a small sum of money was scraped together to pay for supplies. Finally, the two travelers left London in July 1839 on a journey that was to change the course of archaeological history. Had Mitford not been chronically seasick, Layard would never have found a lost civilization and would probably have led a life of respectable anonymity.

Layard and Mitford traveled by horse bus, Rhine steamer, and light carriage across Germany to Italy. Layard was so entranced by Venice on this first visit that, many years later, he chose to retire there. A few weeks later, they were deep in Jugoslavia, where they bought saddles. Layard learned how to ride the hard way, but loved it. "The first day we rode 16 hours, the second 14, and the third 26 without stopping except to rest and change," he wrote home in delight. His body, apparently, was constructed of steel.

The Balkans, although fascinating, involved the travelers in some bloodcurdling episodes. At one point, they found themselves surrounded by Montenegran soldiers who smoked long pipes and calmly lounged in the men's lodgings while, just outside the window, they had full view of a circle of forty-five gory heads stuck on poles, trophies from a skirmish with the Turks a week before. Layard seems to have been unmoved by the spectacle. He wrote his nervous, sensitive mother a vivid account not only of the smell, but also of the blood that dripped from the decaying heads. Such chilling details can hardly have reassured his family back home.

By the time the two young men had reached Constantinople, Layard had fallen in love with the East. He was so fascinated by the sights and the cosmopolitan peoples they encountered in official resthouses and on the streets that the trip's hardships seemed insignificant. Fortunately the two men got on well together, despite marked differences in temperament. Mitford was conservative, careful, and a devout Christian. Layard was liberal, rash, and highly impulsive. Mitford watched the birds and animals; Layard visited every Greek and Roman temple he could find. Their diet was simple in the extreme—fish roe, carob beans, and unleavened bread. It cost them about four shillings a day to live as they made their way on horseback down the centuries-old route through Syria to Jerusalem. The Romans had traveled the very same way.

The Holy Land was in such a state of political confusion that Layard's hastily formed plan to travel eastward from Jerusalem to explore the lost city of Petra was regarded by local officials as crazy. Mitford refused to go with him. But Henry's newly acquired enthusiasm for antiquities could not be subdued. Eventually he left Jerusalem with only two camels and a very young Arab to cross country where most travelers survived by buying off the local chiefs.

Layard harbored the romantic notion that the Bedouin nomads of the desert offered hospitality to every stranger passing through their territory. How wrong he was! As soon as Layard entered the narrow defile that led to the mysterious city of Petra, a place hitherto rarely visited by Europeans, a crowd of suspicious Arabs surrounded his camel, demanding money. Fortunately, the chief arrived just as Henry was about to draw his pistol. Otherwise, he would certainly have been killed.

The Arabs looked on suspiciously as Layard poked around in the rock-cut temples of Petra and finally allowed him to depart for the mountains of Moab. There his luck ran out. He was attacked and robbed of everything by a group of tribesmen. Incredibly, Layard managed to grab the sheikh as a hostage in the nick of time. After lengthy bargaining, his supplies and simple possessions were restored to him, but the sheikh then "sold" him to another chief, who simply did not believe that Layard had no money or valuables. Layard's new owner was so surprised at his folly in traveling without ample "buy-off" money that he let him go free. After numerous adventures, Layard rejoined Mitford in Aleppo, where they made preparations to journey to Baghdad. Their arduous route would take them to Mosul and through the flat, harsh terrain of the Mesopotamian delta. It would be essential to travel light and sleep in their clothes. On March 18, 1841, the two men set out on a stage of the journey that was to change Layard's entire life.

Mosul, which the travelers reached at the beginning of April 1841, is situated on a flat floodplain of the Tigris River. Across the river lies a range of low hills, some four miles in circumference. These humanly made mounds were all that remained of a vast ancient city. Layard rode over to look at the deserted hills and found them littered with a profusion of potsherds and mud-brick fragments. Unlike most of his educated contemporaries, he had never been captivated by the spell of ancient Greece and Rome. Their classic temples left him relatively cold. But the deserted mounds of Kuyunjik, alleged to be ancient Nineveh, sent him into raptures.

"Desolation meets desolation," he wrote in his diary that night. "A feeling of awe succeeds to wonder; for there is nothing to relieve the mind, to lead to hope, or to tell of what has gone by." These huge mounds made a deep impression on Henry Layard. "A deep mystery hangs over Assyria," he said to Mitford. He insisted on staying in Mosul for two weeks while he brooded over the mounds and visited other sites in the vicinity.

By far the easiest way to reach Baghdad from Mosul was to float down the Tigris on a wooden raft supported by fifty sheepskins. The three-hundred-mile journey took them down a river route that had been in use for thousands of years. Twenty miles south of Mosul, they passed the ruins of another great city, Nimrud, their raft careering over some rapids that, according to the boatman, marked the remains of a dam built by ancient kings. Layard decided at that moment that he would one day explore these ancient mounds. By the time they reached Baghdad, a vague notion had become a fixation.

Colonel Taylor, the British agent in Baghdad, received the two travelers kindly. For two months Layard stayed in a guest house near the British residency. He spent hours poring over the books and manuscripts in Taylor's fine library. Henry was particularly interested in cuneiform, the mysterious ancient script that seemed to crop up everywhere—inscribed both on clay tablets and on great cliffs at Bisutun near Kermanshah. Everything he read increased his determination to dig at Nimrud and find out more about this strange writing.

At the end of their stay, Layard and Mitford joined a caravan that took them to Kermanshah and deep into Persia. At this point the two men parted company. Mitford was concerned about their delays and was anxious to reach India after a year on the road, while Layard wanted to press on into unknown country. Mitford, therefore, left along a safe route to the southeast, leaving Layard to venture off on his own in search of ancient cities and lost civilizations. Layard never reached Ceylon.

An extraordinary interlude in Layard's life followed. He decided to visit the country of the Bakhtiari nomads and attempt to locate the site of the ancient city of Susa. For over a year, Henry lived alone among the fierce and proud Bakhtiari, a tribe of warrior herdsmen. He seems to have been content to wander with them and was adopted by Mohamed Taki Khan as a member of his family when he cured the chief's son of fever. Layard became deeply involved in the Bakhtiari's constant quarrels with Persian officialdom. He took part in their skirmishes and political intrigues and, at one point, was captured by a cruel shiekh named Manuchar Khan who had a reputation for inhuman torture and indiscriminate use of the bastinado. Layard managed to escape and started the ride back to Baghdad, only to be robbed in the desert of his horse and possessions. His life was spared simply because he was English. Eventually he managed to reach the British residency in Baghdad, dressed as an Arab right down to the skin.

Layard was now in deep trouble with his family. His long silences kept his mother in a state of constant frenzy. Finally, Henry's father persuaded the Foreign Office to make inquiries about his son's whereabouts. When the British ambassador in Teheran inquired of Layard from the vizier, the latter replied, "That man! Why, if I could catch him, I'd hang him." This was hardly reassuring to the Layards.

But young Layard was regarded quite favorably in some circles. Colonel Taylor and others were deeply impressed with his knowledge of local affairs and sent him to see the British ambassador in Constantinople, Sir Stratford Canning. Layard was delighted to be off on his travels again and journeyed up the same route to Mosul, where he met Paul Botta, the new French vice-consul. Botta was a charming man, sent out by his government to look into reports of ancient cities in Mesopotamia. Layard spent hours poking around the mounds of Kuyunjik with Botta. The latter had already started to dig into them, but had, so far, found almost nothing.

The diplomatic world of Constantinople was a far cry from the wilds of Bakhtiari. Layard was received with scant courtesy by the British embassy staff, so, leaving an indignant letter for the ambassador, he stormed off to find a ship to England. The ambassador, on reading Layard's angry letter, received him promptly and listened to his tales of the Bakhtiari with great interest. Sir Stratford Canning, a formidable diplomat with tremendous prestige with the Turks, took an instant liking to Layard and retained him as an unpaid personal assistant for many months. Many of his assignments were confidential and dangerous and, true to character, Layard relished the secrecy and intrigue.

But always at the back of Layard's mind were the silent mounds of Mosul, especially when Paul Botta sent him drawings of some of his new and extraordinary discoveries at the ancient city of Khorsabad and elsewhere. He showed the drawings to Canning, in the hope that the ambassador would send him to Mosul and Nimrud in search of the ancient Assyrians. Eventually Canning gave in. He dispatched Henry to Mosul with instructions to spy out the land. The ambassador was prepared to pay for two months' excavations. Layard, acting as Canning's agent, was to keep his investigations as secret as possible. It's difficult to understand why Canning agreed to pay for the excavations, unless, of course, he felt he could make money from Layard's finds.

On November 8, 1845, Layard slipped away from Mosul on a raft. The departure was intentionally inconspicuous, for the French vice-consul, Botta, was both suspicious and anxious to keep a monopoly on all excavations in Mesopotamia on his own behalf. Fortunately, since the British vice-consul in Mosul was a contractor, Layard was able to have his excavation tools secretly made in his workshop.

Nimrud was deserted when Layard reached the site. His foreman went to look for laborers while the others slept. All night Layard tossed and

5-3. The ancient mound of Khorsabad, excavated by Paul Botta.

turned on his hard mattress, visions of vast treasures, buried palaces, and great warriors floating through his dreams. At dawn, his dreams gave way to reality and Layard, accompanied by six laborers, confronted the huge and silent mounds of Nimrud.

The site consisted of a long line of narrow mounds, dominated by a conelike pyramid. The pyramid, once the great *ziggurat* temple, had been worn over the centuries into a conical earthwork of mud brick over 140 feet high. The first problem was to decide where to start digging.

Layard chose a spot where a fragment of limestone stuck up above the ground. Within a few hours, the workmen had cleared the remains of a chamber about twenty-five feet long, with an inscribed marble floor covered with cuneiform writing. The room was filled with rubbish and yielded some magnificent ivory figures of a king, some crouching sphinxes, and beautiful flowers. Another trench on the southern side of the site revealed a long, inscribed wall that obviously formed part of another huge structure. In his first few days of excavations, Layard found not one, but two, royal palaces. Several years were to pass before Layard was to know that the Northwest Palace, where he first excavated, had been built by the great Assyrian King Ashur-nasir-pal II (883–859 B.C.). No one had yet deciphered cuneiform writing, nor could anyone read Assyrian inscriptions.

Since there were over nine hundred acres of Nimrud to be excavated, Layard wisely decided to concentrate on the western side of the site. He also decided to concentrate his search on sensational sculptures and art objects. These, he realized, were the sorts of things that excited popular interest and generated future financial support.

As the excavations went on, Layard heard rumors of avid curiosity among local officials in Mosul. Every local ruler was on the lookout for treasure, and treasure seemed to be what Layard was digging for. When a workman smuggled a tiny piece of gold leaf found in the Northwest Palace into a Mosul bazaar, rumors of major caches of gold spread like wildfire. So, while Layard continued to look for sculptures, others were after his gold.

After three weeks of work, the workmen in the Southwest Palace unearthed a wall covered with elegant bas-reliefs of battle scenes and a siege. These were executed in an even finer style than those that Botta had found at Khorsabad. Layard glowed with excitement. Every detail of the siege was represented in astonishing detail. There were long-haired women begging for mercy, a warrior setting fire to the gates of the city, a wounded man falling from the walls. The charioteers and regal horses that pranced across the slabs were ample reward for the months of frustration and uncertainty Layard had experienced. He realized now that he had found a flourishing ancient civilization fully as important as that of the ancient Egyptians.

At this crucial moment, Layard received news that the suspicious and gold-hungry local ruler had withdrawn his permission for Layard to excavate at Nimrud. Instantly Layard galloped to Mosul and sought audience with the pasha. The pasha was evasive. "I have learned that your site is a Moslem burial ground," he said. "The law forbids anyone to dig into ancient burial places."

In vain, Layard argued that there were no signs of recent burials on the mounds. But the pasha, who feared the French vice-consul, was adamant. With false amity the pasha declared, "Your life is more valuable than old stones. What grief would I suffer if anything happened to you?"

There was nothing Layard could do but return to Nimrud and make drawings of his discoveries. There he was confronted with a startling sight: his men were busy moving modern gravestones onto the site at the pasha's order! A local chief with whom he had become friendly was supervising. "We have destroyed more real tombs of the true believers in making sham ones than you could have defiled," bemoaned the chief.

The sympathetic locals let Layard do some quiet digging on the grounds as he was recording the sculptures already uncovered. These surreptitious excavations led to more exciting discoveries, including some gigantic winged bulls and nine-foot-high human figures. Wisely, Layard left these figures in the ground until his relations with the authorities improved.

Just as Layard had begun to despair over the possibility of any future progress, the sultan of Turkey abruptly replaced the pasha with a new governor who was not only pro-European, but a just and efficient administrator as well. The new pasha encouraged Layard to excavate and issued instructions that every assistance be given to him. This, since the local tribesmen had contemplated raiding the excavations, was a distinct advantage. Layard pressed on with the dig as fast as he dared, despite sporadic troublemaking by other Mosul bureaucrats who were convinced that golden treasure was slipping out of their grasp. In the intervals between making further discoveries of sculptures in the Southwest Palace, Layard carefully cultivated the local nomad chiefs to protect himself even further.

It was a wise move, for rumors of treasure had spread fast and Layard's small huts on the mound were a tempting target.

One day as Layard was returning from a diplomatic visit to a local sheikh, he was overtaken by two horsemen riding at a frantic pace. "Hasten, oh Bey," they cried, "they have found Nimrud himself." Layard spurred his horse to a gallop as the riders sped on to spread the word. He found his workmen clustered around an impromptu screen of cloaks and baskets that they gleefully lifted as he approached. An enormous human head sculptured in alabaster rose out of the ground to greet the astonished Layard. "The expression was calm, yet majestic," he wrote in his diary. The workmen were terrified when they first came across this astonishing apparition, half human, half bull, emerging from the ground like a strange monster. At least one man took to his heels, never to return. When he burst into the bazaar at Mosul, the town began to seethe with strange rumors of a new god and of heresy emerging from the earth. The pasha eventually summoned Layard with some concern and suggested he slow the pace of excavations for a while.

Meanwhile, Layard had found a second bull opposite the first, obviously the two sides of a great gate, and was quite content to take it easy for a time. Thousands of Arabs converged on the mound from miles around to stare at the strange bulls with human heads that guarded the gates of Nimrud. Layard himself admitted he spent hours contemplating "these mysterious emblems, and musing over their intent and history."

Layard knew that his discoveries would amaze the world and that much more lay under the ground. But he lacked the financial backing to finish the work. He had now been excavating for nearly six months at a total cost of eighty English pounds. To pass the time, he threw a huge spring party for all his Arab friends. The tribesmen flocked from all directions to the mound, which at that season was covered with green grass and wild flowers, to gaze at the great figures and dance to the sound of drums and pipes. Over five hundred Arabs joined Layard in dancing and feasting for five days. Although people in Constantinople considered such conduct "immoral," Layard was wise enough to know that the goodwill of the locals depended on such displays of hospitality. And, unlike many of his archaeological contemporaries, Layard never had any trouble with his laborers.

In May of 1846, Layard finally received a permit from the sultan of Turkey that allowed him to excavate freely wherever he wished. At last he was able to proceed with his discoveries. He drew on family funds to continue and tunneled deep into the Northwest Palace. The deeper he dug, the more exciting and perfect the sculptures became. The rooms of the palace were decorated with bas-reliefs of kings and horsemen, with servants and scenes of the chase. As each figure came to light, the Arabs would dart forward and either curse it or kiss it, depending on its sex. Slowly Layard

5-4. Discovering the human-headed lion at Nimrud.

began to saw away the bas-reliefs and to pack them in padded crates. They were then carried to the river on buffalo carts and floated downstream to Baghdad.

Layard himself worked frantically, making drawings of sculpture after sculpture in intense heat that often exceeded 110° in the shade. Gone were the spring flowers of a month before; the plain had shriveled under the relentless sun. Layard realized it would be necessary to move to the cool highlands for the summer months, but, before leaving, he paused to look at the human-headed bulls once more. "Their meaning was written upon them," he wrote. "They had awed and instructed races which flourished 3,000 years ago. Through the portals which they guarded, kings, priests and warriors had borne sacrifices to their altars, long before the wisdom of the East had penetrated to Greece." Now all that remained were desolate piles of rubbish covering a long-lost civilization.

When Layard returned to Mosul in October 1846, he found letters from the British Museum awaiting him. It had taken over the financing of the excavations from Canning, but on a scale so niggardly that Layard gasped with horror. The trustees of the Museum made no offer to send out an artist or other experts as the French had done. They had a bargain in Layard and they seemed to know it. He was working with minimal resources at a time when all the European nations were racing to dig up as much as they could in the Near East, many of them with abundant funds. It was sheer luck that the British Museum obtained as many finds as it did. With its backing, Layard was able to raise his labor force to one hundred thirty men. He built a mud-brick house for himself and barracks for his laborers on top of the Nimrud mound. He now headed a considerable party and was often sought out to mediate disputes among quarreling tribes.

By this time, tales of Layard's wisdom and bravery had spread all over Mesopotamia. He was almost an uncrowned ruler among the nomad tribes. His main labor problem was simple worker boredom. To relieve the monotonous routine, the workers devised strange forms of amusement. One day Layard found a group of horsemen driving a large flock of sheep from Nimrud village across the plain at full speed. To his great surprise, the men were emitting bloodcurdling war cries and flourishing swords. One of the men explained that they were bored with digging. "An Arab is an Arab," he cried. "We should be with our swords and mares in the desert. We are pretending that these sheep are taken from the enemy and we are driving them to our tents!"

The excavations continued to yield astonishing discoveries. Layard now realized he was dealing with two periods of occupation. The new finds included a black obelisk erected by Shalmaneser III, the son of Ashur-nasir-pal II, which was decorated with 210 lines of cuneiform. As the finds were dug out, they were packed for shipment downriver. One day, however, the valuable ropes and packing materials needed to prepare the shipments were mysteriously missing. Layard promptly called on the shiekh he felt sure was responsible for the theft, refused to believe his protestations of innocence, and boldly abducted him. By the time the uncooperative chief arrived at Nimrud, he was ready to confess. The packing materials were returned without delay and the shiekh released. There was no more trouble.

Considerable numbers of visitors were now making their way to Nimrud. The news correspondent J. A. Longworth wrote a memorable account of the excavations for the London *Morning Post*. He wrote of the awe he felt at seeing the ancient kings and viziers who had emerged into daylight after centuries of darkness. Layard was soon a famous man as the public eagerly began to follow the progress of his excavations. Longworth encouraged him to think about writing a book on the digs.

While he contemplated this proposition, Henry decided to move the great human-headed bulls from their centuries-old resting place. He had no illusions about the difficulty of the task, for each weighed more than ten tons. After examining some bas-reliefs of Assyrians hauling huge statues with ropes and levers, he decided to follow their example. When everything was ready, Layard climbed to the summit of the mound, high

5-5. The black obelisk of Shalmaneser.

5-6. Lowering the winged figure onto wooden rollers preparatory to its journey to the River Tigris.

above the exposed bulls. The straining Arabs levered one of them on its side with innumerable ropes. As it tilted toward the waiting rollers, the ropes broke and the bull crashed onto the timbers. Layard, seized with fear, rushed to the pit. But, marvel of marvels, the bull was still intact. Overjoyed, the Arabs danced until dawn, gaily prancing back to work the next morning with no apparent ill effects. After further strenuous efforts, the bull reached the river safely and was levered onto a waiting raft, finally ready for its long journey to the British Museum.

The Nimrud excavations were closed down as Layard turned his attention to the secrets of the mound of Kuyunjik near Mosul, still believed to be the site of ancient Nineveh. The Frenchman Paul Botta had worked there for some time. Since his departure, the French consul had hired laborers to put down some haphazard pits. They had found nothing. But Layard was now wise in the ways of Assyrian palace architects and, within a few days, he located a huge palace. Its long and narrow chambers rested on a large platform of mud brick, similar to those that Layard had contemplated for months at Nimrud. The bas-reliefs from this palace were larger than those from Nimrud, although of somewhat inferior workmanship. Winged bulls stood at the entrance to the palace. Layard had only enough time for a cursory examination of this remarkable structure before he hastened home to England, where fame and fortune awaited him. He was certain he had found ancient Nineveh itself and all of its ancient glories.

The once-unknown law student and family black sheep was now a national hero. During two years' arduous excavations, Layard had not only identified the sites of Nimrud and Nineveh, he had also excavated the remains of no less than eight Assyrian palaces. Hundreds of tons of sculpture from the excavations were already on their way to England when Layard himself arrived with his drawings and notebooks. At the age of thirty-one, Layard was well on the way to satisfying his ambitions. The sculptures caused a sensation when they were first displayed and Layard's public lectures were enthusiastically received. The idol of the moment, he was wined and dined. All these popular successes encouraged him to sit down at last and write a book about his discoveries.

Regrettably, Layard's popularity with the public did not seem to extend to the trustees of the British Museum. Although polite, they were rather indifferent to his sculptures and gave no sign of being willing to send him back for more excavations. So he departed, disgruntled, back to a post as an unpaid attaché at the British embassy in Constantinople.

No sooner had Layard arrived in Turkey than his *Nineveh and Its Remains* appeared in the bookstores. It took the public by storm. Layard had the gift of a vivid pen and *Nineveh* proved to be one of those books that every cultured person had to read, if only to say he or she had done so. The printer couldn't keep up with demand. It was a remarkable achievement, for Layard displayed a considerable academic talent and depth of knowledge, far more than might have been expected of a man with no formal training. The London *Times* described *Nineveh* as "the most extraordinary work of the present age." Yet its talented author was stuck in a foreign embassy without pay or work of importance.

This deplorable situation did not last long. Soon Layard was appointed as a paid attaché, then invited to head a new archaeological mission to Mesopotamia. The new expedition was more elaborate and included both an artist and a doctor. In September 1849, Layard and his party finally reached Mosul. His workmen greeted him rapturously; the very same horse was ready for him to ride. Layard felt as if he were coming home.

This time the excavations focused on the great Kuyunjik mounds of ancient Nineveh, which Layard had barely touched two years before. In his absence, the British vice-consul had kept a few men at work to prevent looting. A hundred men were now hired to look for more bas-reliefs. Layard then based himself at Nimrud, where excavations continued for most of the winter. The Northwest Palace continued to yield important finds, including some magnificent copper cauldrons. The excavators at Nineveh uncovered an ancient roadway, deeply rutted with chariot-wheel tracks.

Layard's main preoccupation, however, was with a pair of lions he had uncovered at Nimrud two years before. It was now time to move them

5-7. The figure passes the mounds of Nimrud on its way to the river bank.

to the British Museum. The night before the move took place, Layard and his companions rode to the mound to take a last look at the two guardians in their ancient resting place. Moonlight dramatically highlighted their fine heads. "It seems almost sacrilege to remove them," muttered Layard quietly. Later he wrote, "They had guarded the palace in its glory, and it was for them to watch over it in its ruins."

Both lions were heavier than the sculptures moved two years before. Layard shifted them by tilting each one over on soft mounds of earth which were slowly removed by quarrying underneath the recumbent animals. Just after the first lion was placed on a cart, the heavens opened and, in the heavy downpour, the cart's wheels bogged down in fresh mud. It took three hundred men and a week of hard labor to free the giant creature.

Meanwhile, the excavations at Nineveh were proceeding smoothly, so much so that Layard was able to slip away for a visit to new mounds in northern Mesopotamia. The country was in a state of considerable unrest and his workmen refused to dig in strange territory. Undaunted, Layard collected a mass of information about the nomads who lived in this remote area and had himself lowered over a steep cliff to read some famous Assyrian inscriptions near Bavian. The huge bas-relief of King Sennacherib seemed to sway in the wind as Layard, suspended at the end of a fragile rope, tried to copy the inscriptions. He was highly relieved to return to solid ground.

After two months of exploration, Layard returned to Nineveh to find that a whole new series of bas-reliefs had come to light in the depths of the Kuyunjik mound. Among the discoveries was a great gate bounded by two human-headed bulls and some enormous, incomplete human figures. The sculptures had been damaged by fire and a collapsed wooden gate lay between them. Apparently, the city had suffered some awful calamity. On each side, the deep walls of the excavation seemed to crowd in on the huge gateway, more than fourteen feet wide. Layard was deeply moved by these silent figures. "Between them," he wrote, "Sennacherib and his hosts had gone forth in all their might and glory to the conquest of distant lands, and had returned rich with spoil and captives. . . . Through them, too, the Assyrian monarch had entered his capital in shame, after his last and fatal defeat."

The southeastern side of the same palace yielded another imposing entrance, lined by ten huge bulls and six colossal human figures. The bulls bore inscriptions that linked them to Sennacherib. The same palace contained a series of magnificent bas-reliefs that told the story of the king's siege of the city of Lachish. Layard immediately recalled the Biblical siege of Lachish by Sennacherib's generals, which took place when Hezekiah refused to pay the Assyrians tribute. As more and more clues came to light, historians were able to link Layard's Assyrians and their palaces with the Biblical kings who had tormented the Hebrews. The public interest generated by these and other Mesopotamian discoveries was immense, for Nineveh and other excavations were living proof that the Biblical stories had, indeed, been based on historical fact.

By this time Layard's funds were again running low. Just as he was contemplating closing the digs, the workmen at Kuyunjik uncovered a room in the palace that contained a vast collection of terra-cotta tablets covered with minute cuneiform. Layard realized that this was a treasure house of vital information, probably the archives of the kings of Nineveh. Within a few weeks, he had filled six packing cases with tablets. There were still many more awaiting shipment. History has judged these archives to be one of the most important of all Layard's finds, for they were literally packed with vital information about the day-to-day concerns of the Assyrian kings.

The political situation was now so unsettled that it was obviously wise to scale down the excavations. Layard himself accompanied several rafts to Baghdad. En route, one of them was suddenly attacked by marauders, but the men put up a strong resistance and Layard and his precious cargo reached the city safely.

Although conditions were very difficult, Layard was allowed to do some digging into ancient Baghdad itself. All he found were masses of mud bricks, hardly worth the expense of excavation compared with Nimrud. What was the use of continuing, questioned Layard, "if Alexander the Great, after employing 10,000 men for ten months to clear away rubbish from the ruin, was obliged to give up the attempt?" So he contented himself

5-8. Layard suspended at the end of a rope recording Sennacherib's inscription.

5-9. Layard at work on the archives at Kuyunjik (Nineveh).

by traveling around the neighboring country and observing the Marsh Arabs tunneling their way through dense reeds in their tiny wicker boats. He recalled the Kuyunjik sculptures with their scenes of Assyrian wars conducted in small wicker boats just like those he now observed. Truly, Mesopotamia had deep roots, extending back thousands of years into prehistory.

Unfortunately the unhealthy swamps gave Layard a fever that seriously weakened him. By April 1851, he had had enough and made his way back to London. Although Layard himself felt he had achieved but little, his excavations, conducted with minimal financing, had resulted in quite extraordinary discoveries. "I had opened no less than seventy-one halls, chambers, and passages, whose walls, almost without exception, had been paneled with slabs of sculptured alabaster recording the wars, the triumphs, and the great deeds of the Assyrian kings," he wrote of Nineveh. "By a rough calculation about 9,880 feet, or nearly two miles, of bas-reliefs, with twenty-seven portals formed by colossal winged bulls and lion sphinxes, were uncovered in that part alone of the building explored during my researches."

Thousands of drawings, an entire Assyrian archive, and magnificent bas-reliefs and sculptures were on their way to the British Museum. But Layard was frustrated, for only a small portion of his discoveries could be shipped home. The rest were left to the mercy of looters and the local people. Had the British government been prepared to spend more, the discoveries sent to England would have been even more spectacular and much more could have been saved for posterity. Nevertheless, the clay tablets from Nineveh alone were sufficient to lay the foundations for modern Assyriology.

Henry Layard received a hero's reception in London. It was the year of the 1851 Great Exhibition, a symbol of Britain's emerging preeminence in the world of industry, trade, art, and culture. He was a man of the hour, feted everywhere and welcomed in the homes of the great and famous. The only people who did not seem to approve were the trustees of the British Museum, with whom Layard argued passionately about his finds and the future of the excavations. He considered the authorities niggardly and shortsighted. They, in turn, distrusted their maverick former employee and his enormous popularity.

The public adored Layard. Within two years, *Nineveh and Babylon* followed Layard's earlier book as a best-seller. Everyone read it and all the reviews were favorable. A large folio of drawings of bas-reliefs from Nineveh was published at the same time and is now a rare collector's item. Layard had the gift of literary eloquence, an ability to write moving and evocative descriptions of excavations and personalities, crises and great discoveries. He ranks among the most remarkable of all early archaeologists, not only

5-10. King Ashurbanipal of Nineveh hunting lions.

because of his discovery of the Assyrians and Sumerians, but also because he was able to make these ancient peoples accessible to the general public through his writings and drawings. Londoners could now imagine Assyrian kings strutting to war or sitting in judgment over their subjects. Further, they could gaze on drawings of Ashur-bani-pal as he went hunting or of Assyrian boatmen crossing the Tigris in wicker and bitumen boats. A shadowy Biblical civilization had suddenly come alive through archaeological excavation. Perhaps Layard's greatest achievement was that he laid the foundations for the great excavations that were to take place in Mesopotamia later in the nineteenth and twentieth centuries, excavations that could only build on his astonishing finds.

Nineveh and Babylon was Layard's last archaeological book. In 1852, powerful friends persuaded him to pursue a political career, a profession in which he was far from comfortable. Some time later, Henry became a much-admired diplomat, serving in both Constantinople and Madrid with great distinction. He never returned to the brooding mounds of Nimrud or Nineveh and his interest in archaeology seemed to wane. His life was now consumed by great affairs and by an ambition to succeed in other, less academic spheres. Still, by the time Layard died in 1894, he ranked among the archaeological immortals. He lent an eloquence to archaeology that has yet to be surpassed. In his own memorable words: "The great tide of civilization has long since ebbed, leaving these scattered wrecks on the solitary shore. Are those waters to flow again, bearing back the seeds of knowledge and of wealth that they have wafted to the West? We wanderers were seeking what they had left behind, as children gather up the colored shells on the deserted sands."

6

Heinrich Schliemann and ANCIENT TROY

What memories the name of Troy brings back! The miseries we Achaeans put up with there! Raid after raid across the misty seas in search of plunder at Achilles' beck and call, fight after fight round the very walls of royal Priam's town. . . ." The occasion was a royal banquet. Veteran King Nestor was entertaining noble visitors from the island of Ithaca off the west coast of Greece. Inevitably, the conversation turned to fresh memories of bloody campaigns, to raids and wars fought over the lush plains of distant Troy, hundreds of miles to the north. Nestor himself had played a prominent part in the wars. His memories and those of thousands of his fellow soldiers were soon enshrined in folklore and song, passed on from generation to generation of traveling minstrels who would recount these much-loved stories the length and breadth of Greece, in royal palaces and remote farmsteads alike.

Hundreds of years later, in the tenth century B.C., the epics were written down for the first time. The long poems that made up the story were grouped into two great works: the *Iliad* and the *Odyssey*. Popular legend ascribes the authorship of these magnificent works to the poet Homer. But whether he was a single individual or a group of poets is unknown. Homer's stirring tales of the long siege of Troy, of heroic deeds by brave chieftains, and of divine plots and human frailty became a cornerstone of classical Greek literature.

The *Iliad* tells the story of the final stages of the ten-year siege of the ancient city of Troy, situated in northwest Turkey. Many years before, the Trojan prince Paris had abducted and himself married the lovely Helen, wife of King Menelaus of Sparta. Menelaus and his brother Agamemnon, intent on recovering Helen, formed a holy alliance of dozens of Greek chieftains to wage war against King Priam's Troy. The *Iliad* opens with the Greek camp in turmoil. The mighty hero Achilles, a warrior essential to the Greek cause, is sulking in his tent after a quarrel with Agamemnon over a slave girl. As long as Achilles refuses to fight, the Greek forces are seriously weakened. The dramatic stanzas of the *Iliad* relate how the gods intervene in the war and recount the battles that bring the Trojans to the fences of the Greek camp. Achilles finally emerges from isolation when his friend and lover Patroclus is killed by Hector. To avenge his friend, Achilles slays Hector in single combat. The book concludes with the funeral of Hector, some time before the fall of Troy.

The blow-by-blow battle descriptions of the *Iliad* are richly embroidered with detailed accounts of weapons, customs, ornaments, and dress—all the panoply of a fully developed civilization. The sequel to the *Iliad*, the *Odyssey*, begins some ten years after the fall of Troy. All the heroes have returned home, with the exception of Odysseus of Ithaca, a crafty and skillful warrior-politician who has inadvertently angered Poseidon, the god of the sea. It was Odysseus who invented the brilliant stratagem of the wooden horse, the means used to smuggle Greek soldiers into Troy. As soon as the Trojans had dragged the massive horse into their city, Greek soldiers emerged from its cavernous depths and opened the gates to their comrades waiting outside. Troy fell soon thereafter. When the *Odyssey* opens, we learn that Odysseus is now condemned to wander aimlessly on the oceans of the world, after all his companions have perished. Odysseus' final adventures and his secret return to his beloved Ithaca are related in the *Odyssey*. Once in Ithaca, Odysseus kills off the suitors who are courting his faithful wife and, of course, lives happily ever after.

The *Iliad* and the *Odyssey* contain all the crowd-pleasing ingredients a good epic needs—bloodshed, scheming gods, lust, sex, high living, and, best of all, a wonderful narrative. It's not surprising that, a century ago, both volumes could be found on most educated people's bookshelves. But were the epics true? Had the Trojan War ever taken place? Did Agamemnon, Achilles, and Odysseus ever exist? Was there once an actual city of Troy? These questions intrigued everyone who read the poems. Although expert scholarly opinion leaned toward the belief that Homer himself probably had not existed and that the epics were compiled by the combined efforts of many bards, some classicists fervently believed that Troy was a real place and that Homer had been writing true history.

Now we turn to the story of Heinrich Schliemann, a man so firmly convinced of the existence of ancient Troy that he set out to find it.

Heinrich Schliemann ranks as one of the most extraordinary archaeologists of all time. He was born in 1822, the son of a Protestant minister in a rural parish in northern Germany. As he later wrote, in an autobiographical memoir that was only loosely based on truth, even as a child he possessed "a natural disposition for the mysterious and marvellous." The village of Neu Buckow abounded in legends and folktales that Ernest Schliemann often told his children. The Schliemann house itself was haunted: a ghostly maiden would rise each night from a small pond nearby. Then, of course, there was the terrible robber baron buried in the churchyard. He had killed a cowherd by frying him alive in an iron pan. When cornered, Henning Bradenkirl had committed suicide. For centuries, the story went, his left leg, clothed in a black silk stocking, had protruded from his grave. The young Schliemann, when not planning where next to dig for buried treasure, spent hours contemplating the tombstone.

Ernest Schliemann was deeply interested in the classics. He was fond

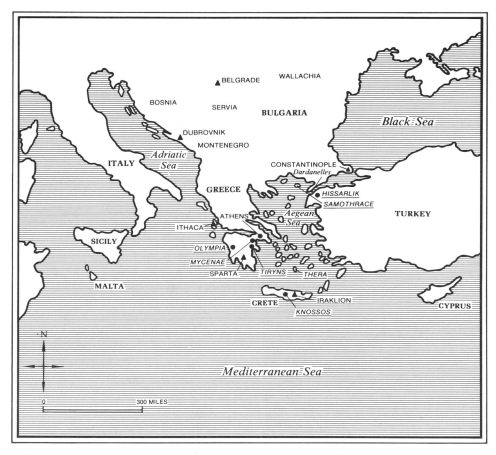

6-1. Locations and sites mentioned in chapters 6 and 7.

of a good story, especially the tale of the Greeks and the Trojans, which he often repeated round the fire on a winter's evening. His excitement rubbed off on his son, and young Heinrich became a champion of the Trojan cause. When the pastor gave his eight-year-old son a copy of Georg Ludwig Jerrer's *Illustrated History of the World*, Heinrich pored over the illustrations for hours, returning repeatedly to a picture of Troy in flames.

"Father," he cried, "Jerrer must have seen Troy, otherwise he could not have represented it here."

"My son, that is merely a fanciful picture," replied his father.

"Father, if such walls once existed, they cannot possibly have been completely destroyed—vast ruins of them must remain," insisted Heinrich.

Ernest Schliemann quietly disagreed, but Heinrich was persistent. According to his memoir, "One day, when I grow up, I will find Troy and dig it up," he cried. Thirty-nine years later, Heinrich Schliemann found the site of Homeric Troy.

The astonishing story of how Heinrich Schliemann became a world-famous archaeologist, as well as a millionaire, is as remarkable as his discovery of Troy. The Schliemanns were so poor that Heinrich was apprenticed to a grocer at the age of fourteen and was therefore unable to complete his schooling. For five and a half long years, Schliemann sold provisions from five o'clock in the morning to eleven at night. Grinding poverty and long work hours slowly sapped his once-strong desire to continue his learning. One day, however, a drunken miller shopping in the store absentmindedly began to recite a hundred lines of Homer in the original Greek. Schliemann leaned on the counter entranced and, when the miller came to the end of his recital, bought three whiskies for the drunkard so he would repeat the lines.

Things went from bad to worse when a chest ailment cost Heinrich his job. In 1841, he wandered to Hamburg, where, in desperation, he boarded ship for Venezuela, selling his only coat to buy a blanket. En route, the *Dorothea* was wrecked in a North Sea gale off the island of Texel. Schliemann and his companions were lucky to reach shore alive. Destitute, frozen with winter cold, ever hungry, he obtained a humble clerking position in Amsterdam. The hours, at least, were not as savage as those at the grocer's. With astonishing singlemindedness, Schliemann set out to educate himself, setting aside half his annual salary of sixty-four dollars for self-improvement. First, he learned to write properly. Then he settled down to learn English and French. He accomplished his objective in a year by the simple expedient of reading the original languages and learning as much as he could by heart. An extraordinary memory and ability for languages encouraged him to tackle Dutch, Spanish, Italian, and Portuguese next: he mastered each in six weeks.

Schliemann's luck was now turning. His original employers were unimpressed by his new learning, but he was hired by the Schröder brothers, prosperous merchants with extensive connections in the indigo trade with Russia. Schliemann promptly sat down to learn Russian, a formidable task, for there were no qualified teachers in Amsterdam. He learned the Russian alphabet from a dictionary and recited the adventures of the Greek hero Telemachus aloud in Russian. His loud discourses could be heard clearly through the partitions of his cheap lodging house, so he was obliged to move. Desperate for a teacher, Schliemann hired a poor Russian to listen to him for two hours a day. His visitor earned four francs a week for suffering through hours of unintelligible recitation. But, within six weeks, Schliemann was conversing fluently with Russian merchants at the indigo auctions.

6-2. Heinrich and Sophia Schliemann. Sophia is wearing the "Treasure of Priam."

In 1846 the Schröders sent Schliemann to St. Petersburg to act as their firm's Russian agent, a task he fulfilled brilliantly. Within a year he had set himself up as an independent, wholesale indigo merchant. He now applied himself to money making with the same intensity he had exhibited in learning languages. His fluency in Russian and other European languages enabled him to conduct business all over the Continent. In 1850 he ranged even further afield, sailing to California at the height of the gold rush. Schliemann promptly set up a banking agency in Sacramento and accumulated a substantial fortune. Returning to St. Petersburg two years later, he married, had three children, and made another fortune in war materials during the Crimean War. He took time off to learn Swedish and Polish and, later, mastered Latin and Arabic during an extensive tour of the Near East that took him to Petra and the Holy Land.

Classical Greek was next on the list. He began by mastering the modern language in six weeks. Then he spent two years on classical Greek, learning it ungrammatically as if it were a living language. The *Iliad* and *Odyssey* now came alive, as Schliemann learned their mellifluous lines by heart. His obsession with Troy sharpened with time. "In the midst of the bustle of business," he later wrote, "I never forgot Troy, or the agreement

I had made with my father to excavate it." In 1863, a fluent classical scholar with years of preparation behind him, Heinrich Schliemann retired from business at the age of forty-one. The rest of his life was to be devoted to Troy and archaeology. "I loved money indeed," he once remarked, "but solely as a means of realizing this real idea of my life."

While most people would have dashed off to Greece at once, Schliemann took the long way around. He set off on a world tour that took him to Carthage, Egypt, India, China, Japan, and finally North America, where he stopped to visit friends in California before settling in Paris to study archaeology seriously. All the energy that Schliemann had devoted to languages and indigo was now diverted to the search for Troy. In 1868 he set out on a leisured inspection of ancient Greece, the first time he had set foot in the land of Homer.

The energetic newcomer was an archaeologist with a difference. He believed with a fanatical intensity in the absolute truth of the *Iliad* and *Odyssey*. When the *Iliad* told how Achilles had chased the doomed Hector three times around the walls of Troy, Schliemann had no doubt that the chase was historical fact. The Troy described by Homer was a substantial fortress, with "wide streets" and "lofty towers." The walled town possessed at least two named gates. There was a marketplace and a great palace. If Homer's description is at all accurate, there were perhaps as many as fifty thousand people living in or near the fortress. The description of Troy in the *Iliad* is by no means detailed, but Schliemann believed that every bit of information in the Homeric poems could be discerned in the ground.

This was not the first time that Schliemann had flown in the face of established opinion. Most classical scholars were firmly convinced that the *Iliad* was nothing more than the product of poetic imagination. Homer himself was probably a fictional character, the Trojan War part of a world that never existed. The Greece of Homer was depicted as a sophisticated land. But, pointed out the learned classicists of Schliemann's day, the earliest Greeks to appear in recorded history were an unsophisticated, poverty-stricken people. How, therefore, could one square the Homeric account with historical fact? They concluded it was useless to look for the actual site of the Homeric city. But Heinrich Schliemann was a dreamer, a romantic at heart who was so wrapped up in the *Iliad* that he was certain the site of ancient Troy could be found. This faith, nurtured from childhood, brought him archaeological immortality.

Schliemann began his search for the lost city far to the north of Greece, near the mouth of the Dardanelles. He reached the Troad—the territory surrounding ancient Troy—by ship, then hired a Greek guide to take him out to the Trojan plain on horseback. Riding bareback in his smart business suit, Heinrich Schliemann gazed for the first time on the land of his childhood dreams. The problem was to locate the ancient city.

Heinrich Schliemann was not the first person to look for Troy. A few explorers had ridden out to the village of Bunarbashi at the south edge of the plain, famous for its springs and overshadowed by the rocky heights of Bali Dagh. Some people thought this was the site of Troy, although Austrian excavations in 1864 had yielded nothing. Schliemann was unconvinced. Instead of a cold and a hot spring rising by the banks of the river Scamander, as Homer had described, he found forty cold springs. Furthermore, Bunarbashi lay eight miles from the sea, whereas the Greeks had obviously camped far closer to Troy than that, for they traveled to and from the besieged city several times a day from their coastal camp. Hasty test excavations near the springs and on the citadel confirmed his hunch. Bunarbashi was not Troy.

Next Schliemann wandered through the hills on either side of the Trojan plain, looking for old town sites. The search was fruitless until he came to a hill named Hissarlik, three miles from the Hellespont. At this point Schliemann was introduced to Frank Calvert, the United States vice-consul at the Dardanelles. Calvert not only owned half the mound, he had also dug into his property in search of Troy. Calvert and Schliemann soon became fast friends, partly because each had made a fortune out of the Crimean War. The consul, however, was in deep trouble with the British, who had accused him of profiteering and condemned him to death in his absence. So, unable to return to England, Calvert lived in great style in the Troad, devoting some of his leisure to archaeology. He had been convinced for some time that Hissarlik was Troy. Most exciting of all, his excavations had revealed traces of stone walls deep in the Hissarlik mound.

Schliemann wandered over the deserted mound, looking for confirmation of Calvert's theory. The topography was flat enough for substantial buildings, the town mound small enough for Achilles to have run around it thrice without undue effort. There were no springs, but, as Calvert pointed out, these could have dried up since the town was abandoned.

Impetuously, Schliemann rode down to the sea and reconstructed the battles that raged between the city and the Hellespont. Homer in hand, he marshalled his arguments in favor of Hissarlik, dismissed the speculations of his contemporaries as irrelevant, and decided to dig into the mound.

It was not until two years later that Schliemann returned to Hissarlik. His marriage had been a complete failure and, with characteristic efficiency, he visited the United States and obtained a quick divorce in Indianapolis. In April 1870, he returned to Hissarlik, sank a trial trench at the north-western corner of the mound, and discovered the remains of a huge stone wall sixteen feet below the surface. Nothing more could be done until he had received a permit from the sultan of Turkey allowing him to excavate on a large scale.

Schliemann was now a man possessed, perhaps because he realized he was on the threshold of immortality. Now totally in love with Greece, he sought a Greek wife to help in his work. Old Greek friends, among them his language tutor, Father Theokletos Vimpos, were importuned. Soon he was interviewing likely candidates, finally settling on the young and beautiful Sophia Engastromenos, the daughter of a shopkeeper. She was seventeen, Schliemann forty-seven, yet the marriage was a success. Sophia was set to work to learn the classics and several languages. Together they waited impatiently for the sultan's permit. To Schliemann, his lovely wife may have been the living embodiment of the dazzling Helen of Troy, so often in his dreams.

The Sublime Porte in Constantinople was not to be hurried. Schliemann's permit finally came through in September 1871, leaving barely enough time for any excavations that summer. Immediately the Schliemanns set out for Hissarlik, only to encounter more frustrating delays at the hands of local officials who insisted on property maps and other minor formalities. Finally, on October 11, 1871, the excavations began.

Conditions were far from comfortable. The only accommodations were in the village of Chilak, over a mile from Hissarlik itself. But bedbugs, poor food, and the ever-present threat of malaria could not deter Schliemann from the task ahead. Eighty laborers recruited from nearby villages set to work with pickaxes and wooden shovels at the northern side of the mound. Six weeks later, with the onset of winter, excavations had to be halted. Even with inadequate tools, the diggers had quarried a large trench thirty-three feet into the mound. Quarrying was an apt description for the digging. Schliemann let nothing stand in his way; stone walls and foundations were ripped out piecemeal. Thousands of pottery fragments, stone implements, and grinders were excavated in the lower levels of the trench. A jumble of stone blocks, perhaps signs of a great city, came from the bottom of the huge cutting.

The 1871 excavations were just the beginning. In March of the following year the Schliemanns were back at Hissarlik with an enormous arsenal of shovels, pickaxes, and wheelbarrows. They built themselves an excavation house on top of the mound. Three foremen and a surveyor were retained to supervise a labor force of a hundred men that grew at times to one hundred and fifty. Large teams were deployed to uncover the successive layers of the mound like layers of a cake. At times the weather was so cold that the Schliemanns shivered in their plank-built house as the wind whistled through the walls and the temperature fell to twenty-three degrees. Even pots of water near the fire froze solid. Although they were able to keep warm in the trenches by day, the evenings were chilly indeed. "We had nothing to keep us warm except our enthusiasm for the great task of discovering Troy," recalled Schliemann later. But their efforts were richly rewarded.

As the excavations penetrated ever deeper into the mound and finally

6-3. The mounds of Hissarlik during Schliemann's excavations. The great trench exposed what he called "Trojan buildings."

reached bedrock at a depth of over forty-five feet, a fascinating picture of an evolving settlement slowly unfolded. Schliemann had started by assuming that King Priam's city was the original town on the hill. Therefore, its ruins were bound to lie at the base of the mound, below the later occupation levels. With characteristic thoroughness, he marshalled his labor force and started to cut a huge trench some 130 feet across through the mound from north to south. Even with modern equipment this would have been a stupendous undertaking. Eventually Schliemann was obliged to scale down his operations, but not before more than 325,000 cubic yards of earth had been excavated from the mound.

The results of the excavation were astonishing. City after city had flourished at Hissarlik, each succeeding series of buildings erected on the foundations of earlier settlements. The debris did not form a single homogeneous mass, but had accumulated in superimposed layers that represented different chronological periods. By the end of the 1873 season, Heinrich Schliemann had recognized no less than seven cities of Troy. By 1890, he had added two more. The earliest city was but a crude and tiny settlement, far too poor to have been Homer's Troy. So Schliemann revised his thinking and proudly announced that the third city from the base was Priam's Troy. What clinched his verdict was the existence of a dense layer of burnt masonry and ash that contained "many treasures" of copper, gold, and silver. This city had been burnt down. Obviously, said Schliemann, this was the Troy that was destroyed by the Greeks at the end of the war. Cities found higher in the mound were obviously more recent.

6-4. Schliemann's trench near the "Great Tower of Ilium." His excavation houses can be seen on top of the mound.

At this stage in his mercurial career, no one could call Schliemann an expert archaeologist. But archaeology was hardly a science at all in the 1870s. The average excavation was little more than a glorified treasure hunt. People were still looting the ancient tombs of Egypt wholesale, with little concern for conservation or accurate chronology. The Troy excavations were started on a large scale without any firm plan beyond a copy of the *Iliad* and some indications from the surface of the mound as to where digging might be most richly rewarded. The sheer scale of the Schliemann operation is mind boggling. His methods were drastic, direct, and costly. The cost was both monetary—the best equipment and a team of workmen that rarely numbered below a hundred—and, regrettably, archaeological. The narrative account of the excavation reads like an army campaign. "The great extent of my excavations rendered it necessary for me to work with no less than 120 laborers," Schliemann notes. A few pages later he blithely admits, "I was forced to demolish many interesting ruins in the upper strata." Temples, fortification walls, burials, and vast quantities of occupation debris were shoveled aside in the search for Homer's city. Nothing was allowed to stand in the way of Schliemann's objective. Without any archaeological experience at all, the Schliemanns tackled the large-scale excavation of an ancient mound with no vast stone structures to guide them. Schliemann was, however, quick to learn. He observed the complex layers of the mound and soon sought out experts to help study the finds.

By June of 1873, the pace of excavation and the difficult living conditions were beginning to take their toll. The Schliemanns had nearly perished in a fire that threatened to engulf the base house, the constant stiff north wind blew dust into their food, and, most nights, they were kept awake by hundreds of shrieking owls and millions of croaking frogs in the surrounding marshes. It was time to call a halt. Besides, the material uncovered so far needed to be studied before excavations could proceed profitably.

As this stage of the excavations drew to a close, efforts were concentrated on the third city. One hot morning, the diggers were working twenty-eight feet below the surface when Schliemann suddenly stiffened. Gold glittered in the morning sunlight, gleaming from a pile of loose earth. The workmen had not yet spotted it. Schliemann rushed for his wife and told her to send the men home for the day on some pretext. She demurred. "Pretend it's my birthday," he whispered. As soon as the delighted men had left, Schliemann jumped down in the trench with a large knife. Oblivious to the huge stone blocks that teetered above him, he cut into the soft earth. Sophia stood close by with her shawl at the ready. Quickly Heinrich shoveled the priceless finds and the earth containing them into the red shawl. No one witnessed this climactic moment of the Troy excavations. "The sight of so many immeasurably priceless objects made me foolhardy," wrote Schliemann later. "I did not think of the hazard."

The laden shawl was soon carried safely to the base house where, breathlessly, the Schliemanns spread their treasure on a rough wooden table. There were gold pendants and earrings, ivory and buttons, chains and brooches. Inspired and ebullient, Heinrich Schliemann decked his twenty-year-old wife in part of the golden treasure. "You are truly Helen of Troy," he cried. Schliemann never doubted that he had found King Priam's own treasure. "Apparently someone in Priam's family had hastily packed away the treasure in boxes," he reported. "Then, on the walls, this person met his death either directly at enemy hands or when struck by

6-5. Schliemann's illustration of the "Treasure of Priam," almost certainly assembled from many isolated finds.

a flying missile. The treasure lay where it fell, and presently was buried under five or six feet of ashes and stones from the adjacent royal house.''

The discovery of Priam's treasure sounds like one of the great moments of archaeology. Alas, there is a real question as to whether the event actually took place. There are strong reasons to suspect that the Schliemanns assembled their "treasure" from many isolated gold finds during their excavations.

At this crowning moment in his career, Schliemann was downright unscrupulous. One condition of his permit was that he had to give half of his finds to the Turkish government and, of course, the treasure came under this condition. But, determined that European scholars should have access to the treasure, Schliemann quietly smuggled it out of Turkey with the help of his wife's relatives. The priceless gold pieces were hidden in a garden shed in Greece.

For days the Schliemanns quietly studied and cataloged the find, bringing the collection to their house in small lots. Every piece was photographed separately. Then, on a feast day when the streets were quiet, the whole collection was brought to the laboratory. The photographer took portraits of the treasure and of Sophia decked out in the ornaments of prehistoric Troy. Then, six months before his book on Troy was to appear, Schliemann wrote a full account of the discovery of the treasure for a German newspaper. In the article he freely admitted that the treasure had been smuggled out of Turkey. The gold pieces, he announced, would be housed in a new museum to be built in Athens at his expense.

The Turks were incensed by the announcement. Rumors of smuggling by the Schliemanns had already been circulating in Constantinople. Official protests were lodged in Athens. The Greeks, anxious to avoid a confrontation with the sultan, rejected the offer of the museum and refused Schliemann the permit to dig at Mycenae that he had requested. Local newspapers accused Schliemann of forging the treasure. Heinrich and Sophia were ostracized by their friends. The furor was at its height when Schliemann's *Trojan Antiquities* appeared in January 1874. It was a handsome and comprehensive narrative of the Schliemann excavations. *Trojan Antiquities* received mixed reviews. The British were enthusiastic, but the German scholars, who refused to believe that Troy existed, murdered the book. Schliemann was castigated for being unscientific and for pulling down priceless temples. Some reviewers openly theorized that Priam's treasure had come from the bazaars of Constantinople. But the general public was captivated.

Despite all the protests of conservative scholars, Heinrich Schliemann was now an international celebrity, accepted as a first-rate archaeologist in his own right. The destitute grocer's clerk was the darling of Europe, his every move observed and duly reported in the press. Some men would have been content to rest on their laurels, but not Schliemann.

◄ **6-6.** Mycenae: Stairway leading down to and through the walls to the spring. Mycenaean stonework in the form of pointed arch.

The scandal over the treasure dragged on for months. Schliemann wrote to Constantinople offering to pay all the costs of the new excavation season at Troy. He received no reply. Then the Turks resorted to the courts, claiming half the treasure. After prolonged maneuvering, the court fined Schliemann two thousand dollars. He promptly offered the Turks eight thousand as well as the fine, an offer that was only accepted in April 1875. Needless to say, his future relations with Constantinople were never easy.

For some time now, Schliemann had had his restless eyes on Mycenae, anxious to dig into the palace and burial place of the legendary King Agamemnon, leader of the Greeks at Troy. Mycenae lies at the north corner of the plain of Argos, a fertile area famous in Homer's time for its horses. The giant stone blocks of its vast fortifications had long been a familiar landmark. In A.D. 170 the Greek traveler Pausanias visited Mycenae. He marvelled at the massive walls and the entrance gate with its carved lions. Nearby lay great subterranean structures that, wrote Pausanias, were the treasuries of the kings. Agamemnon and his royal companions reposed in royal tombs inside the walls of the citadel.

Agamemnon had inherited the wealthy kingship of Mycenae from descendants of Atreus. Such was the prestige of Mycenae that Agamemnon was the logical person to lead the expeditionary force against Troy. His prolonged absence of a decade left his queen Clytemnestra alone at Mycenae. She was promptly seduced by Aegisthus, son of one of Agamemnon's nephews. Aegisthus now plotted to inherit Agamemnon's kingdom. When warned of the king's return, the queen and her seducer invited the returning warriors to a great banquet. Agamemnon and his companions were slaughtered at the table. Aegisthus survived as ruler for seven years before Orestes, Agamemnon's son, killed the usurper and the queen as well.

Schliemann had such faith in Homer that he believed that Agamemnon's bones actually lay inside Mycenae's walls. Once again he put his trust in ancient writers rather than modern authorities. Accepting Homer as historical truth and Pausanias as his guide, Schliemann applied for a permit to dig at Mycenae. After long delays, the Greeks agreed. The famous husband and wife team settled in at Mycenae for a large dig in 1876.

No one expected Heinrich Schliemann to repeat his spectacular Trojan discoveries; he had been too successful already. Surely, for once, he would fail. Two years before, the Schliemanns had sunk some discreet trial pits to see where the deepest deposits lay. They had noted that the thickest accumulations of occupation deposit lay inside the citadel, where the inhabitants withdrew in time of war. All Schliemann's archaeological

6-7. The Lion Gate at Mycenae.

instincts, well developed by many months of digging at Troy, sent him inside the citadel.

While the experts shook their heads, sixty-three men were put to work in three parties. Twelve men began to clear the lion gate; forty-three dug a huge trench immediately to the southwest of the entrance inside the walls; a further eight cleared a "treasury" near the gate, whose entrance was partly exposed.

The excavations inside the gate soon turned up thousands of painted vase fragments. Then a curious, circular structure, built of a double row of stone slabs set on edge, came to light. Nearby were nine "tombstones," several of them decorated with armed charioteers. Immediately Schliemann remembered the Greek playwright Euripides' description of Agamemnon's grave. According to Euripides, the circle of stones was an assembly place for the elders, built in such a way that the heroes' graves were in the middle of the circular arena. With an astonishing and highly unscientific faith in his ancient sources, and even before he had dug below the grave stones, Schliemann announced that he had discovered the burial places of Agamemnon and Atreus.

The first grave was uncovered four months almost to the day after the excavations began. For days the Schliemanns labored inside the stone circle. They found five graves containing fifteen bodies lying in soft earth and ash. Sophia spent hours on her knees separating delicate ornaments from the soil. The fifteen skeletons were literally smothered in gold ornaments, the greatest archaeological treasure ever found until the discovery of the tomb of Tutankhamun in 1921. The wealth and variety of the Mycenae ornaments far exceeded that of the treasure of Priam. Delicately hammered embossed plates of gold, delicate crowns and vessels, and dozens of small ornaments were found in the graves. Several gold death masks with clipped beards and mustaches came to light. Schliemann and the world were excited. In a torrent of articles and books, the discoveries at Mycenae were revealed to a delighted public. Almost daily, the London *Times* carried detailed descriptions of the Mycenae excavations. When the graves were finally unearthed, Schliemann promptly telegraphed to the

6-8. General view from Shaft Grave Circle at Mycenae.

King of Greece: "It is with great pleasure that I announce to Your Majesty that I have found the graves which, according to tradition, are those of Agamemnon, Cassandra, Eurymedon, and their companions."

And the public believed him. Even those who scoffed at his finds, who thought them to be Byzantine or the work of "Orientals," were forced to take Schliemann's researches seriously, even if he was apt to jump to sensational and controversial conclusions. The excavations did far more than bring Homer to life: they brought prehistoric archaeology into the public consciousness to a degree never before deemed possible. The entire world vicariously participated in the Mycenae excavations; two ruling monarchs and a prime minister were kept posted on every phase of the dig. The king of Brazil himself visited the dig and dined in the treasury of Atreus. "I want the world to experience our excavations," Schliemann once said. "If I find I am wrong, I admit it, so people can see me thinking." He succeeded brilliantly.

There seemed to be no end to the wonders from the Mycenaean graves. One of the bodies was so well preserved that some of the nonskeletal parts still remained. The body was squashed almost flat and much compressed, but the gold ornaments were perfectly preserved. News of this unusual discovery spread like wildfire. From miles around the local people arrived to gaze on the long-dead warrior. Schliemann was at a loss to know how to preserve the mummified remains before they crumbled to dust. He commissioned an oil painting of the grave while a local druggist mixed some alcohol and gum arabic to harden the body. After great efforts, the body was lifted out in a block of soil. The laborers insisted on carrying the precious find to the storeroom on their backs, followed by a large crowd. So much gold came from the excavations that the Schliemanns lit watch fires at Mycenae to prevent looting and warm the soldiers who were guarding the excavations around the clock. These were, Schliemann was fond of saying, the first watch fires to be seen at Mycenae since Agamemnon's time.

Schliemann completed his account of the dig within a few months of returning to Athens. *Mycenae* was little more than a diary of the excavations and an essay on Schliemann's conviction that he had found the bodies of Homer's heroes. His claims were immediately disputed by German experts. They felt that the burials—and, indeed, both Mycenae and Troy—predated the time of the Homeric epics. We now know that Schliemann had, in fact, discovered the prehistoric Mycenaean civilization, a society that provided many of the ingredients which later went to make up classical Greek culture. The magnificence of the Greek Bronze Age was revealed to a delighted world for the first time. It would be years before the true significance of Heinrich Schliemann's discoveries at Mycenae was fully understood. In the meantime, the world was ready to admire and praise his achievements. British Prime Minister William Gladstone

6-9. Golden mask of a bearded man from Shaft Grave V, Mycenae.

accepted with alacrity an invitation to write a preface to *Mycenae*, in which he spoke of his "strangely bewildered admiration" at the discoveries. It never occurred to Schliemann that his theories might be wrong. One has the impression that he felt he was God's messenger, sent to bring the truth about Homer to a waiting world.

Heinrich Schliemann himself remains a somewhat enigmatic figure. He has been characterized as a megalomaniac who was, perhaps, also a mythomaniac. His admirers called him a genius, his enemies, a lunatic. But behind the facade of ruthless, single-minded dedication was a kindly and thoughtful man. His second marriage was apparently a real love match. Sophia helped him become a warm and loving person with a lively enthusiasm for life and for people. The Schliemanns' house in Athens was a comfortable, hospitable place. Guests were greeted by the great man himself and were entertained by his gentle and gracious wife. It was only when the talk turned to archaeology that Schliemann's fanaticism would bubble to the surface. A glint would come to his eye as he spoke of Troy or of long days at Mycenae under the hot sun. The trivia of archaeology and the controversies of Homeric scholarship could easily engross him for hours.

Hissarlik now beckoned, for the way had been cleared for further excavations just before the Mycenae dig began. A short 1876 season had been unproductive. The local governor was highly uncooperative, delaying Schliemann on flimsy grounds for two months and then grudgingly allowing him to start work under the eagle eye of one Izzet Effendi. Izzet was so obstructive that Schliemann returned to Athens in despair. In disgust he wrote a furious letter to the editor of the London *Times* in which he denounced Ibrahim Pasha's conduct before, as he aptly put it, "the tribunal of the civilized world." The Constantinople papers picked up the story and the governor was abruptly transferred to another province.

The two eventful years of Mycenae turned Schliemann into a respected elder statesman of archaeology. Other scientists were now glad to work with him. The 1878 Hissarlik excavations started in bitterly cold March weather. "It was only possible to keep warm by exercise in the trenches," wrote Schliemann in his diary. But the chill did not prevent him bathing in the sea every morning before dawn, returning to Hissarlik on horseback before the day's work started. This, he claimed, prevented him from catching cold. He was now working with the great German scholar Rudolf Virchow, who studied the geology of the Trojan plain and the mound. His awesome scholarly knowledge helped Schliemann greatly as he struggled with the details of the excavations. Virchow, too, was responsible for Schliemann's giving Priam's treasure to Berlin after his plans for a museum in Athens were aborted. The treasure vanished during World War II and recently turned up in Russia.

In later seasons, from 1882 to 1890, Wilhelm Dörpfeld, an archae-

6-10. Sophia Schliemann poses in front of the beehive tomb which she excavated at Mycenae.

ologist and architect trained in the German excavations at Olympia, worked alongside the master. Dörpfeld was of a new generation of archaeologists who had grown up with the pioneers and were now improving on their methods. Together the two men decided initially that the so-called third city was, in fact, part of the second city. Toward the very end of their work, Dörpfeld produced irrefutable evidence that the sixth city coincided most closely with the Homeric settlement, a conclusion that Schliemann was planning to test with a huge campaign of excavations in 1891.

Schliemann has often been criticized for his large-scale excavation methods. To reach his ultimate objective, he would not hesitate to plough through buildings and delicate strata. In his defense, it should be noted that he was a pioneer in mound excavation. Dörpfeld refined Schliemann's methods, applying techniques that had evolved through the application of common sense, as well as sound organizational and business principles, to the excavations. He preserved not only valuable gold objects, but also simple, prosaic items, such as pottery. These artifacts often shed more light on the past than the more spectacular, headline-making finds. Above all, Schliemann was never afraid to take expert advice in the field.

Hissarlik remained a dominant theme in Schliemann's archaeological career for the rest of his life. But the demands of Troy did not prevent him from excavating elsewhere as well. His last great excavation was at another famous citadel, that of Tiryns on the plain of Argos, not far from Mycenae.

The stone fortifications of Tiryns, like those of Mycenae, had been known for centuries. Greek archaeologists had considered them medieval and of no particular interest. But classical writers, Schliemann's prime source of inspiration, were familiar with Tiryns. Pausanias had referred to it as one of the wonders of the world, a place built by giants. Schliemann believed it was related to Mycenae, took Pausanias as his guide, and started digging.

The 1886 digging season saw the sixty-four-year-old archaeologist attacking Tiryns with such zeal that he unwittingly destroyed the local farmers' crops. The excavations had hardly begun when the foundations of an elaborate palace came to light on the summit of Tiryns, a palace that far surpassed the grandeur of others of its type already discovered. Schliemann had done it again, this time with an architectural treasure.

The foundation stones of the palace itself were up to eleven yards thick and sixteen yards high. An outer courtyard with stores and workshops also lay inside the massive, fortified walls of the great citadel. The palace itself had been graced with a pillared main hall, various courts, antechambers, even a bathhouse. Its walls had been decorated with fine wall paintings. Thousands of clay vessels bore designs similar to those found at Mycenae and elsewhere, especially on Crete. The geometric designs on this pottery even turned up on vessels found in far-away Egypt and over wide areas of eastern Greece and the Aegean. Schliemann was now convinced that he had found the traces of a widespread culture, perhaps of Asian origin, that had been centered on the Aegean and especially on the large island of Crete.

His thoughts now turned to that island, the legendary home of the terrible King Minos and his fabled Minotaur, part man, part beast. It was to Crete that the Athenian Theseus had journeyed to slay the Minotaur. The palace of the Cretan king was thought to lie at Knossos, a rubble- and pottery-strewn hillside planted with olive groves.

A permit to excavate on Crete was relatively easy to obtain, but the landowners were reluctant both to sell their land and to have Schliemann digging around in their olive groves. Strenuous bargaining brought the price for the land down from ridiculous levels to a more realistic price of about fifty thousand piastres. It then transpired that the land was owned by several Turks, only some of whom wanted to sell. One landowner tried to play Schliemann off against another.

In disgust Schliemann called off any deal and returned to Athens. For the rest of his life he was planning to return. "I want to crown my career with one great project," he wrote, "namely with the excavation of the prehistoric, royal palace at Knossos, on Crete, which I believe I discovered three years ago."

He was never to realize his dream. In December 1890, Schliemann was alone in Italy, preoccupied with his plans and in pain from an ear infection. On Christmas day he suddenly collapsed in a Naples piazza. Fully conscious but deprived of speech, he was carried to a hospital where he was turned away. Never a fastidious dresser, Schliemann did not look like the millionaire he was. He was dumped at a police station where the officers found a scrap of paper in his pocket with a doctor's name on it. The physician was summoned and made arrangements for his transfer to a hospital. No one believed that such a poorly dressed man could afford hospital fees. In exasperation, the doctor exclaimed, "He is very rich," and pulled a purse of gold coins from Schliemann's pocket. It was too late: Heinrich Schliemann died several hours later.

Schliemann's death marked the passing of an era in archaeology. Royal personages, diplomats, politicians, and dozens of scholars paid tribute at his funeral. His archaeology had always seemed an intensely private crusade, conducted with the precious books of Homer in one hand and a spade in the other. The sheer force of his enthusiasm had seemed to wrest great discoveries from the ground. A whole new generation of archaeologists had been inspired by his work, men like Arthur Evans, soon to discover the Minoan civilization, and Flinders Petrie, one of the greatest Egyptologists of all time. One archaeologist wrote, on hearing of Schliemann's death, that "the spring had gone out of the year." The once-controversial figure was now a man universally beloved and admired.

Schliemann's achievements were awesome: the discovery of Troy and of the glorious Mycenaean civilization of Bronze Age Greece. He died believing that he had proved the historical accuracy of Homer, that the *Iliad* was real history. To Schliemann, archaeology was simply digging to find history in a systematic way, using the best people and resources available—and no one can fault that way of looking at the field. Perhaps the best epitaph we can give Schliemann comes from Homer himself: "It is almost as though you had been with the Achaeans yourself or heard the story from one who was." Schliemann's greatness lay in his unique ability to turn prehistory into public property.

7

Arthur Evans and THE MINOANS

Heinrich Schliemann's death prevented him from fulfilling his final dream: to excavate on mysterious Crete. Archaeological genius that he was, he recognized that its olive-covered hillsides harbored the secrets of yet another lost civilization. Fortunately, another great archaeologist carried on where Schliemann left off. Arthur John Evans, an Englishman who never set foot on Crete until his fortieth birthday, followed a Greek legend and a handful of ancient seals to find the Minoan civilization.

Like the excavations at Troy and Mycenae, Evans's explorations on Crete were inspired by Greek legend, in this case by the romantic myth of Theseus and the dreaded Minotaur, a terrible half-human monster kept by King Minos of Crete. According to legend, King Minos sent his son Androgeus to compete in the Athenian games. Androgeus won so many laurels in the competition that, in a fit of jealousy, King Aegeus had him murdered. Minos exacted a terrible revenge for his son's death. After his fleet sacked Athens, he demanded a ghastly tribute. Every nine years the Athenians were to send seven youths and seven virgins to be sacrificed to the Minotaur. Without fail, the king's messengers arrived each ninth year and demanded this tribute from the cream of Athenian youth. The third time they appeared, however, Aegeus's son Theseus was in town after a long absence abroad. Already famous for his heroic deeds, Theseus boldly joined the party and offered to kill the Minotaur. Amidst great lamentations the black-sailed ship departed for Crete. Theseus arranged with his father that his ship would carry white sails on the return trip if he managed to kill the Minotaur.

Upon their arrival, Theseus and his companions were imprisoned in the Palace of Minos. As the story goes, King Minos's daughter Ariadne fell helplessly in love with the handsome young Athenian and managed to smuggle a sword to the prisoner. Then, while Ariadne held one end of a ball of wool, Theseus unrolled the other and made his way into the depths of the dreaded Cretan labyrinth where the Minotaur lived. A terrible battle between Theseus and the monster ended in the Minotaur's death. Theseus made his way out of the labyrinth by rewinding the ball of wool and, with Ariadne by his side, hastily set sail for Athens. In his elation he forgot his promise to Aegeus to carry white sails. When King Aegeus saw the black-rigged ship approaching, he jumped off a cliff in despair.

Schliemann's excavations at Troy and Mycenae had convinced many

7-1. Sir Arthur Evans in 1907.

that the Homeric epics were true. Now they wondered about Theseus and the Minotaur. Had King Minos and the Minotaur actually lived? Was there a great palace with a labyrinth where human sacrifices were performed? The only way to find out, as Schliemann had realized, was to undertake an excavation on Crete to find the fabled palace. Fortunately, the task fell into the hands of a trained and exceptionally gifted archaeologist.

Arthur John Evans was born in 1851 into a family that revered archaeology. His father, a prosperous paper manufacturer and early champion of prehistoric archaeology, collected prehistoric artifacts and was a respected geologist. He embodied the best type of Victorian patriarch, for, as he often stated, he firmly believed in "Peace, Prosperity, and Papermaking." But while John Evans was content to stay at home in England, his son Arthur was ever restless, eventually spending much of his time in the Balkans and the Mediterranean.

Young Arthur Evans was familiar with archaeology from his earliest years. At age seven he was drawing coins. (At the same time, he announced he would become a poet and an astronomer.) At ten, he accompanied his father on geological excursions. Teenage Arthur, although a familiar sight at learned lectures in London, was a far from ideal student. At school he was considered "dirty" and "untidy." Arthur, in return, found his teachers equally objectionable and complained that his Oxford University lecturers were dull. During summer vacations, to dispel the tedium of school, he wandered all over Europe, mostly on foot. An incurable romantic, he once bought a red-lined cloak that made him look like a revolutionary. A friendly customs officer advised him to take it off if he valued his safety.

Soon Arthur was venturing far off the beaten track. He reached the Balkans, a politically volatile country, after a "most weird journey beside people in sheepskin mantles and hats like Cossacks." He walked high mountains, wandered through deep forests, and encountered "wild looking Wallachs" dressed in shaggy skins. As he knowingly told a friend, "The women may be readily distinguished from the men by showing more of their legs and less of their hair."

For the rest of his life, Arthur Evans was never happier than when miles from anywhere and deeply immersed in local society. He fell deeply in love with the Balkans, both with the people and with their complex politics. It was hardly surprising that such an experienced traveler should feel at loose ends after graduating from Oxford in 1875. Arthur, although he had made some reputation for himself as an adventurer, was generally thought of as his father's son, for John Evans was a man of considerable repute. With typical determination, Arthur resolved to strike out on his own. He envisioned a life of travel and literary pursuits, a career he planned to combine with coin collecting and some archaeological research.

Evans's credentials for such a lifestyle were impressive enough. Under the tutelage of his father, Arthur had already developed an instinct for style and an encyclopaedic knowledge of archaeology. In addition, he was gifted with clear reasoning and an ability to grasp the wider significance of archaeological discoveries—qualities vital to a man who was to discover a lost civilization.

Lost civilizations were far from Evans's mind when, after spending a postgraduate summer at the University of Gottingen in Germany, he embarked on a long journey by foot through his beloved Balkans. The Balkans had been a concern of European statesmen for generations, for delicate balances of power could be upset by even a trivial rebellion in southeast Europe. Still, few ever bothered to master the intricacies of its volatile politics. Arthur plunged into this political morass with such enthusiasm that he was arrested by the Austrian police as a spy. Such was the power of a British passport that Evans was free within an hour. A few weeks later, he passed deep into Yugoslavia, walking from town to town until he ended up in Dubrovnik on the Adriatic coast. Evans soon made the ancient walled city his headquarters in the Balkans.

Summers do not last forever. When Evans returned to Oxford he was penniless and without a job. To make a bit of money, he wrote a racy account of his Balkan travels that appeared to popular acclaim in 1876. He was now considered an authority on the Balkans, so much so that the *Manchester Guardian* newspaper sent him back to Dubrovnik in 1877 as a special correspondent to report on the unrest caused by Austrian rule in what is now Yugoslavia.

Evans was in his element. Letter by letter he documented the mercurial fluctuations of Balkan politics for the *Guardian*'s readers. The letters further established Evans's literary reputation, especially his dramatic accounts of the suffering caused by the rebellions. He described refugees with "pinched haggard faces, lean bony frames, scarred by disease and bowed down with hunger."

The "mad Englishman" was welcome everywhere, although some suspected him of being an English spy. He visited princes, rebel leaders, war dances, and refugee villages. Arthur's new wife, the daughter of a historian, soon became accustomed to bearded messengers and secret late-night meetings at their villa in Dubrovnik. The smoky crosscurrents of political intrigue flowed through the Evans house. To keep his readers ever intrigued, Arthur, armed with nothing more formidable than a walking stick, would frequently dash off into the mountains in search of new trouble spots or fresh atrocities.

In the intervals between rebellions, Evans collected artifacts omnivorously. He was continually bargaining for himself, for museums, and for his father. In addition, a few surreptitious excavations in cemeteries and abandoned ruins enhanced his reputation as an archaeologist. His microscopic eyesight enabled him to peer at the most intricate inscriptions with ease and, as a result, he began to appreciate small objects in a way not possible for many of his less keen-sighted colleagues. And it was tiny seals that would eventually lead Evans to the most spectacular discovery of his long career.

Increasingly the Austrian authorities found the *Guardian*'s special correspondent a public nuisance. His anti-Austrian statements sparked official reaction and, in March 1882, Evans was hauled off to prison. For six weeks he languished in jail while his family and the Foreign Office bombarded the Austrians with petitions for his release. He was lucky to escape a long prison sentence. As it was, Arthur was expelled from Dubrovnik forever. His reaction to six weeks' imprisonment was typical Evans: "Stone walls do not a prison make / Nor iron bars a cage / But they make a very tolerable imitation of one, I can assure you."

With the Balkans closed to him, Arthur Evans was again without a job and casting about for a career. After an unproductive year and a half in Oxford, Evans managed to get himself appointed Keeper of the Ashmolean Museum in June of 1884. This curious institution was to be his base for the next quarter century.

The Ashmolean was an anachronism in a university that specialized in such things. In 1677 scholar-astronomer Elias Ashmole had presented Oxford with a large collection of "curiosities." The university built a handsome museum for the gift and then entirely neglected the collections for two centuries. Not that they were not of great interest: the Ashmolean owned some of the first American Indian artifacts ever seen in Europe, as well as Captain Cook's South Sea relics and great collections of fish, birds, and mammals from the Pacific.

Traditionally, the Keeper of the Ashmolean was expected to do virtually nothing. But not Arthur Evans. He plunged into the job energetically and began to bring order to the chaos that was then the Ashmolean. Some influential collectors, including John Evans, closed ranks behind the ambitious young curator and helped him create new displays and acquire no less than two thousand new objects in five years. The university was astonished.

The long hours of slow-moving committee work bored Evans to tears. But it was the only way he could save the Ashmolean. Plans for a new building were eventually pushed through innumerable boards. All this dogged administrative work was sandwiched between extended periods of travel, for Evans was always on the move, always off to Mediterranean lands where he collected and geologized. The Assistant Keeper of the Ashmolean answered all queries by saying, "The Keeper, Sir, is somewhere in Bohemia." Curiously, nobody at Oxford seemed very worried about Arthur's extended absences, presumably because he was less of a nuisance that way.

In 1893, the year Evans finally succeeded in obtaining a new building for his beloved museum, his wife Margaret died of tuberculosis. "She was," he wrote to a friend, "a helpmate such as few have known." Arthur buried himself in his work, feeling increasingly restricted by the monotony of museum routine. He was now a year older than Schliemann had been when he retired from business to look for Troy. A small, pugnacious man, he peered at the world through eyes that were happiest examining the minute artistry of prehistoric craftspeople. Evans's rather insignificant appearance belied his genius, his extraordinary energy, and an intuition that would eventually lead him to the greatest achievement of his life.

No one quite knows when Evans first became aware of Crete and its influential role in Greek prehistory. He had met Schliemann in 1883 and heard him lecture in London. He had peered curiously at the dazzling artifacts that this "odd little man" with a passion for Homer displayed to his learned audiences. Schliemann had always preferred a simplistic explanation for his finds at Mycenae and Tiryns: both were simply Homer come true. Arthur Evans, not content to accept this version, quietly formed a detailed synthesis of the finds from Mycenae in his own mind. He had always thought of Mycenae as a Bronze Age site, a far earlier settlement

7-2. An almond-shaped seal in agate gives the impression of a fish swimming in seaweed. One of the many such artifacts studied by Arthur Evans.

than the legend of Agamemnon and Homeric times. Exotic imports from all over the Aegean had poured into Mycenae, objects that Arthur had also purchased in antique stores throughout Greece, on the Aegean islands, and in the Balkans. Where had all these objects come from? Had the Mycenaeans fabricated the minute seals and engraved gemstones that were so common in their palaces? What were the origins of writing in the Aegean and who was responsible? Evans resolved to find out.

Many people believed that the Mycenaeans were illiterate, but Arthur's keen perception caused him to think otherwise. Browsing in the antique dealers' collections in Shoe Lane, Athens, Evans became interested in the dozens of engraved gems and seals so commonplace in these shops. Every one of the three- or four-sided stones bore symbols similar to the scratchings he had seen on jars from Mycenae. More such symbols had been found on Mycenaean vessels discovered in Egypt. Evans haunted the dealers' stores and bombarded them with questions about the seals. "Crete," they said, "they are found in Crete." Like a terrier, Evans quickened on the scent. Perhaps, he speculated, Crete had been a staging post in the gradual diffusion of writing to Mycenae and Europe. There was only one way to find out: he decided he must excavate on Crete.

Arthur Evans visited Crete for the first time in March of 1894, his mind full of seals and complex symbols. He arrived in Iraklion much the worse for wear from seasickness, but felt at home at once. The architecture reminded him of his beloved Dubrovnik, and the villages seemed familiar and friendly. Crete was soon to become his second home. Iraklion's market proved a gold mine. Arthur purchased twenty-two Cretan gems for one and a half piastres each and a fine Mycenaean ring. Three days later he engaged a guide to take him to Knossos, the olive-covered hillside where Heinrich Schliemann had always wanted to excavate.

The road out of Iraklion led through a pleasant landscape of gently sloping hills and scattered olive groves. Soon they came to a low spur of land to the west of the road where Knossos lay, brilliant with purple and white anemones in the spring sunshine. For hours Evans combed the hillside, copying strange marks off of stones he found protruding from the ground. Someone brought him a piece of a stone vessel. To his astonishment, it was of Mycenaean type. His surface finds that day were such that he was certain that spectacular results could be obtained from a dig. Without further ado, the lone Englishman set out to do what many others before him had failed to accomplish: to purchase the site—lock, stock, and barrel.

Knossos was owned by several landowners, some of whom had tried to cheat Schliemann until that astute gentleman went elsewhere. Since that time, a French archaeologist had applied to dig at the site but had never started work. So Evans had a clear field—if he could purchase the land. He promptly succeeded in persuading the owners of a quarter of the property to sell it to him outright. He then boldly formed the "Cretan Exploration Fund," an organization that existed only in his imagination. The fund, he assured the owners, would raise enough money to buy the rest of Knossos. The negotiations dragged on for two years while the landowners tried every scheme in the book to raise the price. Evans finally invoked an obscure legal statute to force them to sell. Eventually Knossos changed hands in 1896 for a sum just under a thousand English pounds.

By then Arthur Evans had ridden from one end of the island to the other in search of antiquities. Accompanied by a muleteer guide, he scrambled up and down hillsides, through rough watercourses, and into small villages. He found seals similar to those discovered at Mycenae for sale in even the smallest of village markets. At one village Evans spent two days trying to buy seals from a woman who wore them as charms, but she quietly refused, pointing to her child. "If I part with the stone," she explained, "he'll die."

Evans returned to England in a rare state of excitement. He had found traces of at least two writing systems on Crete, both preserved on his precious seals and gems. The solution to the ancient writing problem lay, he knew, at Knossos. Crete had nurtured a great civilization that predated Schliemann's Mycenaeans yet had strong ties with the Greek mainland. Determination to excavate Knossos fired Evans to feverish fund-raising activity. Back in Crete again, he haunted the site as negotiations for its

7-3. (*preceeding page*) The Palace of Minos at Knossos, showing portions of the site reconstructed by Arthur Evans.

purchase dragged on. One day, while eating lunch on a hillside overlooking the settlement, Evans turned to his companions. "This is where I shall live when I come to dig Knossos," he told them firmly. And he did.

Just as Knossos passed into British hands in 1896, the Cretans rose in savage revolt against their Turkish masters. Evans had to leave for his own safety. It was a year before the Great Powers intervened in the dispute. As soon as the revolt died down, Evans rushed to the island. He wrote long letters to the *Manchester Guardian* full of Turkish atrocities and the plight of the villagers. Anxious to help, he traveled all over the island distributing relief supplies and, of course, at the same time buying antiquities. Prince George of Greece, the new ruler of Crete, was so grateful to Evans for his assistance that a permit to dig at Knossos was forthcoming within a few months. Arthur turned his attention from partisan politics to the greatest intellectual and archaeological challenge of his life.

Knossos was obviously a very complex site, and Evans had never excavated systematically in his life. His digging experience was confined to a few small digs, most of them little more than collecting forays. Fortunately, he had the sense to see that he needed experienced assistants. Architect Thomas Fyfe was engaged to prepare drawings and a Scotsman with flaming red hair and an uncertain temper named Duncan Mackenzie came along as Evans's excavation assistant. Mackenzie was to remain at Knossos for more than thirty years. He dealt with the workmen in a fluent but curious Greek spoken with a strong Scottish accent. Soon he became godfather to their children and a witness at innumerable weddings. Evans also started off on the right foot by insisting on both Christian and Muslim workmen. Although the two groups had been shooting at one another only a few months before, the experiment worked and Knossos was never beset with the labor problems that affected so many digs of the time. Thirty workmen were engaged under Mackenzie's supervision. Evans decided where to dig, examined every find minutely, and kept voluminous notes.

The Knossos excavations began in March 1900 and continued intermittently for thirty years. On the very first day, the excavators came across buildings and artifacts and, on the second, Evans was summoned excitedly to examine an ancient house with faded wall paintings. Within a few more days, the site was transformed into a veritable labyrinth of rooms, passages, and foundations. Evans was ecstatic; obviously, they had found a palace—a very unique palace. "It's an extraordinary phenomenon," he cried, "nothing Greek, nothing Roman. . . . Maybe its greatest period goes back to at least well before the pre-Mycenaean period."

The discoveries had only just begun. A hundred men were put to work clearing the palace rooms. In the process, they found thousands of artifacts in the foundations. Great storage jars, hundreds of small cups, even a complex drainage system came to light. The dozens of incised clay tablets bearing Cretan writing especially pleased Evans. At the beginning of April a magnificent wall painting of a male cupbearer emerged from the soil. That same night, the night watchman's dreams were troubled; he complained of spooks, lowing and neighing. But Evans was entranced by the "noble profile of the face." He admired the figure's full lips and "the waist of the smallest." The figure was carefully backed with plaster and transported to Iraklion's museum in triumph. As Arthur fingered the tablets and gems, the ornaments and frescoes, he was certain that he had located the ancient civilization of Minoan Crete, the historical basis of the Theseus legend, even if Minos and Theseus themselves had never actually existed.

Overjoyed, Evans announced his discovery of the Minoans in a telegram to the London *Times*, at the time the only place to announce a really sensational discovery. The term "Minoan" seemed natural to him—in commemoration of the legendary king said to have lived at Knossos. The Evans family was jubilant. Old John Evans sent his son a welcome gift of five hundred pounds with the joyful message: "Dies Creta notanda!—a joyful Cretan day of note."

The site now extended over more than two acres. In April 1900 laborers uncovered a room with a ceremonial bath. Nearby stood a stone throne still upright and intact. Stone benches lined the walls. Fine paintings of wingless griffins formed an imposing background to the royal presence. It was here that the queen of Knossos may have sat, in her personification of the mother goddess who brought fertility to the land. Evans sent for Emile Gillieron, a Swiss artist who had vast experience in ancient inscriptions. Together they set to work to interpret the Knossos frescoes. There was much to piece together: frescoes of people marching in solemn procession, olives in flower, a young boy gathering saffron. A great, painted stucco relief of a charging bull stuck in Evans's mind. "What a part these creatures play here," he wrote. Bulls were everywhere—in frescoes, on vases, on gems. Was the Minotaur a great bull? Arthur's mind boggled at the possibilities.

Every day Evans and Mackenzie rode out to the site on mules from Iraklion. Arthur always rode at breakneck speed, spurring his beast along the rough tracks. Eventually he acquired a fast horse, which partially assuaged his lust for speed. The day began by checking the previous day's work. Nothing was hurried or skimped. Page after page of notes in Arthur's tiny handwriting documented every layer, every find, every room. It was just as well that the excavators were careful, for the palace became more complex daily. It was quite an extraordinary structure. The great central courtyard was entered from the north through a huge, pillared hall. Rows of narrow storage magazines lay to the west of the courtyard, each opening onto a narrow passageway. At one time many of them had been lined with

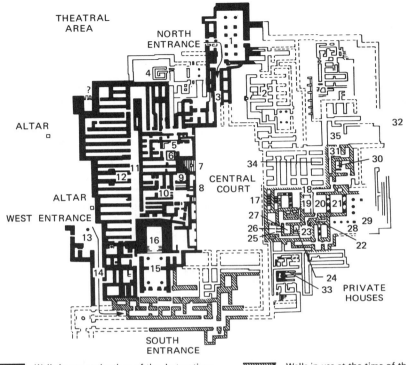

THEATRAL AREA

NORTH ENTRANCE

4

3

ALTAR

?

2

32

35

31

30

5

6

11

7

34

CENTRAL COURT

18

12

9

8

17

19 20 21

29

ALTAR

10

27

28

WEST ENTRANCE

26

23

22

25

13

16

24

14

15

33

PRIVATE HOUSES

SOUTH ENTRANCE

▬▬▬ Walls in use at the time of the destruction: ground floor (central court) level

▨▨▨ Walls in use at the time of the destruction: lower levels

─── Earlier walls and foundations; some may have been in use at the time of the destruction

╌╌╌ Conjectural walls

1 Pillared hall	19 Light well, Hall of the Double Axes
2 Northeast magazines	20 Anteroom, Hall of the Double Axes
3 North entrance passage	21 Main living room of the Hall of the Double Axes
4 Northwest lustral basin	
5 Throne room	22 Private staircase
6 Lustral basin	23 Bedroom
7 Stairway to upper floor	24 Bathroom or sleeping place
8 Triple shrine facade	25 Service room
9 Room with cists in floor (temple repositories)	26 Lavatory
	27 Treasure chamber
10 Pillar rooms	28 Colonnade
11 Corridor of the west magazines	29 Terrace
12 West magazines	30 Store of lapis lacedaemonius (Spartan basalt)
13 West entrance	
14 Corridor of the Procession	31 Schoolroom
15 Monumental doorway	32 East entrance
16 Stairway to upper floor	33 Shrine of the Double Axes
17 Grand staircase to residential quarters	34 Loom-weight basement of the earlier palace
18 East/west corridor	35 Court of the Stone Spout

7-4. Plan of the Palace of Knossos. (From Sinclair Hood, *The Minoans*, London: Thames and Hudson; and New York: Praeger, 1971, p. 63.)

lead to house valuables. Huge supplies of grain must have been kept in these storerooms. Arthur estimated that as much as seventy-nine thousand gallons of olive oil were once stored in the palace.

The western side of the courtyard also led to the royal staterooms and the ceremonial precincts. It was here that the throne room with its ceremonial bath was found. All the baths in the palace were oddly reminiscent of Victorian hip baths.

Two staircases of imposing design led to the state rooms, which formed a second story above the shrines to the west of the courtyard. A western entrance to the palace led through a paved courtyard past huge pictures of young men leaping over bulls. But the king and queen actually lived to the east of the central courtyard. Here the ground slopes away sharply, so that the palace had three or four stories built downward onto the slope. A great staircase led from the courtyard to the living quarters below. Since the complex framework of wooden beams and large pillars that formed the staircase had collapsed into the living quarters, it took

7-5. Residential area of the Palace of Knossos, looking down from the central court before the upper floors were restored. The porch of the Hall of the Double Axes is left center, the bedroom at bottom right.

Evans and Mackenzie months to sort out the jumble of rubble. Fortunately, Fyfe was on hand to prepare architectural drawings. The Knossos excavation was one of the first digs where an archaeologist insisted on having an architect on the site at all times.

The royal living quarters lay below the staircase. In the "Hall of the Double Axes," decorated with Cretan double-axe symbols, traces of wooden thrones were found. The floors were paved with limestone, and sheets of gypsum lined the walls up to a height of eight feet. The rest was plastered and painted. The royal bedrooms, complete with bathroom and toilet facilities, lay nearby, with an elaborate drainage system crisscrossing below them. Many features of the palace seemed remarkably modern, quite unlike the Greek or Roman palaces of classical antiquity.

The residential areas of the palace looked out over the valley of Kairatos, where the royal gardens probably lay. On the northeastern corner of the palace, the craftspeople had their quarters. Great pottery storage jars were found near a jar maker's workshop. The noise, dust, and clay emanating from its busy workbenches must have sometimes bothered the scribes and fresco painters who worked quietly nearby, recording the deeds, policies, and dealings of the king.

Arthur Evans was a celebrity by 1901, the recipient of honorary degrees and a lecturer much in demand all over Europe. The Palace of Knossos was to absorb most of his energies for the rest of his life. A major concern was to keep as much of the site as possible in his own family. A legacy from a relative in 1908 made him financially independent for the first time. "We may as well keep some of Knossos in the family," he wrote. "I must have sole control of what I am undertaking. My way may not be the best, but it is the only way I can work." Still, there were probably times when he regretted Knossos, for the workload was overwhelming, the site was malarial, and the expense simply enormous.

Evans was not content with excavation alone. With typical impetuosity, he resolved to reconstruct at least some of the buildings of the palace. This was, to put it mildly, a controversial undertaking, for many archaeologists believed that nothing should ever be rebuilt for fear of making false reconstructions. Others felt that nothing short of complete reconstruction should be the archaeologist's goal. Evans believed in limited reconstruction. By judicious rebuilding and restoration, he could show both Cretans and tourists something of the marvels of the palace of Minos. One suspects, too, that he wanted a more tangible symbol of his Minoan discoveries, something that would be appreciated by a wide audience, not just readers of learned dissertations.

On the whole, Evans's reconstruction is a fair one. The wooden colonnades were replaced with concrete pillars colored to conform with Minoan decor. Thomas Fyfe was invaluable, for his plans were so accurate that some buildings could be reconstructed at the same time that they were

7-6. The Throne Room in the Palace of Knossos, as reconstructed by Arthur Evans.

being dug. Soon, restored walls were rising alongside trenches where workmen still labored. Colonnades and window frames were replaced, other walls set back in place, and the great staircase rebuilt from fragments found in the digs. The frescoes were a harder proposition. In the throne room, for example, Evans made detail changes that some consider to be inaccurate. But such cavilings are academic, for the overall effect of the palace is achieved. For over half a century the reconstructed walls have resisted war and earthquake, heat and storm to bring prehistory alive for the thousands who visit Knossos each year.

As one sits among the colonnades on a quiet summer's evening, time seems to slip away. In a few moments one is back in prehistory, hearing the tinkle of sheep bells and the distant barking of dogs as smoke from evening cooking fires wafts across the palace. It's easy to imagine the soft footsteps of the palace guard, a ripple of laughter from the potter's quarters, quiet talk from a group of young noblemen seated in the cool shade of the great courtyard. Without Evans, such magical moments would be impossible.

The visitor to Knossos is immediately struck by the incredible complexity of its ruins. A remarkable jumble of artifacts came from the excavations. Apart from the frescoes and architecture, Evans had to sort out thousands of potsherds, metal and stone ornaments, clay tablets, seals, gems, even burials to build up a coherent picture of Minoan civilization. When was Knossos founded? What was the chronological framework for the Minoan civilization? What did the people look like and how did they make their living? The answers to these questions were pieced together from the information painstakingly recorded in Arthur's notebooks and from the vast repository of Knossos finds.

From 1900 to 1935 Evans commuted between Knossos and Oxford, where he now began to write up the history of the Minoans, a task that occupied him for the rest of his long life. By 1906 he had wearied of his daily ride from Iraklion to Knossos, so he built a steel and cement house on the very slope he had chosen ten years before as his headquarters. The Villa Ariadne was to be his Cretan home for over thirty years. There he laid out the large collections of Minoan potsherds and began puzzling over Minoan chronology.

Happily for Evans, the Minoans had been aggressive traders and their society had dealt with many nations. The Knossos storerooms contained all types of exotic treasures, including occasional Egyptian vessels of known age that could be matched to vessels found in Egypt itself. In addition, the great Egyptologist Flinders Petrie had dug up Mycenaean pottery at Ghurab near Thebes that he dated to between 1500 and 1000 B.C. By using this important cross-reference, Evans produced a provisional time frame for the Minoans that could be cross-checked against Egyptian chronology. His original classification, a chronology that he refined progressively for the rest of his life, was published in 1905.

The first occupants of Knossos, suggested Evans, were simple farming folk who had no metals. He boldly dated them to ten thousand years ago, a pure guess. These early Cretans lived in small wooden huts and kept cattle, sheep, and goats. Evans did not have access to radiocarbon dating methods. Had he been able to use them, he would have dated the first Knossos people to between 6000 and 3500 B.C.

By 3000 B.C., Evans continued, rapid technological and economic changes were afoot. The "Early Minoan" period of Cretan civilization began with the beginning of the Bronze Age on the island. Immigrant peoples arrived from the eastern Mediterranean, bringing with them metallurgy, new pottery styles, and extensive trading contacts. There were signs of political upheaval. The Cretans seemed to have taken refuge in caves, as if warfare and raiding had disrupted the rhythm of agricultural seasons. The villages of the newcomers were not much different from those of their predecessors. Small, one-storied houses were packed together in tiny settlements. Some of the larger villages soon acquired small palaces, often associated with relatively humble shrines or temples. The Early Minoan period lasted for over a thousand years, as trading activities expanded and the Minoans began trading with other nations.

With the "Middle Minoan" and the "Late Minoan" periods, two eras that Evans dated at between 2000 and 1250 B.C., the Minoan civilization achieved the height of its glory. By this time Crete was densely populated. The Minoans founded colonies on several Aegean islands and, possibly, also on the Greek mainland itself. Wealthy traders and nobles lived on country estates and in elaborate palaces. Luxury, almost to the point of ostentation, was important. Cretan art overflowed with flamboyant color and lushness.

During its heyday, Cretan civilization was completely self-supporting. Wheat and barley were abundant on Crete; meat and milk came from large herds of cattle, sheep, and goats. But olives and grapes were the most important staples on the island. Since these two crops flourish in two different types of terrain, it is possible to grow them alongside one another without wasting land. Both olive oil and Cretan wine were widely exported by the Minoans in their seagoing vessels. The valuable oil and wine were carried far and wide through the Aegean and further afield in gaily painted Minoan jars, perhaps an export in their own right. Cretan jars and pots have been found as far afield as Egypt, Cyprus, and Syria. Many other necessities, such as foodstuffs and cloth, were exported in the same ships. Cretan wool and perhaps timber may have been exchanged for Egyptian papyrus.

As Evans pored over the Knossos collections, he realized what a huge variety of imported luxuries had flowed into the palace storerooms. Tin and copper came from Italy or the Aegean islands, gold and silver from western Turkey. Syrian ivory, Egyptian amethyst, and even lapis lazuli from Afghanistan were worked into ornaments and fine tools. Scarabs from the Nile, beads, pendants, ostrich eggshells, and Mesopotamian gems and seals were stockpiled in the palace treasure houses. All this trade was highly regulated and conducted with the aid of bronze scales used for weighing gold and silver.

Life at Knossos reflected the wealth and power of the Minoans and the cosmopolitan nature of their civilization. But the wall paintings at Knossos convey a strangely pastoral existence. Youths and young girls wander through meadows blooming with flowers. Birds flock by reedy streams, while gentle winds blow through fields of thyme. It seems a peaceful world, one where the Cretans lived in complete security, protected by their rugged island coasts and a powerful fleet. None of the palaces have any fortifications, so different from the massive walls that encircle Mycenae or Tiryns.

The Minoans themselves were literally beautiful people. They placed great emphasis on youthfulness and physical fitness. Palace clothes were, of course, much more elaborate than those worn in the countryside. The men were bare chested, with a small loin cloth around the hips. This was worn in various styles—as a kilt or folded under the groin like a pair of

7-7. A priestess modelled in faience (glass paste), dating from a late period in Knossos' history. She holds two snakes. A lioness sits on her head.

shorts. A codpiece often bulged in front of the kilt. This stylish costume was sometimes replaced by a long kilt adorned with tassels and worn with a wide belt. Cloaks of wool or animal skins were worn in cold weather.

The women wore long skirts held up by long waist girdles that were knotted down the front. Sometimes priestesses wore flounced skirts with elaborately checkered patterns woven into the cloth. Short- or long-sleeved bodices rose to a high peak at the back of the neck. But the breasts were left exposed, often thrusting forward provocatively from the cut of the bodice. The styles of Cretan fashion changed from generation to generation. Sometimes the women's clothes were cut tight and emphasized every curve of the body; other times, the skirts flowed more easily and were covered with aprons. Lips, cheeks, even nipples were painted with cosmetics.

Arthur Evans puzzled for a long time over the religion and cosmology of the Minoans. The only clues to their religious beliefs were the paintings and sculptures found in the excavations, like a picture book without a text. The chief deity appeared to be a goddess, perhaps a goddess of fertility. She presided over the cycles of planting and harvest, over the annual death and birth of the natural vegetation. But animal-headed gods were worshipped too. Many seals depict bull-headed humans. Bulls obviously

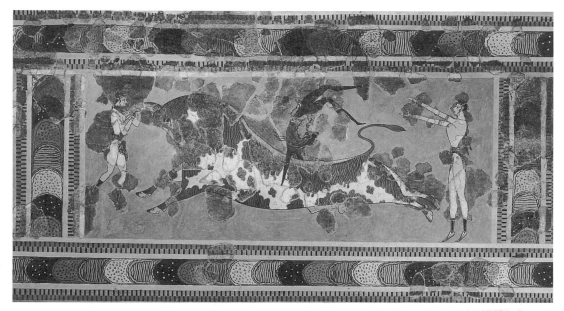

7-8. The bull-leaping scene from the Palace of Knossos. The figures on the left and right appear to be women.

occupied a central place in religious life. At certain times of the year, youths played with bulls, vaulting gracefully over their pitching horns, as depicted on the walls of the palace. Evans was fascinated by the bull rituals. Were they elaborate dances, religious ceremonies, or the very sacrifices commemorated by the Athenian legend of Theseus hundreds of years later? Was the Minotaur a giant bull kept by the king? Unlike Schliemann, Evans refused to link Minoan civilization directly to the legend of Theseus. He remarked only that "the old traditions were true. We have before our eyes a wondrous spectacle—the resurgence of a civilization twice as old as that of Greece." In other words, the legend of Theseus and the Minotaur had some basis in fact. There was a labyrinth, a great Cretan civilization, and perhaps a huge bull which was the centerpiece of elaborate annual dancing rituals. Perhaps Theseus himself was a legendary symbol of the conquerors from the Greek mainland who finally overthrew Minoan civilization.

The legend of Theseus spoke of the utter destruction of the Minoans. For years Evans puzzled over the sudden ending of this Cretan civilization. The palace of Minos had been rebuilt many times during its long life. Earthquakes and fire had destroyed earlier structures, but each time a new palace rose on the ashy foundations of the fallen buildings. The latest occupation of Knossos, however, ended suddenly and the palace was never rebuilt. Everywhere he looked Evans found signs of interrupted daily life, of a sudden catastrophe. As the excavations revealed more and more of the palace, Evans became convinced that a great earthquake had tumbled Minoan civilization, a conclusion that many of his colleagues challenged.

His mind was full of ancient earthquakes as he lay reading in bed at 9:45 P.M. on June 26, 1926. Suddenly, the basement of the Villa Ariadne shook and groaned as a tremor rocked the house. For a minute and a half Evans lay still, feeling almost seasick from the motion. "A dull sound rose from the ground like the muffled roar of a bull," he later wrote, "while through the open window came the more distant jangling of the chimes of Candia [Iraklion] Cathedral." Roofs crashed to the ground, women and children screamed. A cloud of dust rose above the swaying trees. There was widespread damage to local villages, but the reconstructed palace came through well. Evans was fascinated. "It is something to have heard with one's own ears the bellowing of the bull beneath the earth," he told some guests at the Villa. This was the beast who tossed the earth with his horns, the great Minotaur whom the Cretans sought to appease with constant sacrifice. Arthur Evans was convinced he had lived through a reenactment of the death of the Minoan civilization.

Evans was now an old man with but one preoccupation—to publish the results of the Knossos excavations. As the annual dig continued, he started work on a monumental description of his findings. *The Palace of Minos* appeared in several volumes, the first in 1921, the last in 1935 when Evans was eighty-four. It is a chronological survey of Minoan civilization and of the great palace at its center. Stage by stage Evans unfolded his detailed story, pausing in the final volume to bid farewell to his beloved palace. In the book he admits his one great failure: he had failed to decipher Minoan script, the original and ultimate objective of all his Knossos researches. But no one minded, for his achievements at Knossos far outweighed the significance of the four scripts he had found in the palace.

Arthur Evans died in 1941 at the age of ninety. His restored palace was to survive further earthquakes and all the turmoil of the Second World War. Other scholars have carried on where Evans left off. Minoan chronology has been modified by radiocarbon dating and new excavations. But some mysteries still remain. The Cretan scripts, for example, continue to be the subject of considerable controversy. In 1952, Englishman Michael Ventris announced a decipherment of Linear B that indicated these particular tablets were written in Greek. His decipherment is still debated, however, and it is still uncertain whether we can read Minoan writing. Many of the tablets are probably little more than storehouse inventories. One of Arthur Evans's primary objectives in going to Crete is still very much an issue among archaeologists.

The earthquake that shook Evans's house in 1926 led him to believe that Knossos met a violent end. Many people have argued with his interpretations of the closing centuries of Knossos, but most scholars agree that a major natural disaster—perhaps an earthquake and fire—hit the palace in about 1500 B.C. Dramatic finds on the island of Santorini, eighty miles north of Crete document another catastrophic natural disaster that must have had a major impact on Minoan life. Greek archaeologists have found a Minoan colony there, a village complete with two-story houses and still-furnished rooms decorated with brightly painted friezes. Sometime in the late seventeenth century B.C., a massive earthquake and volcanic explosion buried the village under many feet of volcanic ash. The center of the island of Santorini literally blew into space in a violent eruption that generated enormous tidal waves and deposited thick layers of volcanic ash over hundreds of square miles of ocean and on the exposed slopes of northern Crete.

The scale of this great natural disaster beggars the imagination. The only modern analogy is the explosion of Krakatoa in southeast Asia in August of 1883. Tidal waves from that cataclysm killed over thirty-six thousand people on the low-lying coasts of Java and Sumatra. Knossos is less than a hundred miles from Santorini. The effects of the eruption must have been devastating to some coastal settlements in Crete, although tidal waves would not reach Knossos itself. Perhaps choking ash from the explosion mantled some valuable agricultural land, rendering it effectively useless for cultivation. Minoan civilization may have been weakened by the Santorini explosion, but it continued to flourish until the late sixteenth century B.C., when warrior farmers, perhaps from mainland Greece, established sway over the kingdom and decorated the walls of Knossos with military scenes. Seventy-five years later, the palace was finally destroyed, perhaps by invading Mycenaeans from the mainland.

Some scholars believe that the Santorini explosion was so violent that it provided the historical substance for the legend of Atlantis, a lost continent that sank below the sea and killed thousands of people in the process. Is the legend of Atlantis a folk memory of one of the greatest natural disasters ever to affect humankind—the destruction of Minoan civilization? Perhaps we shall never know. But the cupbearer and long-forgotten processions painted on the walls of Minos's palace remind us not only of one of the world's great civilizations, but of the remarkable man who rescued them from a historical oblivion that could have been as profound as that of Atlantis itself.

8

PYRAMIDS, PYRAMIDOLOGISTS, and PYRAMIDIOTS

The pyramids of Giza have graced the banks of the Nile for nearly five thousand years. They have withstood wars and famines, the best efforts of treasure hunters and quarrymen, and the onslaught of tens of thousands of tourists. Even today, they remain somewhat of a puzzle. Why did the ancient Egyptians build these vast monuments? And why the pyramid shape with its angle of fifty-one degrees, fifty-two minutes to the ground? Were these strangely shaped structures sophisticated astronomical observatories as well as the burial places of the early pharaohs? How did the Egyptian kings manage to recruit the enormous labor forces necessary to erect their huge tombs? Even with unlimited human resources, construction of the Pyramids represents an incredible engineering feat, for they were built without the assistance of iron tools or wheeled carts. These and many other questions have provoked centuries of vigorous scholarly debate.

The sheer scale of the Great Pyramid boggles the mind, for it seems to dwarf even modern Cairo at its feet. It is built of over 2.3 million large rocks, covers 13.1 acres, and rises to a height of 481.4 feet above the plain. Each side is approximately 755.79 feet long. Our awe is heightened by the long shadows that the pyramids cast at dawn and dusk, when their dark profiles overshadow the settlements at their feet. During the heat of the day they seem to swim in a brown haze like airy structures floating in eternity.

If the outside of the Great Pyramid seems impressive, its interior is downright confusing, a bewildering maze of narrow passages and hidden chambers. The entrance, on the Pyramid's north face, is about fifty-five feet above the ground and twenty-four feet to the east of the center of the face, presumably to guard against tomb robbers. A long passage approximately three and a half feet wide descends from the entrance to the deep core of the Pyramid and then down even further into the basement rock below the structure. Three hundred and forty-five feet further on, the corridor levels out and leads into an unfinished subterranean burial chamber, apparently abandoned in favor of a funerary chamber located in the main body of the Pyramid itself. Some time after the Pyramid was constructed, workmen cut a hole in the roof of the corridor sixty feet from the entrance and then laboriously tunneled their way through the core of the Pyramid toward its center. After 129 feet of arduous quarrying, they widened their passage into the magnificent Grand Gallery, 153 feet long

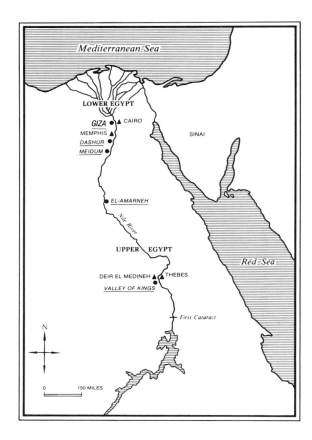

8-1. Locations and sites mentioned in chapters 8 and 9.

and 28 feet high, a chamber they lined with polished limestone. The Grand Gallery leads to the King's Chamber, obviously the burial place of the pharaoh, for an empty sarcophagus weighing three tons still rests there. Two long, narrow shafts lead from the King's Chamber to the outside of the Pyramid. Five closed compartments above the roof of the chamber apparently serve to relieve the massive weight of the rubble core above it.

If the Great Pyramid seems awesome and mysterious to us today, it's not difficult to imagine how less sophisticated travelers of earlier centuries must have viewed it. Controversies about the Great Pyramid began as long ago as 450 B.C., when the Greek traveler Herodotus wrote an account of the building of the Great Pyramid, an account he said he obtained from Egyptian priests. He told how the stones were raised to their places "by means of machines formed of short wooden planks. . . . The upper portion of the Pyramid was finished first, then the middle, and finally the part which was lowest and nearest the ground." We know now that the ancient

8-2. The Pyramids of Giza.

Egyptians used thousands of laborers with rollers and sledges to move the quarried stone blocks from the Nile to the building site. Huge brick and earth ramps provided a pathway for bringing each block to its proper place on the Pyramid. As construction proceeded, the ramps were raised until the summit was reached. Then the builders started to cover the Pyramid with polished limestone casing stones. As these were added course by course to the exterior, the ramps were slowly removed until the shining Pyramid stood free and clear of ramps and scaffolding. Were the "short planks" Herodotus mentioned the sledges and rollers used to shift the thousands of huge blocks?

In Herodotus's time, the Great Pyramid still bore many of its fine casing stones. When Herodotus, visiting the site, stooped to peer at a hieroglyphic inscription on the casing stones near the ground, his guide informed him that it recorded "the quantity of radishes, onions, and garlick consumed by the laborers who constructed it." The gullible Herodotus was fascinated by this revelation and spent hours more poking around the Pyramids. The tourist guides, recognizing an easy dupe, regaled him with lurid tales. Apparently, they said, Cheops ran out of money to complete the Pyramid, so he sent his daughter out to work as a whore to contribute her share. Not only did she raise the money, she made every client contribute a stone block toward her own personal pyramid, which was eventually erected without incident nearby. The thousands of Roman tourists who relied on Herodotus for their Egyptian history must have thought the pharaoh and his daughter a brazen pair.

Century after century, travelers gazed on the Pyramids and speculated about their history. Some early Christians believed them to be the vast granaries erected by Joseph to store grain against the seven lean years spoken of in the Scriptures. The Arabs who followed thought the Pyramids were treasure houses of long-dead kings. In A.D. 870 Caliph al-Mamun directed his engineers to find the entrance to the Great Pyramid. Meticulously they searched the exterior. "There is no entrance," they reported. "Then quarry into the boulders," ordered the caliph.

The engineers began to tunnel laboriously into the stones. Suddenly, a hundred feet in, they broke into a corridor. They made their way back to the ancient entrance through this passageway and broke it open. Within a few days, they found the King's Chamber—but it was bare. While the would-be tomb robbers hammered at its polished granite walls in frustration, the caliph mused on the Pyramid's elusive treasure. "Why," he asked the engineers, "is the interior empty when there are so many obstacles to overcome?"

Not everyone was interested simply in treasure. Others ascribed to the Pyramids a deeper and more mysterious purpose. The Arab chronicler Abu Balkhi thought the Great Pyramid was a place of refuge from divine judgment, a sort of early fallout shelter. Some Christian travelers fell on their knees at the sight of the vast monuments, amazed at what they thought to be a divine revelation. "The Almighty arranged for this great and wonderful plan to be portrayed in symbol long before the Bible was written," cried one astonished observer. As might be expected, extraordinary superstitions surrounded the mysterious structures. The Great Pyramid was said to be full of horrible vermin, and a naked woman with huge teeth supposedly seduced visitors with her spells and drove them insane. Bold was the scholar who dared set foot in the bat-filled chambers of the Great Pyramid.

One of the first people to investigate the Great Pyramid at all scientifically was the Englishman John Greaves, who came to Giza in 1638. Greaves was a bookish mathematician, more at home in a library than in a dusty pyramid. But he had become obsessed with the origins of scientific measurement and with techniques that would enable scientists to measure the size of the earth. Ever since Ferdinand Magellan had circumnavigated the globe, people had been searching for a way to measure the earth's circumference. All the stories Greaves had heard of the Great Pyramid convinced him it had been built upon what he called "higher and more weighty considerations"—in other words, he believed the Pyramids had been constructed as an observatory for measuring the earth and as a repository of sorts for the standard units of linear measurement. He decided to test his theory by actually measuring the Great Pyramid.

Armed with a special ten-foot rod divided into ten thousand equal parts, Greaves gingerly lowered himself into the entrance of the Great Pyramid. As he crawled through the piles of dust and rubbish, huge bats, some over a foot long, circled his head. In desperation, he fired his pistols to scare away the creatures, the shots reverberating along the narrow passageway. Cordite mingled with the almost unbearable stench of bat dung and vermin. For several hours, John Greaves crawled through the chambers, marveling at the close fit of the limestone blocks of the interior walls. He laboriously measured the King's Chamber and the stone sarcophagus in it, which he found to be 6.488 English feet long. "The structure," he wrote, "hath been the labour of an exquisite hand." Outside, he climbed to the summit to admire the panoramic view and estimated the summit of the pyramid to be 499 feet above the ground, an almost correct guess. Greaves returned to England convinced the Pyramids constituted a giant observatory.

No one really studied the Pyramids thoroughly until Napoleon decided to conquer Egypt and control the Nile. He set sail for Egypt in May 1798 accompanied by thirty-five thousand soldiers and 175 scientists. Napoleon was bent on colonization as well as conquest, his objective being to civilize the Egyptians with the expert assistance of his savants, a group gathered from all over France. Principal among these were Edné Jomard, a young antiquarian, and Vivant Denon, a skilled artist and diplomat with a reputation for good living, pornography, and vivid writing. It took Napoleon but a short time to defeat the Mameluke Turks in a famous battle waged near the Pyramids and, within a few days, the savants were crawling through the bat-filled chambers of the Great Pyramid.

Denon and Jomard found that the bat population of the pyramid had increased since Greaves's day. Bat dung clogged the narrow passages. As the scientists crawled through the tight corridors, swarms of infuriated bats clawed at their half-naked bodies and flew into the flaring torches, their wings frizzling in the heat. Denon and Jomard fought off the striking bats with little success, gasping for fresh air. Finally, dripping with sweat, they paused in the Grand Gallery to discharge their pistols. Thunderous echoes reverberated in the hot, cavernous interior. As soon as possible, Jomard gave the signal to retreat.

When they emerged, young Jomard trotted around the Great Pyramid to examine the huge piles of debris that had collected around its footings. Then he climbed to the summit, taking an hour to get there. After admiring the breathtaking view, Jomard tried to measure the height of the Pyramid by means of a slingshot, but was unable to get the shot near the ground. So he measured each step in turn, coming up with a height of 488 feet.

Meanwhile, the savants had put 150 Arabs to work clearing sand from the base of the Pyramid. Soon the workmen hit a huge paved surface surrounding the foundations and two sockets that marked the ancient corners. Army surveyors measured the base and found it to be 757 feet on each side. Jomard then calculated that the slopes were inclined at fifty-one degrees, nineteen minutes. But what did these measurements mean? Rushing back to Cairo to consult the thick tomes the scientists had brought with them, he decided that the Great Pyramid was a huge metric yardstick used by the ancient Egyptians to calculate the dimensions of the earth.

Even when two cynical colleagues remeasured the base of the Great Pyramid and found each side to be two feet longer, Jomard stuck to his guns. The Egyptians were such skilled astronomers, he argued, that they were capable of measuring the circumference of the earth thousands of years before Christ.

Then Napoleon himself got into the act. On August 12, 1799, the general was escorted into the King's Chamber. He had already announced that the Pyramids of Giza contained enough stone to build a wall nine feet high and over a foot thick all around France. After a few minutes, Napoleon asked to be left alone in the chamber. When he emerged, he appeared pale and awestruck, but refused to his dying day to describe what he had experienced in the King's Chamber. "What's the use," he said later, "you'd never believe me."

Most of the tomb robbers and antiquarians who flocked to the Nile after the Napoleonic Wars paused only briefly at the Pyramids before sailing south to Thebes and its rich mummy caves and fine temples. But a Genovese sea captain named Giovanni Caviglio was so excited by Giza that he abruptly retired from the sea and settled down to explore the mysteries of the pyramid.

Caviglio was deeply religious and single-minded in his pyramidical devotions. After shoveling tons of bat dung from a small chamber, he actually set up living quarters inside the Great Pyramid and began to sell antiquities to wealthy tourists to finance his excavations. Convinced that the Great Pyramid contained a secret chamber full of treasure, Caviglio started to tunnel into the solid rock of the Pyramid's interior. Soon discouraged, he gave up digging and contented himself with studies of magic, magnetism, and other esoteric subjects. Perhaps his profits from grave robbing were a consolation to him.

At this point a singularly humorless Englishman named Colonel Richard Howard-Vyse arrived on the scene. Howard-Vyse, a difficult man, was a constant trial to his family. When he wrote from Cairo in 1836 that he intended to study the Pyramids, his family was relieved, although their relief cost them over ten thousand pounds. Howard-Vyse was not one to spare expense: at times, he was paying over seven hundred men to work on his excavations.

Howard-Vyse hired Captain Caviglio as excavation supervisor and Caviglio—at least initially—was delighted with the arrangement. But the two men soon quarreled over money, for Caviglio was by this time more interested in profit than serious scientific inquiry. Contemptuously declaring that the Englishman had "nothing but money," Caviglio retreated to Paris, leaving Howard-Vyse camped in front of the Great Pyramid.

There he was visited by a lady who evidently admired this strict and eccentric man. In her words: "He sat down before the Great Pyramid as a fortress to be besieged." Convinced that the Lord had entrusted him with the great task of interpreting the Pyramid, Howard-Vyse braved summer heat and crowds of tourists to continue his labors, always, wrote his female admirer, "preserving the utmost urbanity, but dealing out the strictest justice in a manner that made a most honorable and lasting impression on the tawny Arabs around him."

But Howard-Vyse's excavation methods were far from honorable. He used gunpowder to blast his way into a series of chambers located above the King's Chamber in the center of the Pyramid. When the dust from the gunpowder subsided, Howard-Vyse could decipher the name of the pharaoh Cheops on the walls. Had Cheops built the Great Pyramid? It seemed entirely possible, especially since the same cartouche—i.e., the oblong design enclosing the pharaoh's name—appeared at the stone quarries where the blocks of the Pyramid had come from. Howard-Vyse also unblocked the small ventilation shafts that "air conditioned" the King's Chamber to a constant temperature of sixty-eight degrees, summer or winter, a great relief to the many tourists who crowded into the Pyramid during the scorching summer months.

After four long years Howard-Vyse returned home and compiled a massive treatise on the Pyramids. Wisely, he devoted much of the treatise to recording precise dimensions and architectural features of the Pyramids, information that astonished everyone who read his book. The colonel laid the foundations for a new field of inquiry, that of pyramidology, the science of pyramids. And many were the pyramidologists who subsequently descended on Giza.

One of the first was John Taylor, a benign and sober gentleman of mature years with an established reputation as a journalist and essayist. Taylor was also a gifted amateur astronomer and mathematician who used these skills to construct scale models of the Pyramids. From these, he derived mathematical formulae that proved, he said, that the Egyptians were familiar with the value of π and had constructed the Great Pyramid to "make a record of the measure of the earth." Thus, according to Taylor, the Great Pyramid had been built to express basic astronomical and geometric laws in simple terms and to perpetuate this knowledge for future generations.

Taylor, a deeply religious man who firmly believed in the Ussherian chronology of the Creation and in Divine Revelation, published his findings in his *Great Pyramid: Why Was It Built and Who Built It*. The volume, which appeared in 1859, attempted to prove that the Lord had revealed the arts of advanced mathematics to the ancient Egyptians. Most people laughed at Taylor. Only an eminent astronomer took him very seriously.

Charles Piazzi Smyth was Astronomer Royal of Scotland when he read Taylor's book. His academic colleagues were horrified when Piazzi Smyth published a paper supporting the theory of Divine Revelation. Piazzi Smyth

◄8-3. The Sphinx and Cheops' Pyramid at Giza.

further argued that the "sacred cubit" used by the builders of the Great Pyramid was the same length as that used by Noah to build the ark. The British inch was almost exactly the same as a twenty-fifth part of the cubit, so, Piazzi Smyth concluded, it had a direct ancestry in the Egyptian unit. When everyone ignored his arguments, Piazzi Smyth decided to go and measure the Pyramids for himself.

Piazzi Smyth and his wife arrived in Cairo in late 1864. They found the sprawling city highly disagreeable—it stank of garlic and human excrement, and barking dogs kept them awake at night. So, their Scottish

8-4. The Pyramids of Giza in the nineteenth century.

sensibilities affronted, they hastened to the Great Pyramid.

While his wife unpacked their belongings and tidied the abandoned tomb they called home, Piazzi Smyth inspected the impressive collection of instruments he had brought along to help him scientifically prove that the Great Pyramid was built by using a special sacred cubit. His measuring bars were specially balanced and constructed with built-in thermometers designed to record even the slightest temperature differences. Piazzi Smyth had also designed a special clinometer, an instrument for measuring angles of elevation, and had even brought a camera with him, at that time a revolutionary piece of scientific research equipment.

For weeks on end, Piazzi Smyth measured and remeasured the passages and chambers of the interior of the Great Pyramid. He took particular pains with the coffin in the King's Chamber which, he believed, had served as an absolutely standard unit of measurement for all Egyptian observations. It was, he said, far better than any standard yardstick of measurement kept in London, for its dimensions did not expand and contract with changes in temperature.

Refreshed with copious draughts of Nile water, guaranteed, he claimed, to cure "the windy melancholy arising from the shorter ribs," Piazzi Smyth now turned his attention to the outer slopes of the Great Pyramid. He spent several eventful nights sleeping on the summit, with the tips of the other pyramids floating eerily nearby. With plumb bob and a five-hundred-inch cord, as well as a sextant and theodolite, Piazzi Smyth carefully measured the altitude, latitude, and longitude of the Great Pyramid. He was amazed at the precise orientation of the structure which, he said, could only have been obtained by a meridian observation of a polar star. But his main preoccupation was with Taylor's conclusions. Was Taylor correct, for example, in believing that "the height of the pyramid was designed to be in relation to the perimeter of its base as the radius of a circle is to its circumference"? After lengthy surveys and profuse calculations, Piazzi Smyth concluded that the Egyptians had built a structure whose basic unit of dimension measurement—the inch—incorporated not only a system for linear measurement but also one for measuring time. Piazzi Smyth went on to claim that the Egyptians were expert astronomers some fifteen hundred years earlier than the Greeks. As soon as Piazzi Smyth paid off his laborers—the best workers were given copper lamps, the worst, mousetraps—he started revealing his conclusions to the world. The sixteen hundred pages of his report were described charitably as being "full of strange hallucinations." One colleague said publicly and in front of Piazzi Smyth that "only a few weak women and a few womanly men believe these theories." Piazzi Smyth's response is not recorded, but he persisted in his beliefs. Eventually, like Taylor, he turned to divine inspiration as the explanation for the Great Pyramid. "Wisdom and metrical instructions" were imparted, he wrote, "to chosen men, by the Author of all wisdom." Piazzi Smyth's earthly reward was abuse and academic oblivion. History has come to regard this sincere pyramidologist as a "pyramidiot."

In 1880, tourists visiting the Great Pyramid were greeted by a strange and outrageous sight. Hastily, respectable gentlemen hustled their wives into the Pyramid or back to the mules. An extraordinary figure carrying a theodolite and binoculars was wandering around the Pyramid. This in itself, of course, was in no way strange—many scientists measured and surveyed the Pyramids. But this gentleman was different: he wore nothing but his pink underwear. The Victorian tourists were horrified, but their horror went unnoticed by this remarkable archaeologist. He was caught up in a colossal task—an accurate triangulation survey of the Pyramids of Giza and their surroundings, something Piazzi Smyth had never managed to complete.

Flinders Petrie was a newcomer to Egypt who relished ignoring the niceties of Victorian etiquette. His one passion was pyramids, a passion developed at the age of thirteen when he came across a copy of Piazzi Smyth's treatise on Giza. Petrie senior was an engineer with a talent for surveying, and his son followed suit. By the time he was twenty-one, Flinders was an expert practical fieldworker who had surveyed over a hundred British earthworks. By this time, too, he had read every reference on pyramids he could find. In November 1880 he finally had the opportunity to visit Egypt. Flinders Petrie sailed for Cairo to begin a career that would eventually culminate in his becoming the foremost Egyptologist of recent times.

Petrie felt at home immediately. He set up camp in an ancient tomb and soon developed a camp routine that he would observe for the rest of his life. He rose from his hammock early in the morning, ate a simple breakfast, and greeted Arab visitors. He did most of his own cooking, for he detested the Arabs' standards of cleanliness. In the evening he wrote up his notes and, as his sole diversion, read before retiring. Day after day Petrie worked around the Pyramids. For up to ten hours at a stretch he peered through his theodolite and laid out his special steel tapes. A large parasol protected him from the midday heat. The survey took months. Petrie was determined to make the definitive survey of the Pyramids, one accurate within a quarter of an inch. He succeeded brilliantly. By digging at the base of the Great Pyramid, he uncovered some of the beautifully fitted casing stones and found that they had been laid on an absolutely straight line that varied by only 1/100 inch over 75 inches. In many places the mortar between the stones was only 1/50 inch thick.

By the time Petrie turned his attention to the interior of the Pyramid, the tourist season was in full swing. Every day crowds of visitors would swarm into the Pyramid and be pushed and pulled by Arabs up the stepped slopes to the summit. Twenty years earlier, Piazzi Smyth had written

8-5. A street in nineteenth-century Cairo.

disapprovingly of "tobacco-stinking gentlemen from some vulgar steamer" and of "whirling dances performed over King Cheops' tombstone with ignorant cursing of his ancient name." Some tourists took lumps of the Pyramid home as souvenirs, others drank from brandy flasks, shouted and yelled, and generally created bedlam. So Petrie waited each day until dark to enter the interior. There he toiled for hours in fetid heat, "clad," as he said, "in nothing, not even a pair of spectacles." The dust was so thick that he choked and suffered from intense headaches. Vandals had blocked up the ventilation shafts again.

But the results were astounding. The walls of the descending passage were so precisely designed that there was an error of a mere 1/50 inch in 150 feet of wall and only 1/4 inch in 350 feet. The design of the King's Chamber showed considerable mathematical skill, for its dimensions were based on the same proportions as those configurations of π that had governed the exterior of the Pyramid. Clearly, the builders of the Pyramid had been expert mathematicians. Petrie concluded that the Egyptians had used a "royal cubit" of 20.63 inches to build a pyramid with a base line of 440 cubits and a height of 280 cubits. He pointed out that Piazzi Smyth's hypothesis—that the perimeter of the pyramid would give one the number of days in the year and was thus a calendar—was based on faulty measurements of the base length of the structure. But he called the structure itself "a triumph of skill. Its errors, both in length and angles, could be covered by placing one's thumb on them."

When Petrie's survey was published in 1883, people were astonished at his achievement. His book was read from cover to cover by dozens of pyramidologists who promptly launched ingenious experiments of their own with the new measurements. A gentleman named John Schmaltz "proved" that a deck of cards was in fact a symbol of the ancient Egyptian calendar. In a book entitled *Nuggets from King Solomon's Mines*, he argued that the 52 cards in a pack equaled the 52 weeks of a year, "the 12 face cards the months, the 13 cards in a suit the lunations, the suits the seasons, the total face value of the cards (counting jack as 11, queen as 12, and king as 13) 364 days, plus the joker as the magic 1.234, for a total of 365.234 days in the year."

The excesses of other pyramidologists were even wilder. Some sought to interpret the Great Pyramid as a prophetic monument. According to Morton Edgar, Colonel J. Garnier, and others, the Great Pyramid contained a six-thousand-year prophetic history of the world which began in 4000 B.C. and extended to A.D. 2045. The prophecies in the Bible were all marked in the stones, the Pyramid's descending passage depicting the gradual decline of humankind toward "ignorance and evil." But there was hope yet. Those who had benefited from Christian teachings would be saved from this fate, for the ascending passage prophesied the ascent of true and humble believers through the Antechamber of Chaos (the modern era) into the King's Chamber, where the Second Coming of Christ would glorify humanity. One pyramid inch on the walls of the passage equaled a year of prophetic time. The first inch represented the Biblical Creation and the Garden of Eden, the last inch, the Day of Judgment. All pyramidologists of this school agreed that the modern era began with the World War in 1914, while the Second Coming was timed for 1953.

One American naval officer who dug sporadically at Giza summed it up nicely when he wrote, "If a suitable unit of measurement is found—say versts, hands, or cables—an exact equivalent to the distance of Timbuctu is certain to be found in the roofing work of the Crystal Palace, or in the number of street lamps in Bond Street, or the Specific Gravity of mud, or the mean weight of an adult goldfish."

The pyramidologists' debates over the Great Pyramid continue to this day. There are many people who still believe the Pyramids are a mysterious and powerful source of cosmic energy. This energy, according to believers, can perform miracles, provide heat and light, and generally illuminate modern life. But although Flinders Petrie's surveys fueled this kind of irrational speculation, they also provided for the first time a scientific basis for the study of the Pyramids. Now, nearly a century later, we know a great deal more about the technological abilities of the ancient Egyptians, as well as about their society.

Unfortunately, there are no surviving contemporary records that give us details of the building of the Pyramids. We can merely extrapolate from other, later records that describe public building projects of a much smaller scale. We can be fairly certain that the engineers who laid out the Great Pyramid on a flattened rocky plateau by the Nile at Giza were not particularly sophisticated astronomers. They used simple astronomical observations of major celestial bodies to position the four straight sides of the Great Pyramid on the cardinal points of the compass—north, south, east, and west. The surveyors used fiber measuring cords to lay out the ground plan in units of 20.62 inches, Petrie's royal cubit. Unfortunately the strings stretched, so there is an error of nearly eight inches between the various sides.

While many details of how the Pyramids were built are now satisfactorily established, we still do not know why the Pyramids were erected in the first place. Without question, they served as burial places for the pharaohs. But why did the kings of Egypt commission such enormous works, projects that took as long as twenty-five years to complete? Surely royal vanity alone is insufficient explanation. If we reject the idea that the Pyramids were spectacular observatories—and most serious scholars do—then can we develop an alternative explanation?

British physicist Kurt Mendelssohn had little interest in Egyptology until he paid a chance visit to the pyramids in the 1960s and ended up spending many months studying their design and the rationale behind

8-6. Modern tourism at the Pyramids.

them. From these studies he has developed a pragmatic explanation for the pyramid projects. Mendelssohn was surprised to find out, as are many strangers to Egyptology, that all the Egyptian pyramids were erected over a very short period of time—only about a century, beginning in 2500 B.C. To complete all this work in such a brief period, he concluded, the builders must have been working on more than one pyramid at a time. It was an eventful architectural century, for the builders had to cope with many new engineering problems. The second pyramid they built at Meidum collapsed during construction. The lateral thrusts of the rubble core were such that the buttresses gave way and probably buried thousands of workmen. So the builders modified their designs and started a new pyramid at Dashur instead. By the time they came to Giza, the architects had solved the thrust problem by using packing blocks to counteract the forces of plastic flow and had reached the classic angle of fifty-two degrees that stood the test of time.

Mendelssohn, in addition to discovering that Meidum had collapsed, carefully considered the human engineering of the construction projects. No one, he found, had any real idea of how many people worked on the Pyramids during the three months when agriculture was at a standstill.

Herodotus claimed that 100,000 people toiled at their construction, an estimate many authorities felt was not unreasonable. While a relatively small number of skilled artisans worked on the Pyramids all year round, the logistics of organizing and feeding armies of unskilled laborers during the peak construction season must have been an enormous undertaking. A permanent organization of bureaucrats and overseers must have been needed to keep the work force in being from year to year. But as each pyramid rose from the floodplain, fewer and fewer laborers were needed. The alternatives were simple: either dismantle the labor organization, a process that would have a number of far-reaching political and economic consequences, or divert the many thousands of laborers to another pyramid project.

Mendelssohn soon realized that once one or two pyramids had been built, a profound change in the living conditions of the Nile's rural population would be inevitable. For a quarter of each year a large segment of Egypt's population was dependent on the country's central government for food and shelter. The pyramid administration had to stockpile surplus grain to feed the workers, grain levied by the pharaoh from the scattered villages of the Nile. As the villages became more accountable to the pharaoh and his government, they gradually evolved from a scattering of settlements into a unified state ruled by a divine king. And the towering Pyramids were the awesome symbol of the power of the pharaoh and the gods he represented on earth. Had the pharaohs and their advisors exploited the advantages of this new economic situation, wondered Mendelssohn? Was it the orgy of pyramid building that strengthened their position and built one of the world's most durable civilizations from hundreds of scattered villages on the banks of the Nile? His hypothesis is certainly a sensible one, far removed from cosmic energy and other improbable theories.

No one knows by what means the pharaohs recruited their labor gangs. The workmen were probably volunteers, for there are no signs of the huge armies that would have been needed to discipline the sweating slaves that Hollywood film producers are so fond of depicting. More likely, speculated Mendelssohn, the Pyramids were built by gangs of peasant volunteers who willingly submitted themselves to the rivalry and discipline of construction-camp life for the good of the state and for the gods. The powerful religious and spiritual forces that motivated this extraordinary army of volunteers will perhaps always be a mystery.

There can be little doubt that Mendelssohn's conclusion is correct: the Pyramids very likely did play a unique role in Egyptian history. Any structures conceived on such a grandiose scale are bound to have had a dramatic effect on the thousands of people involved in their building. But why the pyramid form? And why did the pharaohs choose to be buried under structures that pointed so dramatically heavenward? Perhaps

8-7. Entrance to the Pyramid of Cheops.

American Egyptologist James Breasted was right when he wrote: "The king was buried under the very symbol of the sun god which stood in the holy of holies in the sun temple at Heliopolis and when in mountainous proportions the pyramid rose above the king's sepulchre, dominating the royal city below and the valley beyond for many miles, it was the loftiest object which greeted the sun god in all the land, and his morning rays glittered on its shining summit long before he scattered the shadows in the dwellings of humbler mortals below."

Sometimes on a cloudy day a single ray of sun will pierce the cloud cover and strike the Great Pyramid along the very angle of its sloped side. Witnessing this, one truly grasps the meaning of an ancient Egyptian text: "I have trodden these thy rays as a ramp under my feet whereon I mount up to that my mother, the living being on the brow of Re." Perhaps the Pyramids were a colossal and quite logical gateway to heaven.

9

Howard Carter and
TUTANKHAMUN

I stood in the presence of a king who reigned three thousand years ago," wrote British archaeologist Howard Carter over half a century ago. He had just opened the burial chamber of an obscure Egyptian pharaoh, Tutankhamun. Only a few months after the discovery of his undisturbed mummy, Tutankhamun had become the most famous of all the ancient Egyptian kings simply because, over the years, his tomb had escaped detection by the voracious Egyptian grave robbers. No other archaeological discovery has ever rivaled the golden splendor and magnificence of Tutankhamun.

The tale of Tutankhamun centers around the desolate Valley of Kings near Thebes, for centuries the burial place of Egypt's greatest pharaohs. While early Egyptian rulers had been buried under vast pyramids, the later pharaohs were more circumspect. They were buried in elaborate, rock-cut tombs with carefully hidden entrances. Soon the Valley of Kings was honeycombed with secret burial chambers, each, theoretically at any rate, containing the elaborate and costly worldly goods of the departed pharaohs. Only those who worked on the tombs and the priests who guarded the valley knew the secrets of the royal sepulchres. The greatest of all Egyptian kings slept there, men whose names had been known and feared throughout the ancient world—Ramesses II, Seti I, Tuthmosis III, and many others.

The funerary rites of the pharaohs, their relatives, and their important officials provided employment for hundreds of people. The guards and workpeople lived in a special village at Deir el-Medina near Thebes. Contemporary records give us a fascinating glimpse into life in the Deir el-Medina workshops. We read of absenteeism and of strikes called when rations were issued late. The villagers were kept continually busy— quarrying rock-cut tombs, making grave furniture, preparing the elaborate funerary inscriptions that vaunted the deeds of the dead to heaven and to posterity.

But the people of Thebes not only buried the dead, they robbed them as well. Thousands of richly furnished graves in the necropolis brought untold wealth to those bold enough to steal it. One can imagine the constant plotting that went on, the many attempts to bribe guards and compliant priests. Frequently, small groups of men would assemble at a quiet nocturnal rendezvous. A few words of greeting and they would slip into the darkness. Perhaps a cooperative necropolis guard would stealthily shine a light to show the way to the entrance to an untouched tomb. Sometimes a swift dagger stroke would remove a vigilant sentry. Then the robbers would burrow into the tomb, hastily search the burial chamber for portable loot, and slip quietly away before the relief guard appeared for duty. Within a few days the booty would have been sold or melted down for its precious minerals or gems. It's easy to imagine such happenings. Grave robbing was almost inevitable, for, by taking all their wealth with them, the pharaohs seemed to issue an open invitation to grave robbers. Nearly all the royal tombs in the Valley of Kings were emptied of their treasures within a few generations. Not even the death penalty deterred the tomb robbers. The rewards were too high.

By the time the Romans visited the Valley of Kings only a number of empty tombs remained, so the disappointed travelers did nothing but inscribe their names by torchlight on the tomb walls. During the Middle Ages, hermits settled in the royal sepulchres. Arab treasure hunters followed them. They ransacked every corner of the desolate valley in search of unopened tombs. So did Napoleon's scientists during a lengthy stay in 1799. They counted eleven royal tombs and found a twelfth. It was empty.

Twenty years later the celebrated circus strongman turned tomb robber, Giovanni Belzoni, descended on the Valley of Kings. Belzoni was familiar with the ways of the pharaohs and possessed an incredible instinct for knowing where to dig. Armed with a battering ram and the services of twenty experienced laborers, he soon found the empty tomb of Seti I, a beautifully painted sepulchre, empty except for a wonderful, translucent sarcophagus that had once contained the royal mummy. We know now that royal priests had entered the tomb on at least two occasions to move the royal mummy to safety before grave robbers ransacked the sepulchre and carried off everything portable.

Not even Giovanni Belzoni was able to find an undisturbed royal tomb. Apparently all the royal sepulchres had been emptied in ancient times by tomb robbers working in league with guards and priests. It seemed the pharaohs were robbed as quickly as they were buried. However, the hope that some had been overlooked led generations of archaeologists to comb the Valley of Kings looking for the ultimate archaeological prize—an undisturbed pharaoh's tomb.

The nineteenth century saw a dramatic growth in the tourist trade through Thebes. The town's tomb robbers made so much money from a seemingly inexhaustible supply of mummies and fine antiquities that the authorities in Cairo became suspicious. Their attentions focused on one Ahmed Abd el-Rasul, whose stock of antiquities always seemed to include some unique pieces. In early 1881 Rasul and his brother were arrested and tortured to no avail. But soon afterward a violent family quarrel over the division of the spoils sent Rasul's brother to the police. He confessed everything, recounting how the Rasul family had come across an incredible cache of mummies in a rocky cleft behind Thebes. A few days later he led

9-1. (*previous page*) Howard Carter opens Tutankhamun's shrine.

the police and archaeologist Emil Brugsch to the rocky defile.

Brugsch, after arming himself with a pistol for fear of reprisals from the villagers, had himself lowered into the narrow entrance. As he lit his candles he was confronted by an extraordinary sight: the entire cleft was full of mummies. "The Arabs had disinterred a whole vault of pharaohs," he wrote later. "And what pharaohs! Tuthmosis III and Seti I, Ahmose the Liberator and Ramesses II the Conqueror." Here were the mummies of the greatest pharaohs of all, mingled with an incredible jumble of grave furniture and ornaments, as well as coffins belonging to queens and lesser officials. The Rasuls had stumbled over the secret hiding place of the royal mummies, adopted as a last resort when the Valley of the Kings was deemed unsafe for any pharaoh to lie in. Loyal priests had smuggled the bodies to the secret cache, where they had dumped them hurriedly, perhaps only one step ahead of the grave robbers.

The forty royal mummies and their priceless possessions were carefully transferred to the Cairo Museum. Mohammed Rasul was rewarded for his pains with an appointment as a tomb guard, surely the most incredible piece of official irony in Egyptian history.

With the discovery of this fabulous cache most people believed that the Valley of Kings contained no more royal burials. As more information emerged from the royal finds in Rasul's cache, it became clear that every pharaoh from Tuthmosis I (c. 1504–1492 B.C.) to Amenophis III (c. 1391–1353 B.C.) had been buried there and could be accounted for. But one small gap remained, that of a little-known pharaoh named Tutankhamun who reigned from 1333 to 1323 B.C. His two successors were buried in the valley, but of his tomb there was no sign.

Tutankhamun was born at a time of great political upheaval in Egypt. During the Eighteenth Dynasty, which lasted from about 1550 to 1307 B.C., Egypt occupied a prominent position in the ancient world. It was a great center of international trade, especially famed for its precious raw materials and ever-fertile wheat fields. The green Nile floodplain generated enormous food surpluses that supported all the panoply and show of the Egyptian court and the religion of the great god Amun at Thebes. A huge bureaucracy administered the day-to-day affairs of the state and Egypt's relations with dozens of other nations. Tutankhamun's predecessors had expanded the Egyptian empire far beyond the boundaries of the Nile. Egypt was a powerful military state, her prestige enormous.

The events that shaped Tutankhamun's reign began some seven years before he was born. By that time, the pharaoh Amenophis III had reigned for at least twenty-nine years and was growing old. He appointed his son Akhenaten, at that time known as Amenophis IV, as his co-regent.

Akhenaten seems to have had a strong interest in religion, at that time a complex interest to pursue, for Egypt was a maze of local and national religions and cults. Akhenaten, a strong believer in monotheism, felt the time had come for a single national religion. The god he chose to worship to the exclusion of all others was the sun god, Aten, personified by the solar disk itself.

Akhenaten spent most of his time propagating the religion of Aten, declaring himself the son of the sun god and his co-regent. Accordingly, he changed his name from Amenophis to Akhenaten. A vast temple of Aten was planned at Thebes and the royal capital was moved to a new site between Memphis and Thebes, to a place he named Akhenaten, now known as Tell el-Amarna. While the pharaoh was busy with religious matters, foreign affairs were neglected. Egypt's vassals took advantage of the chaos on the Nile and carried on more or less as they pleased. Tutankhamun was probably born to Sitamun, daughter and wife of Amenophis III, after Akhenaten had been co-regent for eight years.

By this time Akhenaten had but one preoccupation: the obliteration of all religious cults that in any way threatened the preeminence of Aten. Sculptors hacked out all references to Amun and other gods from temples and statues. The temples of Amun at Thebes were ignored and desecrated. Akhenaten himself seems to have become mentally unbalanced to the extent that the very stability of Egypt was threatened. Tutankhamun must have experienced the traumas and tantrums of Akhenaten's court. Fortunately, however, the pharaoh was still surrounded by statesmanlike advisers, one of whom, Ay, had originally served as Master of the Horse and then been elevated to a state adviser to the pharaoh. It seems that Ay paid only lip service to the cult of Aten, being more concerned with the survival of the state than with Akhenaten's peculiarities. Fortunately for Egypt, both Akhenaten and his successor, Semenkhare, died within a short time of each other in 1361 B.C. and Tutankhamun came to the throne. Whether the two were assisted to heaven by the industrious Ay will ever remain a secret.

Tutankhamun was only nine when he became the most powerful ruler on earth. Ay took up the reins of government and served as regent and vizier to the new pharaoh. He also had himself appointed crown prince designate, so that he could legitimately succeed Tutankhamun, a master stroke of intrigue if ever there was one. Acting on the pharaoh's behalf, Ay moved cautiously to restore order and the fortunes of the cult of Amun. Tutankhamun's official inscriptions state how he restored temples that had fallen into ruin, their buildings overgrown with vegetation and weeds. The young king and his equally young queen, Ankhesenamun, were kept busy with the complex round of rituals and ceremonies that custom prescribed for the pharaoh. One of Ay's priorities must have been to restore public confidence in the monarchy after the chaos of Akhenaten's reign.

9-2. (*previous page*) The Valley of Kings.

Then, in 1323 B.C., just as he was of an age to assume the full reins of pharaonic power, the young king suddenly died. He died childless, but two stillborn children, both girls, were mummified and buried with him. The dead pharaoh, although accorded a magnificent funeral, was buried in a smaller tomb than were his predecessors, a tomb originally intended for Ay himself. His faithful vizier succeeded to the throne and ruled Egypt for four years after Tutankhamun's death. Whether he arranged for the young king to be poisoned just when he was becoming a possible political threat we do not know. The process of mummification removed all traces of any foreign substances in the king's body. We can only assume he died of natural causes.

Such, then, is the story of the obscure king whose grave was still undiscovered eighty years ago. Everyone suspected it lay somewhere within the Valley of Kings, even if it had been obliterated in antiquity, and the tantalizing possibility of its presence made the valley one of the Egyptologists' prime excavation targets. A concession to dig in the Valley of Kings was highly prized and was available only to the most wealthy of patrons. From 1899 to 1902 their excavations in the valley were carefully supervised by Howard Carter, a British archaeologist who was chief inspector of monuments for Upper Egypt.

Howard Carter was an artist and draughtsman who first came to Egypt in 1892 at the age of eighteen. His sketches of the inscriptions at Beni Hasan were so widely admired that he was invited to dig with several famous archaeologists, among them the immortal Sir Flinders Petrie, the greatest Egyptologist of all time. When he became chief inspector of monuments, Carter visited the Valley of Kings almost daily. There he met a wealthy American businessman named Theodore Davis, who had just won the concession to excavate in the valley. Davis had come to Egyptology late in life, but was soon pouring money into large-scale excavations. He spent nine years digging in the Valley of Kings, where he found six important tombs and several minor burials. Carter worked with the enthusiastic American on two tombs and had plenty of time to ponder what soon became an obsession—the whereabouts of Tutankhamun's tomb.

In 1905 Carter quarrelled with the government and resigned. For two years he eked out a living as an artist in Thebes. Then one day he was introduced to George Edward Stanhope Molyneaux, Fifth Earl of Carnarvon. The two men—Carter the craftsman and meticulous artist, Carnarvon a wealthy aristocrat of the old school and a man whose cultivated taste in rare books and works of art was well known—took to each other immediately. Lord Carnarvon had first visited Egypt in 1901 at the age of thirty, after a serious motor accident in Germany. Each winter the Carnarvon family took up residence in Egypt so that the earl could avoid the unhealthy damp of the English winter. He began to collect Egyptian antiquities and soon teamed up with Howard Carter. Year after year Carnarvon financed excavations at Thebes, digs Howard Carter supervised on his behalf. The pair made many important discoveries in the vicinity of the Valley of Kings, but the valley itself was closed to them. Each season the two men watched enviously as Theodore Davis uncovered the intact tomb of Queen Ty's parents, the only undisturbed tomb ever found in the valley. But in 1914 Theodore Davis relinquished his concession. In his final publication the wealthy American wrote, "I fear that the Valley of Kings is now exhausted." A year later he died.

In his final season Theodore Davis uncovered a small underground chamber that contained some objects which bore the name of Tutankhamun. He promptly claimed that he had located the remains of the lost pharaoh's tomb. In fact, these few finds were leftovers from an early and rapid theft from Tutankhamun's still-buried tomb nearby. Then Davis made another discovery that seemed of little importance at the time. A small pit containing about a dozen white clay jars came to light. The jars held bundles of linen, some animal bones, and various embalming substances. Davis thought the jars of no importance and turned them over to the Metropolitan Museum of Art in New York, where Hubert Winlock, the Met's Keeper of Egyptian Antiquities, soon realized that the cache consisted of materials used during the embalming of Tutankhamun's mummy. Also found were the remains of a banquet eaten by about eight people, a meal evidently consumed at the time of the funeral.

Winlock did not publish his remarkable findings, but did mention them to Howard Carter. The Winlock discovery set Carter thinking. While he was now certain Tutankhamun had been buried in the valley, he wondered whether it was worthwhile looking for a tomb that could have been obliterated centuries before. The obstacles to further excavation were formidable; huge piles of rubble and sand were scattered over the floor of the valley. Was it worth the effort to shift thousands of tons of soil to search for a mere possibility? These were the days before mechanical earth-moving equipment. The only available tools for the job were adzes and hoes, baskets, and a plentiful supply of very cheap labor. Some sixth sense, perhaps the well-tuned instinct of the experienced archaeologist, caused Carter to embark on what to many seemed a crazy enterprise—a search for a tomb that might not exist.

Although Lord Carnarvon took up Theodore Davis's concession in 1914, it was not until 1917 that work in the valley began in earnest. Howard Carter decided to concentrate on a triangle of ground between the empty tomb of Ramesses II, his son Merenptah, and Ramesses VI. Section by carefully planned section, Carter cleared the valley floor, moving from one sector to another as each was cleared. Except for the foundations of some

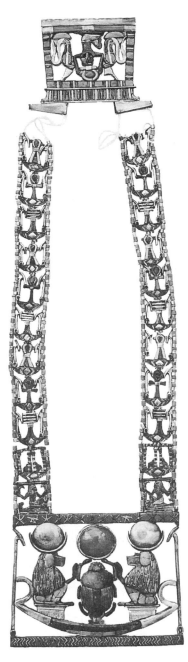

9-3. Necklace of the Rising Sun from Tutankhamun's tomb. Length: 16 inches.

workmen's huts and a cache of alabaster jars, the excavations yielded only endless piles of dry rubble. After six seasons of hard labor, Carnarvon was ready to give up. The excavators had moved 200,000 tons of soil with almost nothing to show for it.

In the summer of 1922, Carnarvon sent for Carter and told him to pack it in. But Carter was not so easily dissuaded. He pulled out a map of the valley and showed his patron a spot they had left untouched in 1917, on the grounds that a dig would have inconvenienced visitors to the tomb of Ramesses VI nearby. The undisturbed area was a small one and would require only one more season to investigate. Carter begged for the chance to dig for one more year and even offered to bear all the costs himself. Carnarvon was so touched by Carter's offer that he agreed to a final season of excavation on the same terms as before. It was a fateful decision for both men.

Carter started work on November 1, 1922, only a few feet away from the spot where he had begun digging six years before. The workmen were instructed to clear the soil away from an area around the entrance to the tomb of Ramesses VI. The very first day more ancient workmen's huts came to light, part of the very same group Carter had partially excavated in 1917. Three days later, as the workmen began to clear away the huts, they came across a hidden step cut in the rocky valley floor thirteen feet from Ramesses's tomb. Since the huts had belonged to the workmen who had labored on the tomb of Ramesses VI in 1143 B.C., the underlying step obviously dated to an earlier period. Twenty-four hours later Carter was gazing at a rocky staircase of twelve steps that converged on a partially exposed blocked and plastered doorway. Breathless with excitement, Carter cleared away some of the rubble and exposed the plaster work. It bore some unbroken seals, the official jackal seals of the royal necropolis. The tomb was apparently intact!

Since the workmen who toiled on Ramesses VI's tomb had built their huts over the hidden entrance, the burial had certainly remained undisturbed since the Twentieth Dynasty. Some of the plaster had fallen away from the doorway. Carter shone his torch into the small, dark hole by the lintel and glimpsed a passageway filled with rubble.

At this supreme moment in his archaeological career, Carter displayed incredible patience and restraint. He filled in his excavation, placed trustworthy guards on the tomb, and sent a historic cable to Lord Carnarvon who was still in England: "At last have made wonderful discovery in the Valley; a magnificent tomb with seals intact; recovered same for your arrival; congratulations." Carter had found the tomb only a few feet from the place where he had started digging six years before.

For three long weeks Carter waited for Lord Carnarvon and his sister to arrive from England by steamer. On November 23 Carnarvon arrived in Luxor. The very next day the entire sixteen steps of the stairway were cleared. As the base of the sealed doorway emerged from the rubble, the two men stopped to gaze at some intact seals on the plaster. They were those of Tutankhamun himself. Although some signs of damage could be detected, the tomb had clearly been resealed by officials of the necropolis. There was a good chance that Tutankhamun's mummy lay in the tomb.

The seals were carefully photographed and removed. Then the doorway was cleared to reveal a sloping tunnel completely filled with stones and rubble. This, again, showed signs of disturbance and later resealing. The rubble was shoveled out. Thirty feet further along the passage was another doorway, again impressed with Tutankhamun's seal. Again, there were signs of illegal entry, so Carter steeled himself for a ransacked and empty tomb. After three hectic days of work, everything was ready for the great moment. Lord Carnarvon and Howard Carter paused before the doorway—a doorway they knew might lead to the greatest archaeological discovery of their careers.

Howard Carter carefully pried away some stones at the top of the doorway. The others waited in restless silence as he passed a candle through the hole to check for dangerous gases. At first Carter could see nothing. His candle flickered as hot air escaped from the long-sealed tomb. But presently, as his eyes became accustomed to the faint light, he saw the glint of gold and a jumble of strange objects. The gold swam in front of his eyes as he gazed absolutely spellbound at the incredible scene before him.

Impatiently Lord Carnarvon waited behind the gazing Carter. The silence became unbearable. Carter was struck dumb with amazement. After holding back for what must have seemed an interminably long time, Carnarvon asked anxiously, "Can you see anything?"

There was a short pause, then came Carter's whispered reply: "Yes, it is wonderful."

A few moments later, Carter stepped back from his peephole, sweating and speechless. Carnarvon grabbed a torch and peered through the hole at the incredible sight behind the stone wall. "It was," recalled Carter later, "the day of days, the most wonderful I have ever lived through, and certainly one whose like I can never hope to see again."

What the two men had seen was the antechamber, the storeroom that lay before the actual mummy chamber. All they had glimpsed in this first look was a tiny part of the entire tomb, but they had seen enough to know that the results of their long search surpassed their wildest dreams.

At this supreme moment in their lives, the two men almost gave in to an overwhelming impulse to burst into the chamber, to open box after box and to handle the extraordinary treasure that lay before them. As Carter later wrote, he felt almost embarrassed, as if he had strayed into someone's private rooms. "The very air you breathe," he wrote, "unchanged throughout the centuries, you share with those who laid the

9-4. The antechamber before clearance.

mummy to rest.'' There was even a farewell garland on the threshold.

As their eyes became accustomed to the darkness, the two archaeologists could pick out individual objects. Three large, gilt couches lay opposite the passageway, carved in the form of monstrous, stretched-out animals. Their gilded sides glittered in the torchlight. To the right stood two life-sized, gold-kilted figures facing each other like sentinels, armed with mace and staff. Between them was another sealed doorway. With a thrill of excitement, Carter realized there was no mummy in the treasure chamber. Perhaps the pharaoh himself lay behind the two sentinels.

Carter and Carnarvon spent hours simply gazing at the antechamber, at painted and inlaid caskets, alabaster vases, carved chairs, a confused pile of chariot wheels, and hundreds of exquisite smaller treasures. As evening approached, they emerged from the tomb, placed a wooden grille over the doorway, and set a guard on Tutankhamun's sepulcher.

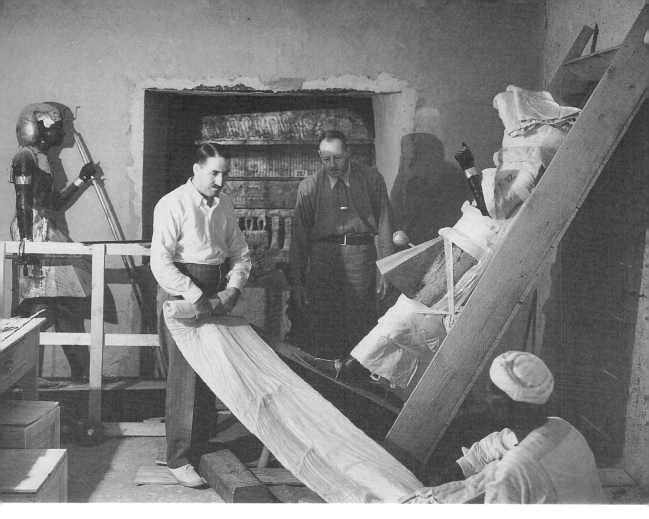

9-5. Carter and Carnarvon wrapping up one of the statues of Tutankhamun in the antechamber for removal from the tomb.

As the party rode home through the darkness, everyone was strangely silent and preoccupied, overcome with the events of the day. Later that night, Carnarvon, Carter, Carter's assistant Arthur Callendar, and Lady Evelyn Herbert quietly returned to the tomb for a long, surreptitious visit. In the small hours, they quietly removed some loose boulders in the sealed doorway of the burial chamber and squeezed their way between the intact sarcophagus and the rock-cut wall. Carter opened the outermost shrine, to satisfy himself that the mummy was intact. Then they withdrew and removed all signs of their quiet inspection. Carter could not help thinking of the arduous, overwhelming work that lay ahead. Perhaps he alone realized that their work had hardly begun.

On November 27 the party returned to the tomb early in the morning. Carter's assistant, Callendar, laid electric cables from a neighboring tomb which enabled them to hang powerful lights in the antechamber. There were clear signs of a forced entry and a rapid ransacking of the treasure chests in the antechamber too. But the robbers never had a chance to reach the mummy itself. Apparently they were disturbed at their work, for they fled with their booty, leaving most of the tomb unrifled. Later the necropolis officials tidied up the damage and repaired the doorways into the tomb, restoration work that cannot have taken more than a day. There were signs of at least two robberies, the first concerned with small portable objects of gold and silver, the second with precious oils and unguents. One thief even left his fingerprints on the inside of the vessel from which he emptied fine oil into a convenient water skin.

These seem to have been the only illegal assaults made on the tomb, for its location was forgotten soon afterward. Unlike other pharaohs, Tutankhamun apparently died unexpectedly, long before the elaborate tomb being prepared for him was ready for occupation. So the necropolis officials cast about for a suitable substitute. Maya, the superintendent of the royal necropolis at the time, ordered the workmen to prepare Tutankhamun for burial in Ay's tomb, a chamber already hewn from the

9-6. Tutankhamun's tomb: the Treasury with the dog-god Anubis in the foreground.

rock. Two centuries later, Ramesses VI decided that his sepulchre would be built into the rock face directly above the forgotten entrance to Tutankhamun's tomb. Thus, quite by chance, the new royal tomb protected the sepulchre until modern times.

First, the archaeologists turned their attention to the antechamber. Obviously, the first step would have to be a complete inventory and photographic record of the jumble of treasure around them. But there was so much to puzzle over and to admire; everything was so fresh and complete. "Any one of the objects," wrote Carter, "would have filled us with excitement under ordinary circumstances, and been considered ample repayment for a full season's work." The artistry of the furniture and jewelry was extraordinary. Tutankhamun's seal lay on all the larger objects and many of the smaller ones. There could now be no doubt as to the identity of the mummy that lay behind the sealed door.

Carter and Carnarvon spent all day in the antechamber, exclaiming at new objects and contemplating the huge task that lay before them. Then, suddenly, they noticed a small, dark hole under one of the burial couches. It was another sealed doorway, again with a hole torn in it. But this time no one had bothered to repair the tomb robbers' damage. Carter cautiously crawled under the couch and shone a light through the hole. Gold glittered in the darkness as the flashlight revealed a jumble of small, exquisite objects haphazardly strewn on the chamber's floor.

This treasure store was much smaller than the antechamber and no one had tidied up after the tomb robbers. Probably a single plunderer had crept into the chamber and ransacked it from one end to the other. He had passed a few objects out through the opening and left the rest in chaos.

The new discovery had a surprisingly sobering effect on the party. Suddenly they faced the immensity of the job ahead. Tutankhamun's tomb was unique, quite outside any archaeologist's normal range of experience. Carter wondered if the job was beyond him.

The first priority was to secure the tomb against unauthorized entry. Carter ordered a gate of tough steel bars, then placed his most reliable guards on watch. Meanwhile, wild rumors were circulating in Thebes: a great treasure had been found in the valley and had been spirited out of Egypt by plane; the burials of several pharaohs had come to light; unbelievable wealth had been discovered for the first time. Dealers' shops and the bazaars buzzed with gossip, and Carter and Carnarvon were besieged with inquiries. To put an end to the uproar, they decided to stage an official opening of the tomb. On November 29, 1922, a large and varied party of distinguished guests assembled at the tomb for a formal inspection of the marvels that lay within. The local correspondent of the London *Times* was present and filed a long dispatch that sent the public into a frenzy of excitement. Howard Carter's problems were only just beginning.

The tomb entrance was filled in as Carter went to Cairo to make thorough preparations for clearing the antechamber. Every object in the tomb had to be recorded and photographed in place. Many pieces were too fragile to be removed without some restoration first. Obviously Carter needed help. Fortunately, expert assistance was not far away. When the *Times* carried the news of Carter and Carnarvon's triumph, offers of help poured in from all over Europe and America. The Metropolitan Museum of Art lent photographers and artists, the Egyptian Antiquities Department offered facilities. Individual Egyptologists rushed to the scene as well, including Alan Gardiner, the world's leading authority on hieroglyphs.

Carter's immediate logistical problems were formidable. He purchased mountains of packing materials, a mile of bandages and a further mile of wadding, thirty-two bales of calico, all kinds of chemicals and photographic equipment, and even a motorcar. So much restoration and packing work had to be done on the site that Carter set up a conservation laboratory nearby in the empty tomb of Seti II. There the contents of the tomb were prepared for shipping to Cairo. In those days there were no tarmac roads to the Valley of Kings, nor were there helicopters to transport delicate finds from door to door. Every statue, every item of furniture, and even the mummy itself had to be carried over dirt tracks by large gangs of men. All Carter had at his disposal were a few lengths of railroad track that had to be laid and relaid again as the precious loads made their slow way to the Nile at Luxor. The alternatives were camels or porters, so Carter used a gang of fifty men to move the precious trucks and the rails. Their progress was slow: they covered only a third of a mile each hour and it took fifteen hours to make the complete journey to the Nile. In addition, the move was made at the height of summer when, at times, the rails became almost too hot to touch. The steamship that carried the finds downriver to Cairo took another seven days.

By December 18, a steel door had been installed and a team of at least seven experts was on hand. During the following months, as Carter began to list the antechamber's contents, he was finally able to appreciate the full range of treasures crammed into this three-hundred-square-foot space. Clearing this cramped area was, as Carter said, "like a giant game of spillikins." It was an exacting job, for many of the most delicate objects were intermeshed with one another and each presented special problems. There were, for example, delicate ornaments of patterned beadwork and funeral bouquets that fell apart at a touch unless first hardened with paraffin wax. Tutankhamun's chariots and funeral couches had been constructed in such a way that they could be brought into the tomb in pieces and then reassembled. Carter's problem was the reverse—he had to disassemble them and remove the separate parts. After three thousand years, the bronze hooks had set hard in their staples and would not budge. It took five people to dismantle the couches. The chariots were even worse, for they had been disturbed by the tomb robbers and been restacked by the priests. The leather trappings were little more than a black, glutinous mass.

It took seven weeks to clear the antechamber. Harry Burton, a photographer from the Met in New York, photographed each object in place. Then two artists added the item to their detailed drawing of the antechamber before Carter and Callendar supervised its removal. Only archaeologists handled the precious finds, both for conservation and for security. Once a day a closely supervised company of laborers would carry a precious cargo of stretchers out of the tomb over to the laboratory in Seti II's sepulchre. What an extraordinary sight each procession was! Painted wooden chests, stools, a golden shrine, even a mannequin to which the king's robes could be fitted, as well as a host of minor objects—fly whisks, bows, vases, a wine strainer—were brought into the bright sunshine of the twentieth century.

Perhaps the finest object was a throne overlaid with gold and richly decorated with glass, faience, and semiprecious stones. The legs were surrounded with lions' heads, and magnificent serpents formed the arms. But the back of the throne made Carter gasp. In a scene inlaid in glass, the pharaoh relaxes on a cushioned throne while the queen, standing in front of him, puts the final touches on the pharaoh's toilet. In one hand she holds a small jar of ointment; with the other, she gently anoints her husband's shoulder. The colors of this charming scene must have dazzled when new. Even centuries later, they glowed with a soft translucence that led Carter to exclaim that the throne was "the most beautiful thing that has yet been found in Egypt."

By this time, the clearance of the tomb was being closely followed by the press. Carter was deluged with congratulatory cables, then with thousands of letters. "They were a curious lot," Carter wrote of his correspondents. There were offers of assistance, as well as inquiries regarding moving-picture rights and fashion-design copyrights. Some told Carter how to appease evil spirits, others sent religious tracts and denounced the archaeologists for committing sacrilege. "An interesting psychological study they would make if one had the time," Carter remarked to a colleague.

Visitors to the site soon became a serious problem. Tourists in the thousands flocked to the entrance of the tomb. Every time a convoy of stretchers left the entrance, dozens of camera shutters clicked. The archaeologists were importuned by reporters in search of sensational stories and by the famous and wealthy seeking guided tours. By now a low wall had been built around the tomb. Each morning, visitors arrived "on donkeys, in sand-carts, and in two-horse cabs." They staked out a claim by the wall and stared. People read, talked, knitted, and photographed everything in sight. At the end of the first season, Carter estimated that a quarter of the archaeologists' time had been consumed with visitors. It

9-7. Tutankhamun being anointed by his wife. The scene depicted on the back of the king's throne.

was difficult to be gracious when there was real danger of irreparable damage to the contents of the tomb. Most annoying were the visitors who pulled every kind of string to get in to see the tomb and then left muttering, ''Well, there wasn't much to see after all.'' The reporters were worse, until Lord Carnarvon gave exclusive rights to the London *Times*. Even so, Carter spent much of his time warding off the public and answering questions.

By the middle of February 1923, the antechamber was swept clean. On February 17, 1923, a party of twenty experts and distinguished people assembled in the antechamber to witness the opening of the sealed doorway. A low working platform was erected, high enough for Carter to reach the top of the doorway. The guests were invited to sit down as Carter advanced to the doorway with a small hammer.

With infinite care, Carter chipped away the plaster from the wooden lintel. After ten minutes of careful work, he was able to insert a flashlight into a small hole. A solid wall of gold blocked the entrance of the chamber. Carter and two colleagues carefully removed the coarse stone slabs that blocked the doorway. As the golden wall came into view, a thrill of excitement passed through the spectators. Two hours later, most of the entrance was cleared. Some agonizing moments of delay ensued as Carter gathered up the scattered beads of a necklace dropped on the threshold by a tomb robber three thousand years before.

The floor of the chamber that lay beyond the threshold was four feet lower than that of the antechamber. There was only a narrow space between the doorway and the huge gilt shrine that protected the royal mummy. Carter lowered himself into the chamber and shone an electric light into the tiny passageway. After removing two alabaster vases that blocked the way, Carter signaled to Carnarvon to join him. Together they squeezed along the passage. They stared at the great gilt shrine, glittering with gold inlay and panels of brilliant blue faience. Its massive bulk— seventeen feet by eleven feet by nine feet—filled almost the entire burial chamber. The walls of the chamber itself had been hastily painted with scenes and inscriptions. Nearby lay the oars the pharaoh needed to ferry himself across the waters of the underworld.

The closed doors of the shrine lay at the east end of the chamber. They were bolted but not sealed. Had tomb robbers wreaked destruction on the sarcophagus that lay within? Eagerly Carter slid back the bolts and swung open the doors. Before him was a second shrine with bolted doors and an intact seal. A linen pall decorated with golden rosettes hung above the inner shrine.

At this point, Carter and Carnarvon paused again, simultaneously experiencing a sharp sense of intrusion. They were, they felt, in the presence of a king to whom they should make reverence. So they closed the doors silently and continued their preliminary examination of the burial chamber. Another surprise awaited them, an open doorway that led to a small chamber containing a marvelous golden shrine guarded by four goddesses of the dead. This shrine obviously contained the canopic jars so important in Egyptian funerary rites. Nearby the jackal god Anubis, wrapped in a linen cloth, sat on his shrine. There were further shrines and chests, too, model boats, another chariot. Carter opened a magnificent casket containing a beautiful ostrich feather fan as fresh as the day it was made.

Their survey of the burial chamber was but a hasty one, for Carter realized the others were waiting their turn. In pairs, the visitors stepped down into the chamber. As they emerged, Carter watched their faces. Everyone, dazzled and bewildered, threw their hands up in front of them as if unable to describe the wonders that lay within. "It was," Carter wrote soon afterward, "an experience which, I am sure, none of us who were present is ever likely to forget." The emotions aroused by the spectacle of the burial chamber made the archaeologists feel they had actually been present at the burial ceremonies of the pharaoh himself.

A week later Carter closed down the tomb for the season and placed it under heavy guard. Two months afterward, Lord Carnarvon was bitten by a mosquito. The bite became infected. Three weeks later, on April 6, 1923, he died in a Cairo hotel. His death created a public sensation, for people thought he was the first victim of the legendary curse of Tutankhamun, a terrible penalty for disturbing the long sleep of the pharaoh. Speculation ran wild, for two other archaeologists associated with the investigation died suddenly soon afterward. Over the years no fewer than twenty-one individuals were claimed by the press to be victims of the curse. But perhaps the more impressive statistic is the number of people who did *not* die. Carter lived to be sixty-six, while the anatomist who performed the postmortem on Tutankhamun lived to be over eighty. All the same, the myth lived on, perpetuated by a rash of Hollywood movies about the curse of the pharaohs. One starred Boris Karloff as a hyperactive mummy. Romantic novelists have made hay with the myth, too. But, whatever one's views on the curse, no one can explain the curious fact that all the lights in Cairo failed at the precise moment that Carnarvon died. And, at that very same moment, his dog in faraway England suddenly howled and dropped dead. Both events are well documented by eye witnesses.

Despite Carnarvon's death, Howard Carter was determined to continue. After prolonged negotiations, the Carnarvon concession was renewed, on terms more favorable to the Egyptian government. In 1924–1925 the objects stacked between the shrine and the walls of the burial chamber were removed. Then the wall between the antechamber and the burial chamber was taken down, so that the delicate work of taking apart the outer gilt shrine could begin. Carter expected to find at least five shrines, one inside the other, but in the end, found only four. Each was removed piece by piece by dismantling the gold-covered planking at the very tongues and grooves where they had originally been joined. It took eighty-four days of intense labor to unveil the magnificent yellow quartzite of the king's sarcophagus. There was so little space in the chamber that the walls of the outer shrine had to rest against the side of the chamber until there was space to move them out.

When a third shrine with sealed doors was revealed within the second, Carter decided to go ahead and open its doors at once. The cords and seals were removed, the bolts slid back. A fourth and even more gorgeous shrine lay within, this time with unsealed doors. With bated breath, Carter drew back the bolts. As the doors swung open, a goddess sculpted on the end of the huge yellow sarcophagus within seemed to raise her hand and wings to ward off the intruders.

Some weeks later, the yellow quartzite sarcophagus stood in the middle of the burial chamber, clear of its four shrines. At this point, diplomacy intervened. A large group of archaeologists and officials gathered to witness the opening of the casket. Blocks and tackles were attached to angle irons along the huge granite sarcophagus lid, which weighed over a ton. As bright lights revealed the inside of the sarcophagus, first impressions were disappointing. The inner coffins were covered with fine linen shrouds. Silently, Carter rolled the shrouds back. As the last was removed, everyone gasped. A fabulous golden effigy of the young king lying on a lion-shaped dais filled the sarcophagus. The metalsmiths had even used two different alloys of gold to render a different flesh texture akin to the grey of death. And, most touching of all, a withered bouquet of flowers lay next to the royal symbols of the cobra and the vulture (Upper and Lower Egypt) on the king's forehead. Perhaps, thought Carter, this was the final tribute of the young, mourning queen. In the silence, he could almost hear the ghostly footsteps of the departing mourners.

In the 1925–1926 season, fully three years after the discovery of the tomb, Carter removed the royal coffins from the burial chamber. The huge, gilt-covered effigy coffin was first. The silver pins that held the lid to the body of the casket were carefully drawn out and a lifting tackle was attached to the silver handles to raise the lid. A second, magnificent, gold-covered coffin lay within, again covered with a linen shroud and withered garlands. There was so little space inside the sarcophagus that Carter lifted the first and second coffins out of their stone cocoon and laid them on planks. Then, daringly, the first coffin was lowered back into the sarcophagus while the second was suspended in midair by fine copper wires for a few breathless minutes.

By this time they were close to the pharaoh's mummy itself. The lid of the second coffin was carefully lifted off, revealing more linen coverings and a third coffin. Another surprise awaited the onlookers. The inner coffin, a little over six feet long, was of solid gold, later found to be about one-

9-8. Tutankhamun inside his sarcophagus.

tenth of an inch thick. Carter was overwhelmed by the incredible wealth of Tutankhamun, at the extraordinary display before him. Small wonder the pharaohs had been robbed in their graves!

At this point, the inner coffins were moved to the antechamber, where Carter proceeded to the ultimate task, that of exposing the royal mummy within the golden coffin. With great difficulty the lid was raised, revealing the mummy of Tutankhamun wearing a golden mask and darkened by the many unguents poured on its bandages. The mummy was covered with necklaces, pendants, and beads, but was obviously in a perilous state because of an overdose of unguents.

On November 11, 1925, at 9:45 A.M., Dr. Douglas Derry, an anatomist from Cairo, began the formal examination of Tutankhamun's mummy in front of a select audience. He started by cutting away the outer wrappings—bandages, sheets, and linen pads. With every incision, he exposed more ornaments. Excitement mounted as Derry started on the bandaged head. The pharaoh was wearing a gold diadem, a broad

9-9. Tutankhamun fishing with a spear from a reed canoe.

headband, and a beautifully decorated skullcap that fit tightly over his shaven head. Then, with a few deft strokes, Derry exposed the features of the long-dead pharaoh.

Tutankhamun gazed serenely at his audience. His "refined and cultured countenance" smiled slightly, the masked lips slightly parted. Everyone was astonished to find just how accurately the contemporary artists had portrayed the king's features. They depicted Tutankhamun as a handsome and finely featured youth, which, his mummy showed, he actually was. The ears were pierced, the skull curiously elongated. The pharaoh's forearms were smothered in bracelets, his fingers and thumbs encased in gold sheaths and rings. A magnificent, gold-decorated dagger lay inside the king's waist girdle. Another, with a virtually unrusted iron blade, lay in a golden scabbard by the ceremonial apron around the pharaoh's waist. Tutankhamun wore gold sandals, with separate gold sheaths for each toe. No less than 143 different objects were placed over, or on, the king's body.

Once most of the wrappings had been removed from the body, the king's corpse was lifted from its coffin. The bitumen that anchored the wrappings to the gold coffin had to be chiseled away. It was then possible for Dr. Derry to examine the pharaoh's body. After a meticulous autopsy, Derry confirmed that Tutankhamun had died when about eighteen to twenty years of age. He was of slight build, perhaps no more than 5' 6" tall. The exact cause of his death is still a mystery.

Many years later a team of anatomists from Cairo and Liverpool universities X-rayed Tutankhamun's mummy. They confirmed Derry's and Carter's conclusions as to the age and stature of the king. Then they analyzed the pharaoh's tissues using a new technique that showed his blood groups were A_2 and MN, identical to those of Semenkhare, whose mummy had been identified some years before. The skull measurements of the two young men, and indeed their facial features, seemed almost identical. The anatomists suggested that the two men were brothers who died within a few years of one another. Unfortunately, Tutankhamun's ancestry remains a puzzling mystery, one of the many that still surround the tomb.

Howard Carter continued to work on the tomb of Tutankhamun until 1928. He cleared the treasure chamber connected to the burial chamber and the small annex to the antechamber. After ten years of strenuous work, he left the valley forever, exhausted and in ill health. Carter died at the age of sixty-six. Although he never completed the herculean task of studying the contents of the tomb, he did complete a three-volume popular account of his discoveries. Meanwhile, Lord Carnarvon's widow had been persuaded to donate all the finds to the Cairo Museum, where they remain on permanent display. She, in turn, was indemnified by the Egyptian government for all the expenses incurred by the family.

Although three quarters of a century has passed since Howard Carter first gazed on the tomb of Tutankhamun, the burial of this obscure pharaoh still seems to evoke remarkable public interest. Perhaps it is the legendary mystery that surrounds the ancient Egyptian kings, perhaps Tutankhamun's mind-boggling wealth, possibly the stirring drama of the discovery itself that generates such rapt interest whenever the young king is mentioned. Wandering through the Tutankhamun galleries in the Cairo Museum, one is conscious of the boy pharaoh's spell. And, as one gazes on the serene, golden countenance of the pharaoh, it's possible for just a moment to imagine oneself—as Howard Carter did—in the presence of a king who lived three thousand years ago.

10

WOMEN IN ARCHAEOLOGY

Women played a vital role in the early development of archaeology, whether traveling to Petra and other remote archaeological sites by themselves at a time when the desert was a dangerous place even for a well-armed party, or working alongside adventurers like Austen Henry Layard. The stories of these early women archaeologists are little known outside the narrow coterie of professional scholars, so it is appropriate to recount some of their remarkable adventures and discoveries alongside those of much better known pioneers. This chapter tells of three great archaeologists—Gertrude Bell, Harriet Boyd Hawes, and Gertrude Caton-Thompson.

Gertrude Bell

"The frail Arab tents falling one by one, leaving the camp fires blazing into the night; the dark masses of the kneeling camels; the shrouded figures binding up the loads, shaking the ice from the waterskins, or crouched over the hearth for a moment's warmth before mounting . . ." Gertrude Bell, like her contemporary Lawrence of Arabia, was one of those English gentlefolk of a century ago who fell in love with the desert at first sight. "One doesn't keep away from the East when one has got into it," she wrote after her first visit to Jerusalem in 1899. Her entire archaeological career revolved around the deserts of the Near East.

Gertrude Bell was born into the family of a wealthy iron master in northern England in 1868. She went to Oxford in 1886, at a time when few women undergraduates attended the university. "She swam, she rowed, she played tennis, and hockey, she acted, she danced, she spoke in debates," we are told—and gained a brilliant modern history degree in a mere two years. Gertrude emerged from the university with an "Oxfordy manner," an insatiable appetite for travel, and an honesty and independence of judgment that often disconcerted her elders. Her travels began in 1892, when she went to Tehran in the heart of Persia. Next she traveled around the world indulging a newly found passion for mountain climbing. After a few seasons, she was recognized as one of the leading female climbers of her day.

Next came the Holy Land, with a seven-month stay in Jerusalem in 1899. This was when Bell discovered archaeology, traveling across the

223

10-1. Gertrude Bell in 1921.

desert to the famous rock-cut city of Petra and the classical ruins at Palmyra, which were still relatively inaccessible. It was then she first experienced "tents with earwigs and black beetles and muddy water to drink." But she chattered away in Arabic to desert chieftains and storekeepers and fell in love with the East. She left Jerusalem with more than six hundred photographs of ancient monuments and spent the next few years studying archaeology in Paris and Rome. At the same time, she worked on Byzantine churches and other ruins in Turkey, publishing a study of the famous Thousand and One Churches at Birbinkilise. This important work established her as a serious scholar and is of vital use to this day, as most of the Birbinkilise sites no longer exist.

But her real love was the desert. In 1909, she set off with a small military escort from Aleppo on the Mediterranean coast on a journey across the Syrian desert to the Euphrates, and then into the territory of the notoriously dangerous Deleim Arabs where the walled Abbasid palace of Ukhaidir was to be found. This was a huge castle set in a fortified enclosure that had never been described scientifically before. Bell spent four days

10-2. Gertrude Bell taking measurements at Ukhaidir, 1909.

planning and photographing the abandoned castle. At every turn, her soldier escort fumbled their rifles as they handled her tapes, for they refused to set them down even for a moment. "I can't persuade them to lay down the damnable things for an instant," she claimed. Ukhaidir cast a profound spell over Gertrude Bell, for her fluent Arabic enabled her to pick up the subtle undercurrents of political revolt and stirring nationalism. She described it in the most famous of her books, *Amurath to Amurath*, which first appeared in 1911. Three years later, her monograph on the site appeared to wide acclaim. "A subject so enchanting and so suggestive as the Palace of Ukhaidir is not likely to present itself more than once in a lifetime," she wrote.

By this time, Gertrude Bell had achieved recognition not only as a traveller and an archaeologist, but as a confidant of desert chieftains. Everywhere she went, she was greeted with ceremonial coffee drinking and confidential gossip. Not that Gertrude was all that popular with British government officials in the region. They regarded her as opinionated and outspoken, which indeed she was. Right up to the outbreak of World War I she was constantly on the move in the Near East, penetrating deep into Saudi Arabia and being locked up in jail by suspicious officials paranoid about spies for her pains. Her intimate knowledge of local political conditions made her a natural for British intelligence in Cairo. She was posted to the Arab Intelligence Bureau in Cairo in 1915.

The military authorities found having a woman among their ranks somewhat of an embarrassment, so they arranged for her to go to Baghdad as a political officer. The British authorities were short staffed and she soon made herself indispensable, flattering local chiefs, interviewing them, putting in a key word where it was needed. The desert people soon regarded her as a pro-Arab member of the political administration, indeed she was sometimes overcome with a "sense of being as much an Asiatic as a European." When her desert friends talked "of tribes or sheikhs, or watering places, I don't need to ask who and where they are. I know; and as they talk, I see again the wide Arabian life."

In truth, Gertrude Bell led a busy, but emotionally empty life, filling her time with all manner of enthusiasms—archaeology, dogs, photography, mountains, and people of every kind. Her intense sympathy for the Arabs stemmed in part from her understanding of the fierce loyalties and friendships of the desert. But as time went on and the makeshift government of wartime days gave way to more formal administration, she was increasingly shunted aside and found herself with less and less to do. It was then that she became involved with archaeology again.

Mesopotamia had been a favorite destination for foreign expeditions ever since the days of Paul Botta and Austen Henry Layard three quarters of a century before (chapter 5). With the end of World War I, scholars from Europe and America were anxious to resume excavations as soon as possible. The Germans wanted to return to Babylon, where they had reconstructed the celebrated Ishtar Gate from a mound of rubble. They were also seeking permission to export the gate in its entirety for display in Berlin. The French sought a permit to excavate in the lowlands, while the University of Pennsylvania Museum and the British Museum had joined forces with an eye to a major excavation at Biblical Ur-of-the-Chaldees to be headed by British excavator Leonard Woolley, already famous for his excavations at the Hittite city of Carchemish near the Euphrates. Bell arranged for all matters archaeological to be referred to her desk and sat down to organize a department of antiquities, new legislation to govern archaeological excavations, and an Iraq Museum for the artifacts from these investigations.

Gertrude was in an unenviable position as she lobbied for the new antiquities laws. The British Museum was so influential that it had even prevailed on the authorities to add a special rider to the peace treaty with Turkey that obligated Britain to create an antiquities law for Iraq. The museum trustees and others lobbied aggressively for liberal permits, while many Iraqis felt strongly that a fifty-fifty division of archaeological finds between the finder and the national museum was too generous to foreigners. Bell was well aware that any less favorable terms would deter overseas excavators. "Our funds available for excavation are funds for the acquisition of objects for the Museum," wrote the Director of the British Museum as the Ur excavations were planned. It fell to Gertrude Bell to administer the new laws, passed just as the Ur excavations began.

Whoever excavated in southern Iraq, ancient Mesopotamia, faced formidable obstacles. British excavator R. Campbell-Thompson dug into ancient Eridu in 1918, using conscripted Indian soldiers. Eridu had long had a reputation as an extremely ancient city, largely because Babylonian legends stated that "all lands were sea; then Eridu was born." It was the fabled home of the Sumerian god Enki. Campbell-Thompson found himself excavating a mud-brick platform some three hundred yards square and forty feet high, with the ruins of a *ziggurat* at one end. "From the ziggurat, as far as the eye can see, there is naught but awful solitude," he wrote. "You look down on somber desert which encircles you for miles." Campbell-Thompson's excavations revealed incomprehensible layers of mud brick and sand. His trenches soon filled with dust as strong winds whipped sandstorms over the ancient city. So he moved across to the city of Ur, fourteen miles away, and set down some small cuttings that revealed finds so promising that the British Museum decided to work this hitherto virtually untouched city instead. They and the Americans chose Leonard Woolley for the task.

Leonard Woolley was one of the last of the renaissance archaeologists. He had attended Oxford with a vague intention of entering the church or becoming a school teacher. Instead, the Warden of New College informed him that *he* had decided Woolley should become an archaeologist, which he promptly did. Woolley learned his excavation along the Nile, in Egypt and the Sudan, then undertook large scale excavations at Carchemish for the British Museum just before World War I. The excavation is famous not only for the discovery of the Hittite city, but also because T. E. Lawrence—Lawrence of Arabia—assisted Woolley on site. At the same time, the two men discreetly spied on a nearby German railroad construction project for the British Government. Gertrude Bell had visited the dig in 1911 and did not endear herself to Lawrence by describing their excavation methods as "prehistoric" compared with those of the Germans. Lawrence dazzled her with erudite conversation. Bell retired in high dudgeon. "Gerty has gone back to her tents," Lawrence wrote gleefully to an archaeological friend.

But she worked well with Leonard Woolley. "A tiresome little man, but a first class digger," she wrote in a letter to her father.

Leonard Woolley started work at Ur in 1922. He worked there for twelve seasons, until 1934. "He was a man of slight stature and no commanding appearance," an anonymous contemporary wrote, "but presence, yes!—even a blind man would have known what manner of man he was." Woolley thought of the Ur excavations on a grand scale. Working with a small team of European experts, he and his devoted foreman Sheikh Hamoudi at times supervised over six hundred workmen. He was the ideal archaeologist for Ur, an excavator who could unravel complicated architectural sequences from masses of mud brick with uncanny skill. With equal facility, he could recover the remains of a long-perished wooden harp by pouring liquid plaster of Paris into small cavities in the ground. Above all, Woolley was gifted with a lively imagination, a sense of the past. Gertrude Bell was captivated by his ability to lead visitors down winding alleys and abandoned four-thousand-year-old brick houses. He actually knew the names of individual house owners from cuneiform tablets found in their dwellings, and would point out minor details of the architecture, even the height of the entry steps.

Excavating at Ur was never easy, partly because of Woolley's overbearing charisma. His wife Kathleen was a gifted artist, a domineering and powerful personality, who never made it easy for the young archaeologists who came to Ur to dig and to learn. The famous detective novelist Agatha Christie visited the Ur excavations and later married Max Mallowan, one of Woolley's assistants and later a distinguished scholar in his own right. It is thought that she drew the characters for her celebrated mystery *Murder in Mesopotamia* from the Ur excavations.

Gertrude Bell was an avid onlooker, who visited the excavations as often as she could. Always smartly dressed, she would arrive at the tiny railroad station near Ur, spending hours at the excavations even on the hottest days. Woolley dreaded her visit at the end of each digging season, for he had to fight hard for his finds with two powerful museums looking over his shoulders. Bell had started the Iraq Museum by keeping the artifacts on a shelf in her home. Then she moved the collections to a few rooms near Iraqi King Feisal's palace. This humble facility paled beside those of the patrons of the Ur excavations, but Gertrude drove the hardest of bargains, taking the precaution of bringing an impartial referee with her in case the going got sticky. Two strong personalities bargained for hours on end. "We had to claim the best things for ourselves," she wrote on one occasion, "but we did our best to make it up to him and I don't think he was much displeased." As for Woolley, he quietly remarked that "in the division we did very well and have no cause for complaint—though I would not say that to Miss Bell."

In March 1926, the government gave the Iraq Museum a more

10-3. Gertrude Bell at Ur-of-the-Chaldees.

permanent home, "rather like the British Museum only a little smaller. I am ordering long shallow drawers in chests to hold the pottery fragments so that you will pull out a drawer and look at Sumerian bits," Gertrude wrote gleefully. Her beloved museum was growing daily and she spent every spare hour cataloging potsherds. She had awesome powers in the eyes of visiting archaeologists. When she visited the Oxford University excavations at the city of Kish, archaeologist Stephen Langdon sunk in gloom, expecting to be shut down within the hour. He was relieved to find that all she was interested in was the finds. "Who decides if we disagree?" asked Langdon as the bargaining began. "I replied that I did," wrote Gertrude, "but he needn't be afraid for he would find me eager to oblige."

Highhanded, even arrogant, Gertrude swept all before her and became increasingly out-of-touch with changing political realities, as superiors disregarded her assessments of affairs. Increasingly, she buried herself in archaeology, for she felt an obligation to the new country of Iraq and its cultural heritage that few others shared. In truth, the debilitating heat and overwhelming workload took a serious toll on her health and mental well-being. Her learning was prodigious, her intelligence legendary. Perhaps her greatest problem was that she never suffered fools gladly, and would run rough-shod over those who disagreed with her or who thought that archaeology was unimportant. "I have a responsibility to archaeology in general," she once wrote, and the perceived magnitude of that responsibility eventually killed her. On July 16, 1926, the fifty-eight-year-old Gertrude Bell took an overdose of sleeping pills. All of Baghdad attended her funeral.

Gertrude Bell made many enemies in her lifetime, for often people could not keep up with her. Her energy was extraordinary and her memorial is the Iraq Museum, with its collections, even in these troubled days, that are among the finest in the world. Bell's reputation among Iraqis is somewhat tarnished today, for many of them feel she gave too much away to foreign excavators. By the standards of the 1990s, this may be true, but she was in an agonizingly difficult position in an era when Iraqi facilities were nonexistent and many artifacts, like the Ur harp, for example, required expert conservation and permanent care under controlled conditions. Bell the scholar tended to put the interests of science above those of nationalism. That so much of Iraq's past, and of the ultimate roots of Western civilization, survives today is in part due to this extraordinary and gifted archaeologist.

Harriet Boyd Hawes

She nursed Greeks wounded in the Balkan War of 1897, ran a massive field hospital for Serbian soldiers during World War I, traveled through Crete on a mule in search of archaeological sites, and discovered the Minoan town of Gournia—all before she was thirty-five. By any standard Harriet Boyd Hawes was a remarkable woman, and an even more remarkable archaeologist considering that nearly a century ago the profession was dominated by a handful of powerful men.

Born in Boston in 1871, Harriet Boyd Hawes grew up with four brothers, an experience that taught her to stand up for herself at an early age. She entered Smith College in 1888, where the faculty worried about her because she spent more time working for social causes than studying. It was here that she developed a passionate interest in the plight of blue-collar workers and met British novelist turned Egyptologist Amelia Edwards, who kindled her fascination with ancient civilizations. For some years, she worked as a poor, but genteel schoolteacher, eventually saving enough money to embark on a properly chaperoned grand tour through Europe in 1895. Harriet was completely captivated with classical Greece and set off a year later to study at the British School of Archaeology at Athens. On the crowded Paris-Marseilles train, "Boyd's luck" put her in a compartment with the internationally famous actress Sarah Bernhardt's sister, a well-connected resident of Athens. Instantly, doors were opened to the busy social life of the Greek capital. Harriet found herself socializing on the fringes of the Greek court. She caused a stir by riding her bicycle

10-4. Harriet Boyd Hawes

through the crowded streets. "I rode my straightest and tried to be as proper as possible," she wrote. One suspects she took a wicked delight in being unconventional, for convention was never a great concern in her life.

In the intervals of an active social life, she wrestled with modern Greek, toured the major archaeological sites, and followed the tumultuous politics of southeastern Europe, then, as today, a maelstrom of competing factions. When war broke out between Greece and Turkey in April 1897, Harriet volunteered for nursing duty at a Red Cross hospital in central Greece a few miles from the front. She was swept into a whirlwind of suffering, as she nursed the shattered bodies of young men still in their teens. She came under fire on several occasions and never forgot the horrible sights she witnessed. "I remember well the half-sick feeling I at first experienced from the horror of the wounds and the smell of the blood," she wrote. But she soon became accustomed to the terrible suffering and the horrific conditions where injured men lay on thin mattresses so closely packed together that it was hard to dress their wounds. After the war, she stayed on to combat a typhoid epidemic among the troops. The Greeks never forgot the diminutive woman who worked among their wounded.

Back in the United States, Hawes applied for, and somewhat to her surprise, received a Yale Fellowship to study inscriptions at ancient Eleusis near Athens. But she yearned to excavate, a pastime considered by the American School of Classical Studies at Athens to be "men's work." By chance, she met a Cretan refugee, who urged her to visit his homeland where ruins were there for the digging. On impulse, she contacted David Hogarth, director of the British School, well known for his diggings in Crete and at the Hittite city of Carchemish in Syria, and legendary for his bad temper before breakfast, and Arthur Evans, who was on his way to excavate at the Palace of Knossos. They both encouraged her to work on the island. When word of her plans got out, Sophia Schliemann threw a lunch so that Hawes would meet Wilhelm Dörpfeld, now director of the Troy excavations, and other archaeological notables.

Harriet arrived on Crete to find there were only twelve miles of roads—archaeologists had to travel on muleback. She explored the rugged terrain around Mirabello Bay on the north coast of the island. "Learn from the peasants," she was told, and learn she did, for they brought in seal stones,

10-5. Harriet Boyd Hawes sorts potsherds at Heraklion.

potsherds, even metal artifacts plowed from their rocky fields and found in caves and in tombs. One farmer led her to a pretty cove called Gournia, where she found traces of massive stone walls and dozens of Bronze Age potsherds. The next day, she assembled a crew of workers. On the hillside they found more artifacts, house walls, and a narrow paved road. Soon Hawes had a hundred men and ten girls at work uncovering what turned out to be a small Minoan town.

Hawes lived with a colony of rats in an old coast guard house near the site, while her workers camped nearby under brush shelters, cooking their simple meals over small campfires. It was tough work that began at six in the morning and ended twelve hours later, with a two-hour siesta at midday. Gradually, Gournia took shape—a compact huddle of small stone houses bisected by narrow paved alleyways. The settlement was unfortified, with steps leading to a public courtyard and what may have been a small palace. Three years of excavations uncovered two or three acres of the town and some seventy to eighty dwellings with up to eight rooms each.

Gournia was a triumph. Back home, Harriet embarked on a short lecture tour for the Archaeological Institute of America, the first woman to appear before its members. "The results of Miss Boyd's work must be considered remarkable," wrote a reporter for the *Philadelphia Public Inquirer* in 1902. "Not only because of their character, but because she achieved them alone." The seasons at Gournia were some of the happiest months of Hawes's life, for she was like a beneficent queen among the local people, treating their medical ills and even setting up a small lending library in the village. It was here, too, that she met her quiet, self-effacing husband Charles Henry Hawes, an inveterate traveler with a taste for anthropology.

Hawes's Gournia monograph appeared in 1909, an oversize book paid for out of her own pocket and by subscriptions from individuals and museums as far afield as Australia. "My first ambition was to produce artistic plates which should take the place of objects which cannot be seen outside of Greece," she wrote. With its beautiful color plates, the site report is a precious rarity today, still consulted by specialists as a definitive source on the excavations.

Had not World War I intervened, Harriet would undoubtedly have returned to Crete, and even to Gournia. First motherhood, then gathering war clouds, changed her life drastically. When German pincers closed around Serbia in 1915, she used most of the family's savings to purchase a ton of food and clothing, then set off for the war zone. She arrived at the island of Corfu off the west coast of Greece on a French torpedo boat in February 1916, representing the philanthropic American Distribution Service. Thousands of starving Serbian soldiers had fled to Corfu. The sick among them were shunted across to the nearby island of Vidos, to lie on damp straw beds under improvised tents at the height of the rainy season.

Hawes crossed to Vidos daily in all weather. Safely inoculated against cholera and typhoid, she delivered essential supplies and prepared light meals over charcoal fires for sick soldiers with "haggard, haunting faces." Many were barely living skeletons. She built a wooden barracks in two weeks, helped organize crucial disinfecting baths for new arrivals, handed out clothing, and took over special responsibility for the "death tent," where dying soldiers lay on dirty straw pallets.

When she returned to the United States, she gave talks only about her wartime experiences, and refused to speak about archaeology. It was, she said, unimportant in these tumultuous times. She pleaded for relief of the suffering, for an end to war. When America entered the conflict, she organized the Smith College Relief Unit, sailed with it to France to help the French wounded, but soon resigned in frustration: it was work for younger volunteers. Undeterred, she worked as a helper at American Red Cross Military Hospital Number 5 near Paris. Calling herself the "Old Lady Aid," she worked the night shift, even nursing the son of a soldier she had cared for years before in Greece.

10-6. East Road, steps from South, Gournia, Crete.

After the war, Henry Hawes became bursar of Boston's Museum of Fine Arts. Harriet threw herself into teaching the history of ancient art at Wellesley College, a course she gave for sixteen years. Only once did she return to Greece, this time with her daughter Mary in 1926. On Crete, Arthur Evans took them on a detailed tour of Knossos, and they journeyed on mules to her beloved Gournia, which she feared had been destroyed. But the site was in good order, and her welcome at the nearby village of Kavousi rapturous. The same headmen greeted her and there were hugs and kisses all around. The magic was still the same in a vastly changed world.

Harriet continued to teach at Wellesley, but turned to socialism and union politics rather than archaeology in her later life. Characteristically, she insisted on traveling in Czechoslovakia as the Nazis marched in. She spent World War II nursing an ailing Henry and growing vegetables for the war effort. Activist to the end, she died, soon after Henry, on March 31, 1945.

Archaeology, adventure, nursing, and politics—these were but a few of the challenges in Harriet Boyd Hawes's eventful life, a life lived with passion and an almost overwhelming integrity. Incredibly, by 1939, she was almost forgotten as an archaeologist. Several publications on Minoan archaeology actually attributed the discovery of Gournia to one of her assistants, Richard Seager, who went on to dig other well-known Minoan sites. Were he alive today, Seager would be the first to correct this strange error. He and his contemporaries knew that this energetic woman was one of the immortals of archaeology.

Gertrude Caton-Thompson

Four years after Gertrude Bell's tragic death, archaeologist Gertrude Caton-Thompson sat in the back of a dilapidated automobile with African river flood water lapping over the floorboards. She gazed ahead at the back of a large mail van towing her car across the narrow ford. Even then, the journey was not over. She had to wade across another muddy torrent while African bearers carried her baggage across on their heads. Another vehicle had to collect her on the other side. As if the rains were not enough, she was soon stricken with a severe attack of malaria. Caton-Thompson was a highly experienced fieldworker with hard-won excavation experience on the banks of the Nile and deep in Egypt's Western Desert, a rarity in a male-dominated archaeological world. Now she was thousands of miles from the land of the pharaohs, in the heart of the southern African bush, about to embark on the greatest challenge of her career—the fabled ruins of Great Zimbabwe.

Great Zimbabwe was a major archaeological conundrum in 1929, rumored to be a spectacular Phoenician palace buried deep in the African bush, the place where word had it none other than the immortal Queen of Sheba had once ruled. These rumors were already four centuries old when Gertrude Caton-Thompson arrived in Africa. When Portuguese explorer Vasco da Gama sailed up the southeast African coast after rounding the Cape of Good Hope in 1497, he and his men came across a flourishing trade in gold and ivory at the mouth of the Zambezi River. They also heard rumors of great stone buildings in the far interior, of a great chief named Mwene Mutapa, the "master pillager." In 1552, Portuguese geographer João de Barros wrote of a land of ancient mines and vast plains in southeast Africa, "in the midst of which is a square fortress, masonry within and without, built of stones of marvelous size, and there appears to be no mortar joining them." A half-century later, missionary João dos Santos, who had worked among the local people, wrote that "the natives of these lands, especially some aged Moors, assert they have a tradition from their ancestors that these houses were anciently a factory of the Queen of Sheba." De Barros and his contemporaries assumed that the stone buildings were the work, not of illiterate Africans, but of a long-vanished civilization, remembered only in the Scriptures. The legend of Ophir in the African bush persisted for generations.

Such tales brought a young German geologist named Carl Mauch to Great Zimbabwe in 1871. He cut some wood from an ancient door lintel and compared it to his cedar pencil. This convinced him that Zimbabwe's doorways were fashioned in part from the famous cedars of Lebanon, that it was the Queen of Sheba who had built the mysterious stone walls! The white settlers who flooded north of the Limpopo River in 1890 made a beeline for the ruins in search of buried treasure and unimagined wealth. They found a series of dilapidated and overgrown stone enclosures overlooked by a low hill that was a maze of vast, rounded granite boulders and ruined masonry.

You need a helicopter to gain an overall impression of Great Zimbabwe, for the relationships between the different stone structures are hard to decipher on the ground. A low granite hill lies at the head of a long valley that funnels moist air up from the distant Indian Ocean, mantling Great Zimbabwe in fog and drizzle for many weeks of the year. It was this persistent moisture that probably gave the site its reputation as a powerful rainmaking shrine. On the summit of the hill is a mass of enormous weathered rocks joined with low granite stone walls. A well-built enclosure wall capped with stone uprights protects the western end of the hill, which is accessible up a steep stairway and a much narrower entrance on the south side, as if the people who lived on the hill were secluded from those in the valley below.

From this Hill Ruin, you look down on a jumble of ruined stone enclosures that once held cattle and huts of mud and thatch. The valley is dominated by the massive, beautifully constructed stone wall of the celebrated Elliptical (Great) Enclosure, once the precinct of Great Zimbabwe's powerful chiefs. The outside wall is built of carefully shaped granite blocks and stands thirty-five feet tall at the highest point. Inside, a narrow defile between this wall and another one inside leads to a solid masonry tower, now thought to be a symbolic grain bin, a symbol of chiefly power. You can still discern the remains of the royal houses and enclosures inside the towering stone walls.

This, then, was the imposing and mysterious stone structure that confronted the puzzled settlers of 1890. They had never seen anything like it, for the local people lived in mud and thatch huts nearby and denied any knowledge of the powerful rulers who had once lived in palaces of stone. Thus, they assumed that Great Zimbabwe was the work of foreigners, of a long-vanished white civilization. After all, they wondered aloud, who could believe that primitive Africans could have built such stupendous buildings. The imperialist Cecil John Rhodes, the settlers' sponsor and sponsor of white settlement in what became Rhodesia, visited the ruins and proclaimed that "Zimbabye is an old Phoenician residence." More than

10-7. Gertrude Caton-Thompson

ten years of sporadic investigations followed, most of them in the hands of a journalist named Richard Hall, who was obsessed with Phoenicians. Appointed curator of Great Zimbabwe in 1902, he embarked on a campaign of fast-moving, unscientific excavation that stripped between three and twelve feet of vital archaeological deposit and priceless artifacts from all corners of the ruins. He was, he said, removing "the filth and decadence" of African occupation. He believed the local people, the Shona, were but squatters in a magnificent Phoenician palace dating to as early as 1100 B.C. Hall did such damage to Great Zimbabwe that he was removed from his post. All subsequent excavation has been a matter of piecing together shreds and patches of occupation layers from places his diggers missed.

By no means everyone was convinced by Hall's extravagant theories. Eminent archaeologists of the day, among them Arthur Evans of Knossos fame and Egyptologist Flinders Petrie, refused to believe such tall tales. They arranged for the British Association for the Advancement of Science to send Egyptologist David Randall-MacIver to Zimbabwe in 1905. Unlike his predecessors, Randall-MacIver was a professional excavator, trained to investigate not only spectacular architecture but the smallest of artifacts as well. Randall-MacIver excavated inside the Elliptical Building at a spot left intact by Hall. He also focused his attention on the tiny glass beads and Medieval Arabian glass discarded by Hall as "rubbish." Far from being useless debris, they were the clues that mattered. They told Randall-MacIver that Great Zimbabwe had been built not by Phoenicians, but by the ancestors of the modern African population some six centuries earlier.

So vicious was the outcry sparked in Rhodesia by Randall-MacIver's findings that no one excavated at Zimbabwe again for a quarter of a century. Randall-MacIver had committed an unpardonable sin in the eyes of the settlers: he had given the Africans credit for a tremendous architectural achievement. This was the political morass into which Gertrude Caton-Thompson was thrust that rainy day in 1929.

Gertrude Caton-Thompson was born in 1888, the daughter of an English lawyer, who died when she was only five years old. Until World War I broke out in 1914, she enjoyed the leisured existence of a well-to-do English family, visiting Egypt and the Holy Land for the first time in 1907. She and her mother walked over the dusty mounds of ancient Jericho and admired the Pyramids of Giza at sunset. These experiences, and others in the Mediterranean, kindled her interest in archaeology, but she did not study the subject seriously until after the war, during which she gained valuable administrative experience working on the requisitioning of merchant ships for convoy duty.

Gertrude studied Egyptology and Mediterranean archaeology at the University of London, learning surveying in a small park "where trees and seats were the only fixed objects; the seats in particular were mainly identifiable by their inhabitants, mostly old ladies in hats, who moved away before their position was safely established." Unlike her contemporaries, she was interested in early prehistory, in the Stone Age, studying stone artifacts as well as pottery and ancient art. In November 1921, she accompanied the great Egyptologist Flinders Petrie to his excavations at Abydos. In Luxor, she met Howard Carter, who complained that he was finding nothing in the Valley of Kings. A year later he discovered the Tomb of Tutankhamun (chapter 9).

While Petrie cleared Old Kingdom tombs, Gertrude searched for Stone Age artifacts in the nearby desert, in spite of having been informed by other archaeologists that there were no such tools to be found in Egypt. She soon discovered more than two thousand 100,000-year-old artifacts as well as learning a great deal about Egyptology, much of it from Flinders Petrie's habit of discoursing on ancient history by lamplight after dinner. This field season established Gertrude as a serious archaeologist and she was soon asked to excavate a cave in Malta and to return to Egypt, where in the 1920s, she acquired an international reputation for her excavations on early farming villages in the desert Fayum, an arid depression west of the Nile.

Flinders Petrie had long proclaimed that the Fayum had once been a great lake formed when the Nile broke into the depression in the fifth century B.C. Caton-Thompson had geological training, which Petrie did not, and realized that there had been more than one lake in the Fayum. She and geologist Elinor Gardner spent two long field seasons to good effect, not only reconstructing the complicated geological history of the ancient Fayum lakes, but finding a series of basket-lined storage pits that contained the remains of carbonized barley and wheat, estimated to date to at least 4,000 B.C., at that time the earliest evidence for prehistoric agriculture in the world.

The Fayum discoveries caused a considerable stir and established Gertrude as an up-and-coming younger scholar. Her growing reputation and close ties to Petrie, Arthur Evans, and other eminent archaeologists led to an entirely different challenge far from the Nile in 1928, an invitation from the British Association for the Advancement of Science to excavate at Great Zimbabwe "to reveal the character, dates, and source of culture of the builders." Gertrude was given a blank slate to work with, the only requirement being that she report on her work to the annual meeting of the Association a year later, when it would gather in Johannesburg, South Africa.

Gertrude knew nothing about Great Zimbabwe and had never traveled south of the Sahara. Her only sources of information were Richard Hall's books about Phoenicians at Zimbabwe and Randall-MacIver's monograph, the latter detailing the first scientific excavations at the site, also undertaken at the invitation of the British Association a quarter century earlier. Eager for a new challenge and intrigued by the archaeological mysteries at Zimbabwe, she accepted the invitation with alacrity. Five months later,

10-8. Jar; Badarian (5500–3800 B.C.).

she arrived at the site, accompanied by two young women, Dorothy Norie, who had architectural training, and an Oxford graduate named Kathleen Kenyon, who was to achieve great fame some twenty-five years later as the excavator of the earliest town in the world at the base of Biblical Jericho.

She started work with twenty African workers, who were paid ten shillings a month (about ninety cents) with a further ten shillings a month for food. Gertrude was horrified by the low government pay scale and supplemented the laborers' wages by offering small rewards for useful finds, a practice common under Petrie in Egypt. This more than doubled most of the men's wages, once the workers had become accustomed to working under a woman's supervision. Experienced in the ways of Egyptian laborers, she simply faced down an attempted strike and kept the men until an hour after dark when they downed tools. She had no more trouble.

So much damage had been done to the ruins by Richard Hall that Caton-Thompson was forced to work with small patches of intact deposit. Zimbabwe had been effectively ransacked for gold and other exotic treasure. Everything else—potsherds, animal bones, iron tools, and house walls—had been shoveled aside. Gertrude examined the Elliptical Building with great care and decided that it was not worth trying to salvage anything there. So she boldly set to work in a complex of ruined enclosures in the valley floor, excavating no less than two thousand square yards down to bare rock in six weeks. In doing this, she followed current practice in Egypt, where everyone worked on a large scale. But, unlike Hall, she kept every tiny potsherd and glass bead, every fragment of brass wire. Her workers uncovered a hard clay floor, some ten to twelve inches thick, under which lay three feet of silt containing three different types of African pottery, clearly separated in stratigraphic layers. These were coarse vessels, decorated with square and round impressions at the neck, later forms being polished with black graphite. Caton-Thompson puzzled over the stone foundations until the very end of the excavation, when she took some calipers and drew circles on the plans. She realized that the ruined walls were the stone openings to nine or ten long-vanished circular mud huts. This clearly suggested that the ruins were built and occupied by Africans, but she found no imports in the enclosures, so the conundrum was unresolved.

After a day off, Gertrude turned her attention to the Hill Ruin overlooking the valley. Again, the deep deposits inside its walled enclosures had been ravaged by Hall and others long ago, but it occurred to her that there might be some undisturbed areas on some of the upper terraces. She sunk test pits into these terraces and found African hut foundations overlying thick middens that contained iron tools, as well as potsherds identical to some of those from the valley below. Her largest test pit turned into a major excavation behind a granite enclosure wall. Here she found the same sequence of potsherds as she had excavated in the valley below, also imported glass beads that a British Museum expert proclaimed to date to the eighth to tenth centuries A.D. Here was the proof that Caton-Thompson was looking for—imported objects far later than the Phoenician date claimed by Richard Hall and others.

By the time Caton-Thompson had finished work on the Hill Ruin, she was convinced that Great Zimbabwe had been built by Africans, not foreigners. Randall-MacIver had been absolutely correct a quarter century earlier: the imported Chinese porcelain and glass was of Medieval date, as was Zimbabwe itself. It took some courage to stand behind these conclusions, for they were highly controversial to the many Europeans who visited the excavations, all of them convinced that Great Zimbabwe was an ancient Phoenician palace. They refused to believe that the local Shona people were capable of building stone structures like the Elliptical Building, let alone the solid conical tower, which Caton-Thompson had tunneled under with the aid of a mining engineer.

Matters came to a head at the British Association meeting in Johannesburg, where she addressed the delegates for an hour and a half. Her presentation was a model of sober reporting, outlining her excavation strategy, describing each trench and the finds therefrom, and the vital sherds of Chinese, Persian, and Arab pottery and glassware that were barometers of overseas trade. Zimbabwe, she concluded, dated to between the tenth and fourteenth centuries A.D. "It is inconceivable," she ended, "to me now I have studied the ruins how a theory of Semitic or civilized origin could ever have been foisted on an uncritical world. Every

10-9. Enclosure wall of the Elliptical Building (Great Enclosure) at Great Zimbabwe.

detail . . . appears to me to be typical African. . . . My respect for, and interest in the . . . ruins is enormously strengthened nearby. Instead of a degenerate offshoot of a higher Oriental civilization, you have here a native civilization . . . showing national organization of a high kind, originality, and amazing industry."

Gertrude's masterly lecture was greeted with incredulity by those who believed in a Phoenician Zimbabwe. None other than the famous anatomist Raymond Dart, celebrated for his discovery of the fossil ape-human *Australopithecus*, stated with great vehemence that she was wrong and that Zimbabwe was much earlier. Public opinion still ran in favor of the Phoenicians, for, it was felt, any later date for the ruins would represent adverse publicity for the colony of Rhodesia where Zimbabwe lay. "Surely facts are what everyone wants and only facts will count today," wrote an editorial writer in the Johannesburg *Star*. The editorial pointed out that Richard Hall was a publicist, not an archaeologist, who, it said, based his work not only on his own excavations, but on those of other credulous early diggers. As for Gertrude herself, she returned to Great Zimbabwe, where she welcomed a committee of experts from the British Association, who inspected her excavations. Everywhere she lectured, she found her audience in polite, and sometimes obstreperous, disagreement. But her scientific reputation was never higher, for, to expert eyes at any rate, this strong-minded woman had solved one of the great mysteries of African archaeology and shown that Great Zimbabwe was indeed the work of medieval African chiefs.

Caton-Thompson herself went back to her beloved Egypt, excavating Stone Age sites in the Kharga Oasis west of the Nile. She only returned to Africa once, to a conference on African archaeology at the Victoria Falls on the Zambezi in 1955. This gave her an opportunity to return at the age of sixty-seven to the scene of her greatest archaeological triumph. All subsequent work on Great Zimbabwe has been based on the research of this woman, who was as tough physically as she was mentally. I had afternoon tea with her when she was in her eighties and underwent an exacting oral examination on central African archaeology, from which it was clear that she kept up with the latest discoveries by people who had not yet been born when she arrived at Great Zimbabwe in a rainstorm.

We can marvel at the achievements of these archaeological pioneers, who carried out major excavations and archaeological surveys with minimal resources in areas far from civilization. They did so knowing that their presence was often barely tolerated in a male-dominated archaeological world. Their discoveries, while less spectacular, perhaps, than those of Austen Henry Layard and Heinrich Schliemann, are nevertheless a critical part of the foundations of modern archaeology. It is not given to today's archaeologists to solve the mystery of an ancient civilization by themselves, or to found an antiquities service on their own.

Nor is it easy for them to go off into remote parts of Greece and dig up a Minoan palace. These remarkable women did these things, and much, much more.

11

The City of TEOTIHUACÁN

ometimes archaeologists' efforts seem puny in the face of the achievements of the ancients. A small team of laborers digs for months under the shadow of a great, brooding pyramid, their trenches yielding handfuls of broken potsherds and long-buried house foundations. These finds seem insignificant compared to the vast structures that surround the diggers. One can almost hear the mocking laugh of the long-dead architects and engineers who built the ancient city. They cannot help but be amused by the archaeologists' humble attempts to understand the magnitude of their own works.

Nowhere do the archaeologists seem more puny than in the magnificent city of Teotihuacán outside Mexico City, where, for centuries, a teeming metropolis ruled much of Mesoamerica, only to vanish into oblivion a thousand years ago. This chapter tells the story of Teotihuacán and of the archaeologists who have pitted their abilities and their meager resources against one of the greatest cities of antiquity.

Teotihuacán is now a household word, a prehistoric city familiar to thousands of camera-toting tourists. Its faithfully reconstructed pyramids and plazas—today thronged not by priests, warriors, and merchants, but by busloads of tourists from all over the world—reflect the city's former glory. The Mexican government has spent a tremendous amount of money on the restoration of Teotihuacán, determined to turn the ancient city into a major source of tourist revenue. But they have a deeper motive as well: a desire to foster a sense of nationalism throughout Mexico. The achievements of the ancient Mexicans are becoming a symbol for the modern nation; their influence can be seen in public architecture, in education, and in philosophy as well. Teotihuacán is a dramatic reminder of Mexico's long and glorious prehistoric past, of a time when the ancient Mesoamericans enjoyed a brilliant and long-lived indigenous American civilization. This symbolism may be lost on the foreign tourist, preoccupied as visitors to the site often are with the city's mysterious past and with the extraordinary authority that brought Teotihuacán's great pyramids into being. Like the Pyramids of Giza in Egypt, Teotihuacán has a forceful impact on the casual visitor. The scale of its architecture is simply overwhelming, the magnitude of the achievement stunning.

Fifteen hundred years ago, Teotihuacán was already known the length and breadth of Mesoamerica. Every traveler to the Valley of Mexico would take time to visit the great city, if only to admire its brightly painted public

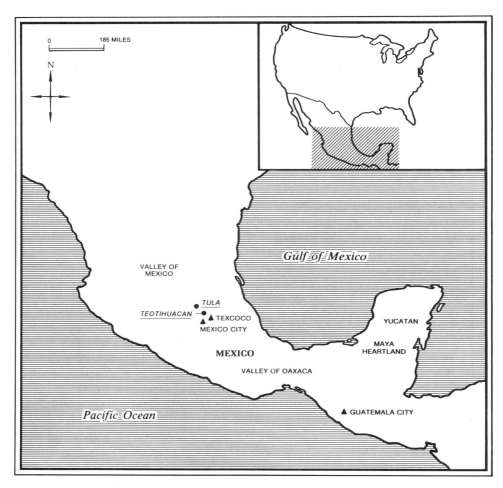

11-1. Locations and sites mentioned in chapter 11.

buildings and stroll down the wide and imposing Street of the Dead that traversed the city's center. Teotihuacán was the largest human settlement in the Americas, with a population of at least 125,000 people. The Mesoamerican world shopped at Teotihuacán, traded with its merchants, and worshipped at its temples. Thousands of scattered villages in the Mexican highlands relied on its markets and specialist manufacturers. At certain times of the year, the entire countryside would flock to Teotihuacán's plazas to participate in the annual public ceremonies that ensured the future prosperity of the great city and the people of the Valley. Yet, within a few short centuries, the city had vanished forever. Only a few crumbling pyramids and temples remained as testaments to its former glory.

The earliest ceremonial buildings were erected at Teotihuacán about 100 B.C. Within a few centuries, Teotihuacán had mushroomed into a huge city dominated by the great Pyramid of the Sun. This sacred, truncated edifice stood 210 feet high and 650 feet square, a vast pyramid of rubble, adobe mud, and earth, all faced with stone. A wooden temple on the summit of the pyramid afforded a spectacular view of the sprawling city below.

The priests who served this temple had a panoramic view of a remarkable urban complex. In the morning, they could look westward, down to the long plaza in front of their pyramid and to the Street of the Dead, an avenue that seemed to stretch for miles into the far distance north and south. Its north end opened onto a large plaza in front of another huge pyramid. In the rising sunlight, this vast structure cast long shadows below. The priests could see the small temple at its summit, but the figures of

11-2. Staircase of the Temple of the Plumed Serpent, Quetzalcoatl, at Teotihuacán.

their colleagues there were dwarfed by the scale of the pyramid under them.

Southward, the Street of the Dead led through another plaza and, as the sun rose higher, the priests could gaze even further in this direction. Their eyes would light on the Temple of the Plumed Serpent Quetzalcoatl. The elaborate serpent carvings on its facade were barely discernible in the dark shadows. But the gigantic, open square in front of the temple already teemed with bustling life. From their lofty perch, the priests could dimly hear the noise of the busy city below.

The Street of the Dead was lined with fine civic and religious buildings. Beyond these, the priests could survey a mass of densely packed houses and apartment complexes interspersed with courtyards and separated by winding streets. A lingering pall of smoke from innumerable domestic hearths generally hung in the morning air. Outside the ceremonial precincts, numerous paths led into the surrounding countryside. Small villages of thatched huts dotted the distant landscape. From the heady elevation of the pyramid, Teotihuacán was truly a wonderful sight.

Any traveler to Teotihuacán first made a beeline for the market. There were several markets in the city, but the largest flourished in a huge open compound off the Street of the Dead, opposite the Temple of Quetzalcoatl. The markets supplied the needs of the entire city. While the priests and craftsworkers lived in dwellings built around small courtyards, the less privileged dwelt in large compounds of rooms connected by narrow alleyways and patios. Most of these people were urban dwellers who bought their staple diet of maize, squashes, and beans in the market. There were few farmers within the confines of Teotihuacán itself, but we know that many rural villages flourished nearby. Most of them were compact and expertly planned settlements whose agricultural activities were carefully supervised by city rulers. These were the villages that produced the enormous surplus of agricultural produce necessary for Teotihuacán's survival. Although we have no definite proof, we can be certain that the villagers used irrigation agriculture, harnessing swamps, lakes, and rivers to fertilize the large acreages of land that were brought under cultivation to feed the nearby urban population. Most of the products of the harvest were sold in the large market off the Street of the Dead.

This market was the center of Teotihuacán's daily life, the place to meet with friends and hear the gossip of the city. Only the market area would provide a visitor with a true measure of Teotihuacán's incredible range of activities. The market itself was organized into sections. In one part, hundreds of stalls displayed ripe maize and every type of food stuff, from fish and game to the most delicate of vegetable relishes. Teotihuacán lay at a hub of the far-flung obsidian (volcanic glass) trade of Middle America. A visitor could pause to handle hundreds of delicate blades and fine knives displayed in the obsidian traders' part of the market. Then there were the potters, whose booths were thronged with strangers buying fine bowls and painted pots in large numbers. Teotihuacán's potters were famous far beyond the confines of their city. Their wares have been found in the lowlands and as far west as the Pacific coast. Feather headdresses, cloaks, live birds, and jewels of every form could also be purchased in Teotihuacán's bustling daily market. The variety of goods must have been truly bewildering to the stranger.

If the market was bewildering, the city itself must have seemed enormous. Today's tourist is exhausted after traversing the Street of the Dead, climbing several pyramids, and wandering through the huge plazas and temples nearby. So great is the city that public buildings at one end are barely discernible from the other. Many of the buildings are identical, laid out in monotonous array. Every religious structure bore a terraced facade embellished with similar painted and sculptured motifs, usually elaborate renderings of feathered serpents and other gods. The artists and architects were not being unimaginative, they were simply responding to a rigid religious symbolism. As a result, Teotihuacán seems dull, until one realizes that the buildings were once ablaze with fresh paint, a vivid counterpoint to the repetitive religious symbolism.

Teotihuacán was a highly organized city rigidly governed by religious

11-3. Wall painting from Teotihuacán.

and secular leaders who had complete control over the minds, spirits, and bodies of their subjects. The priests, an intellectual elite, were skillful astronomers who kept track of the ever-changing cycles of public life, of the seasons for religious ceremonies, and of the endless procession of days, months, and years. The tentacles of religion extended into every household; domestic altars were commonplace even in humble dwellings. Teotihuacán's art was intensely religious, depicting the feathered serpent deity Quetzalcoatl and other gods. However, some wall murals do depict trade and traders; distant foreigners like the Maya from the lowlands are portrayed with slanting eyes and distinctive dress styles. As Teotihuacán reached the height of its powers and warlike leaders began to assume major roles in public life, warriors and priests also began to appear in the murals.

By A.D. 500, Teotihuacán had established a unique position for itself in the Valley of Mexico and possessed a prestige and power unprecedented in Middle American history. But just as its art and architecture were reaching their full climax and trading activities were at a peak, the political, economic, and religious fabric of the city began to unravel. The first strains appeared about A.D. 650. A century later, Teotihuacán was a shadow of its former self. The population had declined so rapidly that the once-proud city was now little more than a series of hamlets extending over an area of about a square kilometer. Some great catastrophe apparently struck the city in A.D. 700, reducing its population to below seventy thousand. Many of its people moved eastward. The city was deliberately burnt and destroyed. Over the years, its buildings collapsed and the pyramids became overgrown with dense vegetation. Teotihuacán's decline was almost as rapid as its rise to prominence. Even so, eight centuries later, Teotihuacán was still revered far and wide as an intensely sacred place. But no one remembered who had built it or that tens of thousands of people had once lived there.

Today, Teotihuacán is receiving visitors again. It ranks as one of the world's most famous archaeological sites, attracting almost as many visitors annually as the Egyptian pyramids. It has taken generations of scholars to reveal its mysteries. Their inquiries culminated in some of the most intensive archaeological researches ever undertaken anywhere.

The Spanish *conquistadors* first came upon Teotihuacán six centuries after its final collapse. Hernando Cortés and his followers arrived at the site in 1520—hotly pursued by thousands of angry Aztec warriors. They were in desperate straits and, understandably, had little time to contemplate their surroundings or the high earthen mounds that surrounded their exhausted camp. But only a year later, Cortés laid siege to the nearby Aztec capital for seventy-five days. Tenochtitlán, with its great palaces and imposing temples, was no match for 450 Spaniards and thousands of Indian allies who hated the Aztec. Cortés ordered Tenochtitlán razed to the ground. Within a few months, Mexico City was rising from the rubble of the Aztec capital.

The newly arrived Catholic priests of Mexico City now had a chance to learn more about the remarkable countryside around them. But Teotihuacán was a complete mystery. According to the local Indians, the great pyramids of the city had been overgrown with dense vegetation as long as they and their forefathers had lived there. No one knew who had built them, although great idols still stood on the summit of the two largest pyramids. Perhaps ancient giants had erected the temples in the long-distant past. The local Indians still revered the idols on the greatest mound, known to them as the Hill of the Sun. In an effort to eradicate any competition to their own Christian beliefs, the Spaniards eventually toppled the silent idols. With savage and systematic care, the missionary friars who brought the Cross to Mexico destroyed priceless Aztec archives and historical records, as well as thousands of idols and shrines. Teotihuacán slept on, consigned to an historical oblivion that lasted for centuries.

Only a handful of dedicated priests tried to find out something about the history of the Aztec and their predecessors. They learned that the Aztec remembered arriving in the Valley of Mexico about two hundred years before the Spaniards. They had overrun the remains of a great Toltec civilization that had flourished in the Valley of Mexico before them. When the sixteenth-century friar Bernardino de Sahagun had sifted through a mass of historical data on the Aztec, he was convinced that a great civilization had flourished near the Valley of Mexico for over two thousand years. The logical capital for this vast empire seemed to be the deserted city of Teotihuacán. This city, wrote Sahagun, was "very rich and well ordered, very wise and powerful, which suffered the adverse fortune of a Troy." Sahagun's conclusions were quietly suppressed by the church and the government.

The few foreign travelers who reached Teotihuacán added little to the legends that surrounded the ancient city. It was difficult, at best, to study ancient Indian cities in a country ruled with repressive severity by the Catholic authorities. When the Italian world traveler Giovanni Francesco Careri reached Mexico City in 1697, he was favorably impressed by his reception. Of course, his reaction is hardly surprising, for he had just completed a harrowing five-month voyage in a crowded ship all the way from Manila to Mexico. One hundred thousand people lived in Mexico City by this time. Careri reveled in the company of civilized gentlemen, among them a scholarly priest named Don Carlos de Siguenza y Gongora. Siguenza had a passionate interest in ancient Mexico. His friendship with Indian nobles gave him access to both oral histories and priceless historical documents. He learned some of the secrets of Aztec hieroglyphs and, with this knowledge, managed to reconstruct a chronology of their kings. All these activities were risky at best, for the slightest breath of heresy—and Indian history was a great heresy—meant the Inquisition. One of Siguenza's most important contacts was a family named Ixtlilxochitl, the nominal lords of Teotihuacán. He visited the city's remarkable ancient pyramids on several occasions and even dug into one of them in a vain attempt to find an internal treasure house.

Careri had one priceless asset as a traveler—he was insatiably curious. So one day he rode out in search of Teotihuacán's past. Armed with introductions from Siguenza, Careri had no difficulty obtaining a noble Indian guide to take him around. Laboriously, the inquisitive Italian climbed two great pyramids, the first named after the moon, the second and much larger one named "The House of the Sun." Careri was immediately reminded of the Egyptian pyramids. Both Siguenza and his hosts told him that great idols had once stood on the summits of these mysterious structures. It was obvious that Teotihuacán had once been an enormous city. But no one could tell Careri who had built the silent pyramids or who had lived in the crumbling palaces and houses that stretched for miles toward the horizon.

When Careri returned to Europe, he sat down to write a six-volume travelogue that contained, among many other nuggets of information, a sketchy description of Teotihuacán. Most writers dismissed Careri as a fraud who had never left his native Naples. How could such primitive people as the Mexican Indians ever have built great temples or designed a vast city? The eighteenth-century Scottish historian William Robertson summed it up in no uncertain terms. According to him, ancient Mexican palaces were a myth; it was unlikely that "men just emerging from barbarity" would dwell in such splendid structures. Further, he found it incredible that such elaborate cities as those reported by the Spanish and Careri could have vanished so quickly and with so little trace. "The Spanish accounts appear highly embellished," he noted. To cap it all, when Don Carlos de Siguenza died, his priceless manuscripts were scattered or destroyed by his superiors.

Although some travelers visited Teotihuacán in the early nineteenth century, among them the English merchant Bullock, who described the Pyramid of the Sun as being "as perfect as the great pyramid of Egypt," little firsthand information was available. When the Boston historian William Prescott wrote his immortal *History of the Conquest of Mexico* in 1843, he of necessity relied solely on tourist accounts. "The traveler, who will take the trouble to ascend its bald summit, will be amply compensated by the glorious view it will open up to him," he wrote. There was nothing much he could say, however, about the people who built the Pyramid of the Sun. He could only comment that "a nation has passed away— powerful, populous, and well advanced in refinement, as attested by their monuments—but it has perished without a name. It has died and made no sign." It was some time before archaeologists could expand on the worthy Prescott's speculations.

Archaeological research into the mysteries of Teotihuacán remained sporadic during the remainder of the nineteenth century. Claude Joseph Desire Charney, a French traveler and writer, visited Mexico in 1858 and spent three years journeying from Mayan site to Mayan site, taking the first photographs of the ruins ever made. Twenty years later, he returned for another visit, this time to Mexico City and Teotihuacán. Unlike most travelers, he was now determined to dig for the secrets of the pyramids. He started by excavating at the ancient capital of the Toltecs at Tula. He found traces of a palace and of a pyramid topped with giant statues. His discoveries were treated with skepticism. It was not until many years later that Tula was firmly identified as the Toltec capital, built about A.D. 900 and destroyed by the Aztec two centuries later. All this happened long after Teotihuacán was abandoned, but Charney was not to know this.

Armed with his Tula excavating experience, Charney now turned his attention to Teotihuacán. He climbed up the overgrown Pyramids of the Sun and Moon, admired the view, and then set about finding a place to dig. There were so many fragments of prehistoric life on the surface that it was difficult to know where to start. Eventually he sank some small trenches in the middle of the modern village of San Juan Teotihuacán and promptly recovered a number of ancient graves, containing over a dozen children and several adults. The children had been buried in pots. Convinced that he had struck the poor quarter of the great city, Charney turned his attentions elsewhere. He moved to the opposite bank of the San Juan River and set his men to work at a spot where walls appeared to outcrop on the surface. Within three days, the excavations revealed a complex of ten rooms that formed part of a large building with courtyards, pillared roofs, and several levels. The thick walls were constructed of stone and mortar, sometimes covered with decorated plaster. Some of the painted frescoes on the chamber walls were still bright with multicolored designs. Charney quietly removed several of the frescoes for exhibition in his native Paris. After numerous adventures in the Mexican lowlands, he returned home, never to come back to Teotihuacán.

The political upheavals that beset Mexico in the late nineteenth century prevented archaeological investigations by foreigners for many years; President Porfirio Diaz's harsh dictatorship discouraged any archaeological activity by non-Mexicans. Thus it was no coincidence when the dictator gave the son of one of his henchmen a permit to dig at Teotihuacán. Leopoldo Batres, son of a military man, had himself appointed Inspector and Protector of the Archaeological Monuments of Mexico. This imposing title gave Batres *carte blanche* to excavate anywhere in Mexico he wished. And, if there was gold at the end of the rainbow, so much the better.

Batres excavated at Teotihuacán for two long periods: 1884–1886 and 1905–1911. His first season was financed by the government at a time when much of the country's population was suffering severely from hunger and poverty; his second used up more money than the entire social-welfare budget for Mexico at the time. Batres spent his first months at the site poking around randomly. He dug near the Pyramid of the Moon and discovered a huge building decorated with striking murals. The paintings depicted brightly painted flowers and animals, gods and priests, as well as elaborate geometric designs. He also dug through numerous large, single-story dwellings that were divided into many small rooms and roofed with stout timber beams and stucco-plastered ceilings. Wherever he dug, Batres came across beautifully finished aqueducts that still brought water from natural springs to all parts of what, he now realized, was once a great city.

Batres estimated that Teotihuacán had extended over an area of at least seven square miles. He also determined that much of the city had been destroyed by fire at some late period in its history. Many dwellings Batres dug had collapsed. Their walls were charred and the rafters had settled into the foundations. Some, he said, even contained the skeletons of the inhabitants, lying where they had been trapped in the holocaust.

11-4. Leopold Batres' view of Teotihuacán.

Yet other homes were still perfectly preserved, buried in fine clay. What had happened to Teotihuacán? Batres was puzzled by a question that has still not been satisfactorily answered.

After an interval during which he tried to find treasures at other sites, Batres persuaded President Diaz to fund another long series of excavations on his mysterious city, under the pretext of restoring Teotihuacán as a great national monument, one that would enhance Mexico's image in the world. Diaz provided ample funds in 1905. Batres started on an ambitious project: the complete restoration of the Pyramid of the Sun.

He began by organizing his workmen in teams. Aided by a steam locomotive and a length of track, they removed thousands of tons of earth from the overgrown pyramid. When Batres started, the Pyramid of the Sun was little more than a huge pile of earth. He realized that no half measures were possible. Either he had to leave the pyramid as it was or expose the huge masonry structure that lay, he thought, under the soil. To achieve the latter, it would be necessary to remove several hundred thousand tons of earth.

It was an extraordinary undertaking, one that took four years and cost the then-colossal sum of forty-five thousand dollars. Batres stripped all the earth and rubble from the great mound. When heavy rains started to erode the adobe, Batres was forced to introduce lime and cement to stabilize the outer surface of the pyramid. He found it was a huge, stepped structure with a temple on the summit dedicated to Quetzalcoatl. Clay figures and numerous ornaments lay under the surface of the uppermost platform. Child sacrifices had been placed at the corners of each level. They crumbled to dust upon exposure to the air. The pyramid was surrounded with a great platform nineteen feet high and one hundred twenty-six feet wide. Beautifully decorated houses lay nearby.

Just as Batres was nearing the end of his work, political unrest caused him to abandon Teotihuacán forever. By that time, he estimated he had removed between twelve and twenty feet of earth from the outer surface of the pyramid. Batres's version of the Pyramid of the Sun was 203 feet high and 745 feet by 684 feet at the base. His many enemies were appalled at the damage. They accused him of having stripped off the outer layers of the pyramid as if it were an onion and of having mangled it beyond repair. When President Diaz was abruptly deposed in 1910, Batres fell from grace, leaving the field open to better-qualified archaeologists.

Batres's successor, a man of very different caliber, had been specially trained at Columbia University under the great anthropologist Franz Boas. Manuel Gamio was a museum man, in charge of antiquities at the National Museum in Mexico City. Powerful American backers paid for his training in the hope that he would one day make scientific excavations at Teotihuacán and elsewhere. Gamio was a talented archaeologist who spent the years of civil war between 1910 and 1917 quietly digging into the huge

11-5. Pyramid of the Sun, Teotihuacán.

piles of rubbish under Mexico City. Unlike his predecessors, Gamio was interested in the minutest of finds, which he dissected layer by layer into a complex chronology of occupation horizons. He found at least three major phases of prehistoric occupation of the Mexico City site—the latest Aztec, preceded by Toltec, with an earlier "Archaic" civilization that had flourished before either Toltec or Aztec. But how did the vast city of Teotihuacán fit into this pattern? Had the Toltecs built it, as Batres and his predecessors believed? Or had an unknown civilization erected its vast pyramids and plazas? Gamio was determined to find out.

Manuel Gamio started serious work at Teotihuacán in 1918. The excavations were conducted along the principles he had followed with success in Mexico City. His first effort was an attempt to establish the chronology of Teotihuacán by studying the architectural styles of the buildings. After sixteen test excavations, Gamio felt confident enough to tackle an even larger project, the excavation of a mysterious quadrangular area of earth-covered mounds known as the Ciudadela, lying to the south of the Pyramid of the Sun.

This was a formidable project, for Batres had already found traces of elaborately decorated temples in the Ciudadela mounds. Like his infamous predecessor, Gamio realized he would have to preserve the temples as soon as he uncovered them; otherwise they would disintegrate in a few days of rain. This part of Teotihuacán, obviously unique, was preserved as a tourist attraction and as a monument to Mexico's new national spirit. Wisely, Gamio employed the services of an expert architectural draftsman named Ignatio Marquina. Marquina's drawings of the newly excavated temples gave Gamio the information he needed to anchor masonry and to replace mortar where necessary as the buildings were uncovered. He uncovered only the inward facing sides of the Ciudadela buildings, so that the facades were stabilized by the earth mounds that covered the rest of the masonry.

The Ciudadela excavations began in 1919. Within a few weeks, the earthen mounds were yielding sculptured serpents' heads. When the diggers started work on the large mound in the center of the Ciudadela,

11-6. The carved facade of the Temple of Quetzalcoatl, Teotihuacán.

they found it consisted of two pyramids, built one against the other. The rear pyramid of the two was the earlier, a vast structure that rose in six steps to a height of seventy-two feet. Gamio had to destroy part of the first pyramid to get at the better-built rear one. But the effort was worth it. As the diggers uncovered each successive stage, Gamio was able to admire the vast, sprawling serpents, some with glittering obsidian eyes, that protruded from each level. These feathered serpents represented the ancient god Quetzalcoatl. A beautifully designed staircase lined by watching serpents led to the summit of the pyramid, where six burials were found.

The entire Ciudadela was a vast complex of buildings over a mile in circumference, covering an area of thirty-six acres. Gamio soon realized that millions of pesos would be needed to excavate the whole of Teotihuacán. And, at best, it would be a controversial undertaking. Already he was being attacked by the aged Batres, who accused him of "grotesque" reconstructions and of being a man "without understanding or conscience." But, while Batres's strictures were ignored, the worldwide depression of the 1930s postponed any further work on a large scale. Although the Swedish archaeologist Sigwald Linne excavated at Teotihuacán in the 1930s and discovered extensive complexes of residence quarters, ball courts, and other public buildings, his work, and that of Pedro Armillas and others who succeeded him, was sporadic. The combined work of these men did show, however, that the mysterious site had, in fact, been far more than a complex of temples. It was a great city with a flourishing market and a vigorous artistic tradition that was reflected in brightly colored wall murals of gods and priests. Still, as late as 1960, no one had any idea who had lived in the city or when it had been built.

Teotihuacán languished until 1960, when the Mexican government was looking around for new sources of revenue. They decided to carry out a major excavation at Teotihuacán and to reconstruct the central part of the city to its former glory as a tourist attraction close to Mexico City. The project ended up costing seventeen million pesos and employing over six hundred workmen. The dig was under the direction of José Acosta and Ignatio Bernal, both experienced archaeologists. Within a few months, they had cleared the plaza in front of the Pyramid of the Moon and started work on the buildings on either side of the Street of the Dead, their objective being to restore the central part of the city. As many of the buildings were in a late and inferior architectural style, Acosta and Bernal boldly decided to tear many of them down to reveal the superior, older buildings that lay behind the later facades. Their efforts were brilliantly successful. Teotihuacán, of course, has become one of the great archaeological tourist attractions of the world and the costs of the excavation have been recovered many times over.

The most ambitious part of the excavation was an effort to reconstruct the Pyramid of the Moon, still an earthen mound that only Batres had tried to excavate—and he had left a huge crater in the middle. Acosta and Bernal were determined not to repeat the mistakes made by Batres. Proceeding with great care, they soon discovered there were at least five stages to the pyramid, linked by a great staircase. Fortunately, one of their colleagues found a cornerstone of the original stairway still in place, so they were able to reconstruct the angle of the steps and replace forty-eight courses. The north side of the pyramid was left in its original state to stabilize the structure.

When all of the work was completed, the visitor could gaze down on the vast complexity of Teotihuacán from the summit of the Pyramid of the Sun and walk up the Street of the Dead to the Pyramid of the Moon. One could obtain a vivid impression of a great ceremonial center, of the great avenue lined by fine temples and palaces. But the city, even when full of tourists, seemed dead. Where had the inhabitants lived? How many people had dwelt in the shadow of the pyramids and temples? Was Teotihuacán just a ceremonial center, or was it a city as well?

The Mexican excavations finally threw some light on the date of the site. When Acosta and Bernal sat down to examine the thousands of pottery fragments and art objects found in their digs, they established that the site had been occupied over a very long time, from about 100 B.C. until as late as A.D. 800. Teotihuacán reached the height of its prosperity around A.D. 500. After that time, the city began a gradual decline and, by the end of the first millennium, was deserted. This chronology differs considerably from more modern interpretations, which place the heyday of the city between A.D. 450 and 750, the decline following with arresting speed. The Toltec peoples who took over political power in the Valley of Mexico made their headquarters at Tula, abandoning Teotihuacán altogether. The Teotihuacanos came under new rulers.

In 1950, a young American archaeologist name René Millon visited Teotihuacán for the first time. He was fresh out of Columbia University, where his lecturers had waxed eloquent about this extraordinary site. Immediately, he came under the spell of the Pyramid of the Sun and the Street of the Dead, silent under the Mexican sun. How had such a center arisen, he wondered? Had it really been an enormous city? Millon decided then and there to devote his career to solving the mystery.

Millon realized at once that he had undertaken an enormous, almost mind-boggling project; the mapping operations alone would take years. The only plans of Teotihuacán had been prepared by a scientific commission appointed by Emperor Maximilian in 1865 and by Manuel Gamio in 1922. Both concentrated on the center area of the site. Millon wisely spent some years becoming more familiar with archaeology in the Valley of Mexico. He studied with Mexican archaeologists and investigated ancient irrigation systems near Teotihuacán. It was not until 1957 that he felt prepared enough to tackle the city itself.

Millon's preliminary surveys convinced him that Teotihuacán had been a vast and highly complex city. Other archaeologists violently disagreed, insisting it was merely an elaborate ceremonial center of pyramids and temples. There was only one way to solve the problem: the entire site must be mapped in detail. Millon blithely took on the task, a research campaign supported by the National Science Foundation. The project is only now in its final stages. "Depending upon one's point of view," he remarked years later, "it is fortunate or unfortunate that I did not realize the implications of what I was undertaking, for surely I would never have taken it on."

In order to record the full extent of Teotihuacán's twelve and a half square miles, the mapping project covered an area of twenty-two square miles around the site. The first stage of the work began in 1962, when a complete aerial photographic record of the site from four thousand feet was made on a cloudless April day. Then the archaeologists took the photographs into the field. It took them five years to transform the air photographs and field surveys into a finished map.

The results were astonishing. Teotihuacán was revealed as an orderly, carefully thought-out city that had been laid out on a grandiose scale. Nearly all its buildings had been erected on a north-south axis, an orientation that gave Teotihuacán a planned appearance, in spite of the many thousands of people crowded into its houses and apartments. The orientation of the city was extended to the east-west axis as well, presumably by means of astronomical observations. No one knows why the north-south orientation of the Street of the Dead was chosen.

The city was divided into four quadrants; the northwest quarter was by far the most densely settled. The southern parts of the settlement impinged on extremely fertile agricultural land. Most of the earliest buildings were erected on the northern edge of Teotihuacán. Apparently, the orientation and length of the Street of the Dead were decided early on, perhaps as early as the second century A.D. The three-mile street seems to have been part of a master plan, but it is unclear to what extent the rulers of Teotihuacán kept to any original plan in later centuries. Probably what happened was that the limits of the city were decided on as Teotihuacán grew into a dense complex of closely spaced, walled compounds.

Teotihuacán was far from an open city. Millon found the remains of walled precincts and large compounds that served to restrict entry into certain parts of the settlement. There do not seem to have been defensive walls, nor are there traces of fortifications enclosing the entire city. But anyone wanting to attack Teotihuacán would have had a difficult time. The narrow streets between the apartment complexes could be covered by rooftop arches, and the dense thickets of cactus and deep, irrigated swamps surrounding the city would hinder a large army of attackers. In addition, the teeming *barrios* of Teotihuacán would have been a strategical nightmare for any raiding party.

Teotihuacán was divided into many neighborhoods. When Millon came to examine the houses in each neighborhood more thoroughly, he found that groups of apartments were set off into distinctive clusters. There were more than two thousand residential compounds in the city. Each consisted of sets of dwelling units, often with a communal shrine and a central patio. The surface finds from the clusters of compounds indicated that people with the same occupations tended to live in the same apartment complexes. Obsidian knife makers, potters, and merchants all seem to have lived in their own precincts.

In the western part of the city, there was even one enclave where people from faraway Oaxaca lived and worked. Millon found numerous potsherds from this area of Mexico on the surface of a residential complex. When the compound was excavated, it was found that the Oaxacan apartments were first occupied around A.D. 400, and the occupation continued for centuries. No one knows what the Oaxaqueros were doing in Teotihuacán. Perhaps they were merchants, although there is no evidence to suggest this. Although the foreigners lived in the standard Teotihuacán houses and compounds, they preserved their own burial customs for centuries. The vessels they used were comparable to those from the great ceremonial center of Monte Alban in the Valley of Oaxaca. Was there a special relationship between the two centers? Were the Oaxaqueros but one of several foreign enclaves in this cosmopolitan city? This is just another of the many tantalizing questions posed by Teotihuacán.

Once the Teotihuacán map was complete, René Millon sat down to compute the population of the city. He began by examining the excavated apartment buildings in an effort to estimate the number of sleeping places in them. Millon devised a series of estimates for apartments of various sizes. Then he measured compounds throughout the city, using his map as a basis for the calculations. The result was a conservative, minimal estimate of 75,000, with perhaps as many as 125,000 people at the height of the city's prosperity. Millon believes these figures are far too conservative, that Teotihuacán may have housed over 200,000 people. But any population figures for the city are little more than intelligent guesses.

Why did this enormous settlement arise in the first place, a city with over five hundred craft workshops, many of them engaged in obsidian-tool manufacture? Millon points out that the Teotihuacán Valley is semiarid today. Its agricultural potential would be by no means exceptional were it not for the springs at the southwestern edge of the city that provided abundant water for irrigation, agriculture, and domestic purposes. Water supplies were canalized throughout the city. But the valley contained another vital resource as well—obsidian. This volcanic glass was widely prized for toolmaking, and we know that obsidian working was a major

11-7. Teotihuacán: an Early Classic effigy vessel from a site near the city. Height: c. 12 inches.

activity throughout the city's history. Teotihuacán Valley lies near the shore of Lake Texcoco, the largest lake in the Valley of Mexico, important both as a communication route and as an economic resource in itself. Thus Teotihuacán occupied a key geographical position and possessed valuable economic resources, both elements of potential political importance. Certainly the Teotihuacanos exploited the potential of their valley brilliantly.

By analyzing both the Teotihuacán map and the thousands of potsherds found at the site, Millon showed how the original settlement a few centuries before Christ consisted of a handful of villages, at least one of which may have specialized in manufacturing various articles from obsidian. By 100 B.C. Teotihuacán had begun to expand rapidly. The scattered villages became a settlement covering more than three and a half square miles. There were obsidian workers in the city and several public buildings with walls of stone. Much of this early settlement, the home of six thousand or more people, is covered by later buildings. Perhaps the people lived in small clusters of houses. We do not know. But Teotihuacán was already an important center of obsidian trading and of production and marketing. Perhaps its religious ceremonies were known far and wide, too.

By A.D. 150, Teotihuacán extended over eight square miles and contained some twenty thousand inhabitants. By now, the Teotihuacanos could worship at several temple complexes on either side of the Street of the Dead. The Pyramid of the Sun and the Pyramid of the Moon, begun at this time, formed the focuses of two major religious complexes. Obsidian trade and manufacture was expanding fast. So was agricultural production, for a rapidly growing urban population had to be fed. Teotihuacán was now so large that anyone seeking to pass through the valley had to traverse the city. It was a city with a diverse population of specialists, priests, and distinct social classes. A revolution in the structure of Mexican society was under way.

Between A.D. 150 and 200, the Ciudadela was erected and became the religious and political center of the city. What is more, the city's rulers seem to have realized that they could now exert religious and political influence over a much larger area of Mexico. By this time, too, the Street of the Dead, with its vast structures, would serve to impress both local dwellers and visitors with the incredible prestige and power of the city's rulers.

The next two and a half centuries saw the erection of hundreds of standardized apartment complexes and a steadily increasing social distance between the Teotihuacán rulers and those they ruled. Thousands of people had now moved into the city, where their activities and living arrangements were closely regimented. It is likely that they were discouraged from ever returning to the countryside, for, within the confines of Teotihuacán, they could be more easily organized and taxed.

Unlike Acosta and Bernal, Millon believed Teotihuacán was at the height of its power between A.D. 450 and 750. The city was actively engaged in trading with communities hundreds of miles away, on the Gulf Coast and in the Mayan lowlands, as well as throughout the Valley of Mexico. The city was now not only an important obsidian workshop, but an international marketplace as well, a place of pilgrimage for Teotihuacanos and foreigners alike. Significant numbers of outsiders now resided permanently in the greatest city Mexico had ever seen.

Then, with an arresting suddenness, Teotihuacán collapsed. Many of the central buildings were burnt during the eighth century A.D. and never rebuilt. Up to this moment, the city was prospering; there were no obvious signs of decline. The city proper was as populous as ever, although the surrounding countryside supported fewer people as more and more rural dwellers flocked to the city. Was Teotihuacán sacked and burned by foreign invaders? Or was the center of the city destroyed by a tremendous fire? If so, why was it not rebuilt? What happened to the thousands of people in the city? Did they disperse to live elsewhere? Why, if the city was besieged, were its inhabitants unable to resist attack? Did more and more people move into the city for defensive reasons? So far, no one has been able to answer these questions satisfactorily.

Millon did determine, however, that Teotihuacán was prosperous up to the very end, although its sphere of political domination appears to have contracted somewhat. Were other centers beginning to challenge Teotihuacán's dominance? The city may have faced a severe ecological problem as well, perhaps generated by a series of dry years and more frequent crop failures. The irrigated fields may have been unable to produce the huge food surplus needed to maintain an urban society. To what extent did the rulers of Teotihuacán overreach themselves and place intolerable strains on the food supplies available to them? We do not know.

Conceivably, those who ruled Teotihuacán were so set in their responses to the city's difficulties that they were unable to act rationally and effectively to solve the critical ecological problems that faced the city. Their society may have faced major internal stresses too, strains that the rulers sought to contain by force and military curbs. Perhaps it is significant that military figures appear with increasing frequency in Teotihuacán's later art styles. Did the Teotihuacanos turn on their rulers in bloody revolt? Did they destroy the temples and gods that oversaw them in a massive act of desanctification that left the mighty city in smoking ruins? Again, we do not know.

There is but one certainty. By the time the Spaniards came to Mexico, Teotihuacán was a silent ruin, a mystery that generations of archaeologists have puzzled over. But, despite the ancient questions it poses, Teotihuacán leaves us with a strangely relevant thought for our own times. Did the city, by its great and spectacular successes, sow the seeds of its own failure by overreaching the limits of its resources? Conceivably it did. In that case, the lesson of Teotihuacán is indeed timely.

Guide to Sources

The literature for this book is scattered in hundreds of books and specialist articles, many of them very specialized. This Guide lists some of the major sources, for those readers interested in delving more deeply into the personalities, sites, and archaeological topics discussed in this book.

Chapter 1

The general reader will have to go far to discover a better introduction to the excitement of archaeological discovery than C. W. Ceram, *Gods, Graves, and Scholars* (New York: Knopf, 1953), which has become a modern classic. It is particularly good on the discovery of the early civilizations. See also Brian Fagan, *The Adventure of Archaeology* (Washington, DC: National Geographic Society, 1985), a lavishly illustrated account of the development of archaeology. A more specialized introduction: Glyn Daniel, *A Short History of Archaeology* (London: Thames and Hudson, 1981), while the same author's edited *The Origins and Growth of Archaeology* (Baltimore: Pelican Books, 1967) contains many excerpts from the writings of early archaeologists. J. P. Droop, *Archaeological Excavation* (Cambridge: Cambridge University Press, 1915) is deliciously amusing reading, while Sir Mortimer Wheeler, *Archaeology from the Earth* (Oxford: Clarendon Press, 1954) is a classic account of good excavation technique. The history of American archaeology is well covered by Gordon Willey and Jeremy Sabloff, *A History of American Archaeology* (New York: Freeman, 1980). Finally, a useful biography: W. V. F. Winstone, *Woolley of Ur* (London: Secker and Warburg, 1990).

Chapter 2

College texts on the methods and theories of archaeology abound. For a short, readable account, try James Deetz, *Invitation to Archaeology* (Garden City, NY: Natural History Press, 1967), which is a minor classic, or my *Archaeology: A Brief Introduction* (New York: HarperCollins, 5th ed., 1994). For more comprehensive accounts: Robert Sharer and Wendy Ashmore, *Archaeology: Discovering Our Past* (Mountain View, CA: Mayfield, 2nd ed., 1992), or Colin Renfrew and Paul Bahn. *Archaeology* (London: Thames and Hudson, 1991), or Brian Fagan, *In the Beginning* (New York: HarperCollins, 8th ed., 1994). The prehistory of humankind is summarized by Robert Wenke, *Patterns in Prehistory* (New York: Oxford University Press, 2nd ed., 1990), or in Brian Fagan, *People of the Earth* (New York: HarperCollins, 7th ed., 1992). For an insightful account of recent developments:

L. R. Binford, *In Pursuit of the Past* (London: Thames and Hudson, 1983). Bruce Trigger, *The History of Archaeological Interpretation* (Cambridge: Cambridge University Press, 1989) is definitive.

Chapter 3

Twenty years after his death, Louis Leakey still has a wide following, indeed, almost a fan club. The most widely read Leakey biography is Sonia Cole's *Leakey's Luck* (London: Collins, 1975). His own autobiographical works, *White African* (Cambridge, MA: Schenkman, 1966) and *By the Evidence* (New York: Harcourt, Brace, Jovanovich, 1974) are useful sources. Mary Leakey chronicles her remarkable career in *Disclosing the Past* (Garden City, NY: Doubleday, 1984). For outside assessments, see Roger Lewin, *Bones of Contention* (New York: Simon and Schuster, 1987) and John Reader's magnificently illustrated *Missing Links* (Boston: Little, Brown, 1981). Donald Johanson and Maitland Edey, *Lucy* (New York: Simon and Schuster, 1981) provides background on recent controversies, also on Ethiopian fossil finds. The Olduvai Gorge discoveries appear in L. S. B. Leakey, *Olduvai Gorge 1931–1951* (Cambridge: Cambridge University Press, 1953), and in subsequent volumes on the human fossils and archaeological finds by Mary Leakey (1973) and anatomist Philip Tobias (1969 and 1990). Jane Goodall, *In the Shadow of Man* (Boston: Houghton Mifflin, 1974) and *Through a Window: My Thirty Years with the Chimpanzees of Gombe* (Boston: Houghton Mifflin, 1990) describes her unique researches for a general audience.

Chapter 4

Ozette: Ruth Kirk's *Hunters of the Whale* (New York: Morrow, 1974) is a popular account written in collaboration with Richard Daugherty. I have drawn on it extensively in chapter 3 and would refer the interested reader to its fine photographs. The Northwest Coast Indians themselves have been much described. Perhaps the most famous survey is Philip Drucker's *Indians of the Northwest Coast* (Garden City, NY: Natural History Press, 1963). See also: Roy Carlson, *Indian Art Traditions of the Northwest Coast* (Burnaby, BC: Archaeology Press, Simon Fraser University, 1983). Elizabeth Colson, before becoming a world-famous African anthropologist, wrote a definitive study of the Makah in 1955: *The Makah Indians: A Study of an Indian Tribe in Modern America* (Minneapolis: University of Minnesota Press, 1953). A general account of American archaeology for beginners may be found in Brian Fagan, *Ancient North America* (London: Thames and Hudson, 1990), and of the controversies surrounding first settlement in the same author's *The Great Journey* (London: Thames and Hudson, 1987). For general accounts that embrace the entire New World, see Stuart J. Fiedel, *Prehistory of the Americas* (Cambridge: Cambridge University Press, 1987) and Brian Fagan, *Kingdoms of Gold, Kingdoms of Jade* (London: Thames and Hudson, 1992).

Chapter 5

Austen Henry Layard, although one of the most colorful archaeologists of all, has been sadly neglected by biographers. Gordon Waterfield, *Layard of Nineveh* (London: John Murray, 1963) presents the great man's fascinating life in detail, especially his later diplomatic career. Nora Benjamin Kubie, *Road to Nineveh* (New York: Doubleday, 1964) is a more superficial account of Layard's archaeological work. Perhaps the best source of all on Layard is Layard himself. Both his popular accounts, *Nineveh and Its Remains* and *Nineveh and Babylon*, are readily available in many libraries, either in the original editions or in a reprinted form. I urge you to read Layard, for he possessed a unique gift for communicating his exciting finds to a lay audience. He was a member of a heroic archaeological generation and his writings reflect the excitement of the age. Seton Lloyd, *Foundations in the Dust* (London: Thames and Hudson, 1980) and Brian Fagan, *Return to Babylon* (Boston: Little, Brown, 1979) discuss the early history of Mesopotamian archaeology and place Layard in a wider context. Two books provide admirable overviews of Sumerian civilization: Samuel Kramer, *The Sumerians* (Chicago: University of Chicago Press, 1963) is a brilliant account of the Sumerians as we know them from their cuneiform tablets; and Harriet Crawford, *Sumer and the Sumerians* (Cambridge: Cambridge University Press, 1991).

Chapter 6

Heinrich Schliemann, like Layard, has for the most part been overlooked by biographers. However, no one should miss Irving Stone's brilliant fictionalized biography, *The Greek Treasure* (New York: Doubleday, 1975). The research behind this book is extremely authoritative and the story line is both vivid and compelling. Archaeology has rarely been so competently popularized. Carl Blegan, *Troy* (New York: Praeger, 1961) is a straightforward, spare summary of this complex site. C. W. Ceram, *Gods, Graves, and Scholars* (New York: Knopf, 1953) also includes a good account of the discovery of Troy. The Mycenaeans and Mycenae itself are well covered by Lord William Taylour, *The Mycenaeans* (London: Thames and Hudson, 2nd ed., 1990). For those interested in consulting the original sources, E. V. Rieu's brilliant prose translations of Homer's *Iliad* and *Odyssey* were published by Pelican Books just after World War II. The best modern *Iliad* is Robert Fagles, *Homer: The Iliad* (New York: Viking, 1990).

Chapter 7

The Evans family constituted an archaeological dynasty of extraordinary distinction. Joan Evans, the last of the dynasty, wrote an account of the family in *Time and Chance* (London: Longmans, 1943). Her book, based on family papers, is very authoritative as well as readable. Knossos is competently surveyed by Sinclair Hood, *The Minoans* (New York: Praeger, 1973) and by L. R. Palmer, *A New Guide to the Palace of Knossos* (London: Faber, 1969). The origins of Aegean civilization are much debated. Colin Renfrew, *The Emergence of Civilization*

(London: Methuen, 1972) is a fundamental but rather technical source for readers interested in this topic. Arthur Evans's *Palace of Minos* (Oxford: Oxford University Press, 1921–1936) requires the reader to wade through a mass of detail, but it is a remarkable work. Mary Renault's fictional recreation of Knossos and the Minoans: *The King Must Die* (New York: Random House, 1963) is a good starting point for anyone interested in prehistoric Crete.

Chapter 8

The Pyramids have inspired an enormous outpouring of popular and technical literature, much of it frankly crazy. Peter Tompkins, *Secrets of the Great Pyramid* (New York: Harper & Row, 1971) wades through the technical literature as well as the fascinating history of research at Giza. I. E. S. Edwards, *The Pyramids of Egypt* (New York: Viking Press, 1972) and Ahmed Fakhry, *The Pyramids* (Chicago: University of Chicago Press, 1961) are the standard works on the structures themselves. Kurt Mendelssohn, *The Riddle of the Pyramids* (New York: Praeger, 1974) offers an ingenious explanation for why the Pyramids were built. No one should miss David Macaulay's enchanting *Pyramid* (Boston: Houghton Mifflin, 1975), an artist's account of how the Egyptians built the Great Pyramid. My own *The Rape of the Nile* (Wakefield, RI: Moyer Bell, 1992) covers the history of tomb robbing and early archaeology on the Nile. Mark Lerner, *The Pyramids* (London: Thames and Hudson, 1994) is an up-to-date, lavishly illustrated account of the Pyramids of Giza and their surroundings. For ancient Egyptian civilization, see Cyril Aldred, *The Egyptians* (London: Thames and Hudson, 2nd ed., 1986), and Barry Kemp, *Ancient Egypt: Anatomy of a Civilization* (London: Routledge, 1989).

Chapter 9

Nicholas Reeves, *The Complete Tutankhamun* (London: Thames and Hudson, 1990) is the ultimate general book on the tomb and the circumstances of its discovery. Its illustrations alone break new ground. Another widely read, if slightly dated, source: C. Desroches-Noblecourt, *Tutankhamen: Life and Death of a Pharaoh* (London: Thames and Hudson, 1963). Both these books contain bibliographies of more technical books and articles on the tomb. Howard Carter is well served by W. V. F. Winstone's recent bibliography, *Howard Carter and the Discovery of the Tomb of Tutankhamun* (London: Secker and Warburg, 1991). Discerning readers will also enjoy Howard Carter's own, very personal account of the discovery: Howard Carter and A. C. Mace, *The Tomb of Tut-Ankh-Amen* (London: Macmillan, 1923–33).

Chapter 10

The literature on early women archaeologists is widely scattered, and, until recently, received little attention. W. V. F. Winstone, *Gertrude Bell* (London: Jonathan Cape, 1978) is the authoritative biography, while Bell's *The Desert and the Sown* (London: Heinemann, 1907) and *Amuranth to Amuranth* (London: Heinemann, 1911) give a good impression of her writings. Mary Allsebrook, *Born to Rebel* (Oxford: Oxbow Books, 1992) gives us a delightful biography of her mother, Harriet Boyd Hawes, while Gertrude Caton-Thompson's *Mixed Memoirs* (Gateshead, England: Paradigm Press, 1983) provides insights into an eventful, and often intensely private, life. For the Fayum: G. Caton-Thompson and E. W. Gardiner, *The Desert Fayum* (London: Royal Anthropological Institute). Caton-Thompson's *Zimbabwe Culture* (Oxford: Clarendon Press, 1931) is still an authoritative source on the site. For an assessment, see Peter Garlake, *Great Zimbabwe* (London: Thames and Hudson, 1973).

Chapter 11

René Millon et al., *Urbanization at Teotihuacán, Mexico* (Austin: University of Texas Press, 1974) contains the maps upon which the study is based and is well worth perusal. Peter Tompkins, *Mysteries of the Mexican Pyramids* (New York: Harper and Row, 1976) surveys the early history of excavations at Teotihuacán, as does Ignatio Bernal, *A History of Mexican Archaeology* (London: Thames and Hudson, 1980). The prehistory of Mesoamerica as a whole is summarized by Muriel Porter Weaver, *The Aztecs, Maya and their Predecessors* (Orlando, FL: Academic Press, 3rd ed., 1991) and by Michael Coe, *Mexico* (London: Thames and Hudson, 1962). See also Jeremy A. Sabloff, *The Cities of Ancient Mexico* (London: Thames and Hudson, 1989) and Kathleen Berrin and Esther Pasztory (eds.) *Teotihuacán: Art from the City of the Gods* (London: Thames and Hudson, 1993).

Photo Credits

Cover English Heritage

Frontispiece Hirmer Fotoarchiv, München

Opposite Table of Contents English Heritage

1-1. Michael Wakely **1-5.** © Society of Antiquaries of London
1-6. The University Museum, University of Pennsylvania,
Neg. #S8-139328

2-1. Brian M. Fagan **2-2.** Jeffrey Chouinard **2-3.** Kathy Schick and
Nicholas Toth **2-4.** The University Museum, University of Pennsylvania,
Neg. #S4-139317 **2-5.** Cambridge University Museum of Archaeology and
Anthropology **2-6.** Harold D. Walter, Courtesy Museum of New Mexico,
Neg. #128725 **2-7.** English Heritage **2-8.** National Museum of Denmark
2-9. Tyne and Wear Museums, Newcastle upon Tyne
2-10. Pitt Rivers Museum, Oxford

3-2. Melville B. Grosvenor © National Geographic Society **3-3.** Institute
of Human Origins **3-5.** *top* Cranium of *Australopithecus africanus* (STS
5, "Mrs Ples," from Sterkfontein. © Transvaal Museum **3-5.** *bottom* from
Phillip V. Tobias, *Olduvai Gorge* (London: Cambridge University Press,
1967). Reprinted with the permission of Cambridge University Press.
3-6. Robert F. Sisson © National Geographic Society **3-7.** Robert Matter
3-8. Cara McAteer

All photographs in **Chapter 4** by Ruth Kirk except **4-6.** by Harvey S. Rice.

5-2. and **5-5.** © British Museum

6-2. and **6-8.** The Bettmann Archive **6-6.** and **6-7.** Kelsey Museum
Archives **6-9.** Hirmer Fotoarchiv, München

7-1. © Society of Antiquaries of London **7-2.** and **7-5.** Ashmolean
Museum, Oxford **7-3.**, **7-6.**, **7-7** and **7-8.** Hirmer Fotoarchiv, München
7-4. Plan of the Palace of Knossos (from Sinclair Hood, *The Minoans*,
London: Thames and Hudson and New York: Praeger, an imprint of
Greenwood Publishing Group, Westport, CT, 1971, p. 63)

Index

Abu Balkhi, 178
Abu Simbel, 14
Achaeans, 125. *See also* Troy
Acheulian culture, 49
Acosta, José, 260–261
Adaptation, culture as, 38
Aegean region, 6, 7, 146
Africa. *See also* Egypt
  Great Zimbabwe, 235–238
  Gwembe Tonga farmer, 36
  Kalahari Desert, 77
  writing and, 31
Ahmose the Liberator, 198
'Ain Ghazal, Jordan, 37
Akhenaten, 198–199
Alps, Bronze Age traveler in, 27–28
Amenophis III, 198
Amenophis IV (Akhenaten),
  198–199
Americas, 6
  colonial Virginia, 32–33
  Maya in, 31
  Pacific Northwest, 81–97
  Teotihuacán, Mexico, 247–266
Amurath to Amurath, 225
Analogy, 51
Arabs, Bell, Gertrude, and, 224–227
Archaeological context
  space, 43
  time, 39–43
Archaeological record, 32–34
  interpreting, 51
Archaeological sites. *See also* Sites;

  specific sites
  excavation of, 4, 5–13
  time periods of, 6
Archaeological Survey of India, 15
Archaeology
  context in time and space, 39–43
  defined, 27–28
  finding and digging sites, 45–46
  goals of, 21–23, 28
  historical review of, 3–23
  prehistorical archaeologists and,
    28–31
  research process in, 44
  specialties within, 28–31
  theory and, 53–54
Argon. *See* Potassium-argon dating
Argos, 146
Armillas, Pedro, 260
Artifacts, 33, 34. *See also*
  Excavation
  analysis of, 49
Ashmolean Museum, England,
  154–155
Ashur-bani-pal (King), 122
Ashur-nasir-pal II (King), 109
Association, law of, 43
Assyria, 3, 6. *See also* Nimrud;
  Nineveh
Astronomy. *See* Great Pyramid
Atlantis, 171
Australopithecus, 69–70
Avern, Frida, 60
Ay, 199–202